KIERKEGAARD
TREACHERY C

This is a major study of Kierkegaard and love. Amy Laura Hall explores Kierkegaard's description of love's treachery, difficulty, and hope, reading his *Works of Love* as a text that both deciphers and complicates the central books in his pseudonymous canon: *Fear and Trembling, Repetition, Either/Or*, and *Stages on Life's Way*. In all of these works, the characters are, as in real life, complex and incomplete, and the conclusions are perplexing. Hall argues that a spiritual void brings each text into being, and her interpretation is as much about faith as about love. In a style that is both scholarly and lyrical, she intimates answers to some of the puzzles, making a poetic contribution to ethics and the philosophy of religion.

AMY LAURA HALL is Assistant Professor of Theological Ethics at the Divinity School, Duke University.

CAMBRIDGE STUDIES IN RELIGION AND
CRITICAL THOUGHT 9

Editors
Wayne Proudfoot, *Columbia University*
Jeffrey L. Stout, *Princeton University*
Nicholas Wolterstorff, *Yale University*

Current events confirm the need to understand religious ideas and institutions critically, yet radical doubts have been raised about how to proceed and about the ideal of critical thought itself. Meanwhile, some prominent scholars have urged that we turn the tables, and view modern society as the object of criticism and a religious tradition as the basis for critique. Cambridge Studies in Religion and Critical Thought is a series of books intended to address the interaction of critical thinking and religious traditions in this context of uncertainty and conflicting claims. It will take up questions such as the following, either by reflecting on them philosophically or by pursuing their ramifications in studies of specific figures and movements: is a coherent critical perspective on religion desirable or even possible? What sort of relationship to religious traditions ought a critic to have? What, if anything, is worth saving from the Enlightenment legacy or from critics of religion like Hume and Feuerbach? The answers offered, while varied, will uniformly constitute distinguished, philosophically informed, and critical analyses of particular religious topics.

Other titles published in the series

KIERKEGAARD
AND THE
TREACHERY OF LOVE

AMY LAURA HALL

CAMBRIDGE
UNIVERSITY PRESS

PUBLISHED BY THE PRESS SYNDICATE OF THE UNIVERSITY OF CAMBRIDGE
The Pitt Building, Trumpington Street, Cambridge, United Kingdom

CAMBRIDGE UNIVERSITY PRESS
The Edinburgh Building, Cambridge CB2 2RU, UK
40 West 20th Street, New York, NY 10011-4211, USA
477 Williamstown Road, Port Melbourne, VIC 3207, Australia
Ruiz de Alarcón 13, 28014 Madrid, Spain
Dock House, The Waterfront, Cape Town 8001, South Africa

http://www.cambridge.org

First published 2002

Printed in the United Kingdom at the University Press, Cambridge

Typeface Baskerville Monotype 11 / 12.5 pt   *System* LATEX 2ε   [TB]

A catalogue record for this book is available from the British Library

ISBN 0 521 80913 4 hardback
ISBN 0 521 89311 9 paperback

To John Fredric Utz

"It is a joy to me to apply this as a small installment on the debt — in which I still wish definitely to remain."

Why, all the souls that were, were forfeit once,
And He that might the vantage best have took
Found out the remedy. How would you be,
If He, which is the top of judgement, should
But judge you as you are? O think on that,
And mercy then will breathe within your lips,
Like man new made.

Measure for Measure, II.ii. 73–79

Contents

List of abbreviations

The following abbreviations occur in parenthetical references to works by Søren Kierkegaard:

CUP   *Concluding Unscientific Postscript.* 2 vols. Eds. and trans. Howard V. Hong and Edna H. Hong. Princeton: Princeton University Press, 1992.

EO   *Either/Or.* 2 vols. Eds. and trans. Howard V. Hong and Edna H. Hong. Princeton: Princeton University Press, 1987.

FT   *Fear and Trembling* (published with *Repetition*). Eds. and trans. Howard V. Hong and Edna H. Hong. Princeton: Princeton University Press, 1983.

JP   *Søren Kierkegaard's Journals and Papers.* 7 vols. Eds. and trans. Howard V. Hong and Edna H. Hong, assisted by Gregor Malantscuk. Bloomington: Indiana University Press, vol. 1, 1967; vol. 2, 1970; vols 3 and 4, 1975; vols. 5–7, 1978.

R   *Repetition* (published with *Fear and Trembling*). Eds. and trans. Howard V. Hong and Edna H. Hong. Princeton: Princeton University Press, 1983.

SLW   *Stages on Life's Way.* Eds. and trans. Howard V. Hong and Edna H. Hong. Princeton: Princeton University Press, 1988.

WL   *Works of Love.* Eds. and trans. Howard V. Hong and Edna H. Hong. Princeton: Princeton University Press, 1995.

All of these works except JP are copyright © Princeton University Press and extracts from them are reprinted by permission of Princeton University Press.

Preface

I am grateful to my professors, colleagues, and students who have read Kierkegaard's frustrating and fruitful texts with me. Vanessa Rumble, at Boston College, was the first teacher to introduce me to Kierkegaard's work. From the first week, reading *Fear and Trembling* and hearing her engaged, close explication, I was hooked. She inspires in her students not only a love for Kierkegaard, but also a passion for the truth about ourselves. At every stage of this project, Gene Outka offered patient, persistent advice, and I learned a great deal under his guidance. May the extent to which I differ with him be a testimony to his generous, ever-charitable, teaching. Margaret Farley, David Gouwens, George Lindbeck, and Cyril O'Regan read a prior manuscript in full. Like Dorothy Day, Margaret bristles when her students at Yale call her a saint, but we do so with the prayer that there may be more like her. Margaret lives the faithful love about which she so perceptively writes. While still in course work, I presented an early version of Chapter 3 at the AAR, and, from that point on, David Gouwens has been an invaluable advisor and colleague. George Lindbeck not only taught me how to read theologically, he took my questions seriously before I even knew how to formulate them. Through his attentive encouragement, he has had an inestimable influence on my development as a scholar. To the extent that I understand Kierkegaard's work as against the tidal wave of German Romanticism, I thank Cyril. His advice and friendship helped many a weary student through her time at Yale.

My colleagues at Duke have been wonderful. Deans Willie Jennings and Greg Jones have given me time, support, and encouragement. Stanley Hauerwas has tried to keep me honest about love, and I am grateful for his friendship. Reinhard Huetter has generously read the first chapter and has tried to keep me honest about Luther. Richard Hays has graciously advised me in ministry and scholarship for eleven years. I am grateful also to Christine Bowie, Steve Chapman, and Laceye

Warner, whose friendship during this project helped to keep me sane. The students who signed on for my very first seminar on Kierkegaard were appropriately cantankerous. Their questions and frustrations forced me ever to clarify my readings, and I am grateful for their help. I wish to thank two research assistants, Margus Sarglepp, who read numerous chapters, made substantive suggestions, and translated a portion of Pia Søltoft's book, and Daniel Barber, who closely read and so astutely commented on the final version of the manuscript. Chanon Ross graciously prepared the final proof and index. Three of these chapters appeared, in earlier forms, in other journals. Chapter 2 appeared as "Self-Delusion, Confusion, and Salvation in *Fear and Trembling* with *Works of Love*," in *Journal of Religious Ethics* 28, no. 1 (Spring 2000). Diane Yeager then edited out my gratitude to her, but she cannot do so now. Her careful reading was indeed a work of love. A version of Chapter 3 appeared as "Poets, Cynics and Thieves: Vicious Love and Divine Protection in *Repetition* and *Works of Love*," in *Modern Theology* 16, no. 2 (April 2000). I owe thanks to Jim Fodor for his careful editing and his encouragement. Finally, Chapter 5 appeared as "Stages on the Wrong Way" in Volume 11 of *The International Kierkegaard Commentary*, Fall 2000. Robert Perkins, the editor of *IKC*, has been my toughest reader, and I am grateful for his persistence. Mark Lloyd Taylor read an earlier version of Chapter 4, and made many helpful suggestions. Would but that I could name and thank all of those nameless readers who, on behalf of journals and Cambridge, wrangled with me from a distance. Please know that I am grateful for your considerable time and effort. Thank you to Lesley Atkin, who kindly read and edited the entire manuscript. I am grateful to the editors of this series for their generosity. Finally, working with Kevin Taylor has been a delight.

I wish to thank my colleagues with whom I studied (and, in some cases, organized for the union) at Yale; in particular, Jennifer Beste, Barbara Blodgett, Jaime Clark-Soles, Shannon Craigo-Snell, Bill Danaher, Eric Gregory, Steve Edmondson, Warren Smith, and Brian Stiltner. David Clough, my friend and colleague, held me accountable for completing the darned thing. Lucy Clough gave me a rhyme that I repeated daily: "She started to sing as she tackled the thing that couldn't be done, and she did it." Thank you, Lillian Daniel, for friendship beyond expectation. Thank you, Rebecca Parkhill and Robert Willett, for friendship and gracious hospitality. Mirela Moga, Betty Baisden, and Tammy Hughes taught my daughter, Rachel, while I learned and taught; thank you for your care and attention. The UMC congregations at Sierra Vista, New Canaan, First and Summerfield, and Trinity kept me in prayer.

Fred, Paula, and Laura Lee Utz offered me a second family. Robert, Carol, Bob, and Rebecca Hall have listened to me talk overmuch about love, but loved me nonetheless. I am grateful beyond words for their encouragement and constant support. Rachel Hall Utz, who was born my first year at Yale, was not a welcome distraction. She was the point. Finally, I cannot begin appropriately to thank John, who read more against eros than any young husband should have to, who cares for our daughter more hours in one day than most fathers spend in one week, and who, in multiple ways, constantly adduces the truth of the book's dedication. There is only one to whom I owe more. To that one, may I dedicate my life.

Introduction

In his otherwise disparaging essay on Kierkegaard's poetics, George
Lukács notes: "he saw more clearly than any other the thousand aspects, the thousand-fold variability of every motive [and] how, if we
look really close, we can see an unbridgeable abyss gaping between two
barely perceptible nuances."[1] This comment well characterizes one of
Kierkegaard's most compelling rhetorical strategies. The reader who
enters a text supposing himself to have a respectable grasp on reality
and its principles finds himself dizzied by the numerous, previously im-
perceptible, possibilities for error. In *Works of Love* Kierkegaard brings
this tactic to bear on our intimate engagements, pressing the reader
to inspect the vast "variability of every motive" and to discover the
"unbridgeable abyss gaping" between what we think to be love and what
love truly is. If appropriately taken by the text, we peer inward at the
multiple, often dubious motives propelling our own engagements, confess
with dismay the irreparable fracture running through our love, and seek
redemption.

Kierkegaard's aim and his form are offensive, his rather unlovely tone
unremitting. As Karl Barth protests regarding *Works of Love*, merely human love is "tracked down to its last hiding-place, examined, shown to be
worthless and haled before the judge!"[2] This complaint, by a theologian
indebted to Kierkegaard, has been magnified and repeated, in various
ways, by subsequent interpreters. The response is understandable. Employing what Barth calls his "detective skill," Kierkegaard shines harsh
light on the distinction between *eros* and *agape*, and we are left, quite
uncharitably, exposed. Barth's own argument with Kierkegaard on this
matter is complicated, but it hinges in part on the concern that *Works
of Love* over-accentuates conflict between the erotic and the Christian.
Kierkegaard misses that the two loves "do not finally confront each other
in equal dignity and power," and that "in *agape*, we have to do with a
superior and triumphant human action." By Barth's interpretation, our

author is preoccupied with error, overestimating our predicament and miscalculating God's power.

When faced with this critique, some of Kierkegaard's apologists have uncovered in *Works of Love* his positive depiction of *eros* redeemed, of desire taken up through God's grace, into the "unity of love" that "overcom[es] the dichotomy" between "sensuous and spiritual love."[3] In this book, I disagree with such an apology, and not merely for the sake of academic argument. Reading Kierkegaard's book of love alongside his intricate tales of love gone awry, we find that, to employ and counter Barth's words, Christian love is neither a "superior" nor a "triumphant human action." Rather, faithful love teeters right on the edge of our infinite culpability and God's radical grace. And what is more, we learn that, for those who live after the fall and before the return, our access to such love is precarious, dependent precisely on what Barth deems preoccupation with error.[4] For Kierkegaard, it is our continued detection and prayerful confession of self-delusion, acquisition, and usurpation that repeatedly returns us to the only context wherein love can draw breath, a relation of infinite debt.

Works of Love is not a book regarding love in general. It is aimed at the reader in particular. As his preface makes clear, Kierkegaard intends for each "single individual" to read the text as it applies, ineluctably, to his own existence (WL, 3). Although Kierkegaard consistently returns to this point, we are tempted, in various ways, to prevent such exposure. Reading the text alongside his narrative works – where narrators and characters attempt, and fail, to love – prevents one such evasion. In the pseudonymous texts, Kierkegaard gives life, voice, and volition to the sketches of blunder and vice in *Works of Love*. For example, our temptation to despair of love's possibility becomes, in *Fear and Trembling*, a knight who gives up the princess; the desire to consume, a duplicitous merman. In *Repetition*, Kierkegaard molds a young troubadour from poetic enthusiasm and forges a voyeuristic detective from cynical acquisition. Through the voice and person of Judge William, in *Either/Or* and *Stages on Life's Way*, Kierkegaard plays out the soporific implications of our false confidence in marriage. And, through the entries of the secretive Diarist (also in *Stages*) Kierkegaard breathes anguished life into our fear of disclosure. His characters are not simply allegorical examples or one-dimensional manifestations of mistaken love. Rather they are like us, complicated and decidedly incomplete. The "lesson," and there is one, is intertwined with our perplexity over the impending conclusion to their and our story. Kierkegaard entices the reader to care about and puzzle over them – and over ourselves. The texts provoke us to realize that our task occurs in the cacophonous intersection of unceasing temporal movement, epistemological bafflement, and vice.

What Kierkegaard intimates in these pseudonymous texts, indirectly and variously, is that the reader must repent. Each story involves a different false start along a wrong route, and the reader must seek instead a relationship with that one who occasions our repentance and our redemption. The common factor uniting all of the irreligious texts is the void that brings them into being. Running underneath and between the disorder of the characters' lives is an absence, the correction for which Kierkegaard commends in *Works of Love*:

When we speak this way, we are speaking of the love that sustains all existence, of God's love. If for one moment, one single moment, it were to be absent, everything would be confused. (WL, 301)

Perceiving with Kierkegaard's characters that our hope cannot lie with our righteous, resolute will, with our incremental tallying of guilt and innocence, or with a coincidence of desire and tangibility, the reader is opened to Kierkegaard's summons in *Works of Love*. We are pushed toward the very source of love that truly "sustains all existence."

The pseudonymous works also disconcertingly suggest that this sustenance to which *Works of Love* points is a far cry from what we normally estimate as security. It is not as if the perceptive reader progresses, leap by leap, from pseudonymous to religious text, from secular to spiritual stage, toward a fixedly joyful expression of Christian love. Those who take up Kierkegaard's call to redemption do not become "yodeling saints," to use one character's phrase (SLW, 259). Although Constantin Constantius, the narrator of *Repetition*, surmises from the outside that faith grants the individual an "iron consistency and imperturbability," the love Kierkegaard elucidates in *Works of Love* is perilous (R, 229). Even we who seek the relation offered in Christ find ourselves decidedly inconsistent and perturbed. Kierkegaard's ability to direct our attention toward "the unbridgeable abyss gaping between two barely perceptible nuances" (to return to Lukács) continually troubles us as we seek to love well. What we think to be apt adoration may be predation; supposedly respectful distance may be a manifestation of fear, or even repulsion; we may think we hear God's call to withdraw from engagement, but the voice may instead be our own self-protective desire to retreat. And, even when we are fairly clear about the task at hand, we rarely, if ever, meet it.

This is not a snag in Kierkegaard's system but a deliberate unsettling which reveals the very impossibility of a Christian system of morality. If there is a "key" to the Christian life (even phrasing it this way weakens

Kierkegaard's rhetorical aim), it is that we recognize our drastic need for forgiveness. The Taciturn Friar from *Stages on Life's Way* puts this point sharply: "from the religious point of view, the greatest danger is that one does not discover, that one is not always discovering, that one is in danger" (SLW, 469). We learn, by reading these texts together, that the virtue most closely aligned to love, for Kierkegaard, is humility: a sense of our original, potential, and actual transgression and of our indebtedness to God. It is through such humility that we are able to approximate Christ's command to love the neighbor with whom we live daily. Knowing the treachery of our intimacy and our infinite need for grace, we are better able to distinguish self from other, to forgive the beloved whose faults most tempt us to despair, and to perceive generously the one whose transgressions we have most frequent occasion to note.

In order to note the "danger" to which the Taciturn Friar alludes, we must become aware of our immediate predicament. We resist the work Kierkegaard intends unless the text hits home, literally. Reading the pseudonymous texts with *Works of Love* proscribes the evasive maneuver of philosophical generalization at the expense of specificity. By presenting the question of existence precisely where boy meets girl (and where boy seduces girl, marries girl, or escapes from girl), Kierkegaard poses the question as the reader's and the interpreter's own. In all of the texts we will consider, Kierkegaard labors to bring us back to our own life and love. The "problem" is thus not merely one of "alterity"; the problem is also the other, before you, and what you wish to do to or with her. Although theory is necessary, given that we are faced with the problem of all the possible others, we must also face up to the problem of that single individual with whom we are to sup. We cannot know the "unbridgeable abyss" resulting from this problem unless we resist the temptation to flee from the question. Interpreting Kierkegaard's book on love with "the girl" always in view is, therefore, not only morally but religiously crucial. Unless the reader faces the quandary that is her existence in relation to his own, he may miss his own call to confession and redemption.

One example may serve to suggest this point, which will become clearer as we proceed. The "concept" of "repetition" in *Repetition* cannot do the work Kierkegaard intends if we wrest it free from the text and send it soaring into the atmosphere. To do so allows us to avoid Kierkegaard's narrative poetics, in which the term is inextricably imbedded. The strange tale itself matters for our accurate understanding of any particular "category" therein. Our author places Constantin Constantius's musings on repetition at the opening of a detailed story, in which two men collude to acquire renewal from the other while remaining at a self-protective distance. In a lovely way, *Repetition*, as a text, prohibits its use as an escape from immediacy, that is, your immediacy, and mine. As we shall see, the thief and the poet who seek to define "repetition" do so while attempting to control, and then avoid, the real other who occasions the problem. Kierkegaard knew this elusive move well, and, in his authorship, he refuses himself and his readers such comfort. Using the poet's own means against himself, Kierkegaard renders the romantic attempt to fly from actuality as a form of cowardice. Just as *Repetition*'s narrator is *denied* repetition while sitting safely alone in the theater, voyeuristically observing others enact, scholars who carefully extract and re-narrate the concept deny themselves the point.

As Kierkegaard wages battle against German Romanticism, one of the issues clearly at stake is this loss of a real reader. As our generation attempts to understand, and use, his terms, we must not forget that his texts represent a painstaking attempt to awaken those who interpret, but do not live. Kierkegaard endeavors, over and over again, to create and engage a reader who will not flee, who will not break away from that which is read. Constantin and the young poet live a lie in part because they are unwilling to enter their own play and face the returned gaze of a real other, whose claim implicates them. If we watch the text perform, without finding ourselves entangled in it, we thwart Kierkegaard's aim and implicate ourselves in his accusation. The warning of *Repetition* exists in each of the other texts we will treat. Each pseudonymous work powerfully tethers text to existence, and *Works of Love* definitely fastens command to life; to read the texts together strengthens his aim. The result intended may be more than the reader can bear, but we are, like their author, not allowed escape. In an attempt to be true to this, Kierkegaard's homiletic intent, I will throughout this book remain close to the twists and turns of each text, pulling back from his prose and his poetry only in order to haul each one of us back in.

At the risk of weakening that effort, I should note here in the introduction that Kierkegaard's provocative work on love answers other philosophical endeavors of his and our time. His effort is historically apt, but not merely so. The echoes of the voices he countered reverberate still, and it is thus worth noting his continual reply. First, by converting duty into an inaccessible law of love, Kierkegaard takes our supposedly resolute will, inspects it for discrepancy, and determines us to be irreparably torn from the ought we should both perceive and enact. Second, by narrating the poetic dream of love as it runs aground in actuality, Kierkegaard displays the dissipation of supposedly liberated play. Finally, by thwarting a Christian return to clarity, coherence, and confidence, he attempts to shut down the system. We will briefly take these answers in turn. Although this is just one possible, and merely suggestive, way to describe his influence, it is a plausible one.[5]

Several of the texts we consider undermine, in obvious and more subtle ways, Immanuel Kant's description of duty met. In *Works of Love*, Kierkegaard gives theological reasons for his resistance. By leading the reader repeatedly back to the command to love the neighbor close at hand, Kierkegaard compels us to confess that Kant's confidence is beyond us. The text is to have a dizzying effect on us, as we twirl around and around a law that is infinitely faceted yet immediately required. Kierkegaard redefines the discrepancy between who we presently are and who we are called to become as a problem of knowledge and of will, for we discover ourselves to be both inadvertently and willfully confused. In the fruitful disorientation resulting from *Works of Love*, we further note that, on the rare occasion when we do perceive the command clearly, we find ourselves unwilling to submit. What emerges is our realization that duty, so construed, is met only in the form of a radical other. In this, Kierkegaard's alternative context, our freedom is not derived from our own meeting of duty. We do not participate in the realm of liberty to the extent that we choose well. Rather, we are freed to the extent that we remain in perpetual relation to the one who truly fulfills such a law, the same one by whose work we become beholden to God. A mere postulate of the divine is therefore insufficient.

Kierkegaard's answer to Kantian duty becomes acute in his treatment of Judge William, in both *Either/Or* and in *Stages on Life's Way*. As we discover that William's wife is the postulate that holds together the beautiful, the desired, and the required, we begin to worry that Kant's rendition of the moral life is inadequately troubled. Reading the three texts together (WL, E/O, and SLW), we may detect Kierkegaard's warning to philosophy: if William's wife can plausibly "fill in" for God, as the lovely *deus ex machina* in this treatise on morality, then William's ethical question is inadequately complex. By reading William's treatises with *Works of Love*, we may note the way that Kierkegaard uses Kant's own prohibition of mere use to thwart the reliability of duty itself. Although it is crucial to note that William is Kierkegaard's own literary construction (and as such is an overly convenient foil), the misunderstanding to which Kierkegaard alludes in these texts is not. William presents a culturally malleable Kantianism that haunts his and our time. By gravely underestimating God's command, we not only use others with ignorance and impunity; we also eschew the requisite crisis and avoid an encounter with God.

If staid marriage does not resolve the predicament of existence, neither does poetic license. Kierkegaard forecloses this philosophical turn as he depicts the illusion of poetic idealism. In *Works of Love*, he exposes as frivolous the attempt to decorate the fissures remaining in Kant's work with perpetual, freed enjoyment. George Pattison persuasively argues that Kierkegaard seeks, in the Seducer's Diary of *Either/Or*, to defy the answer Friedrich Schlegel gives in his own life and in his Romantic text, *Lucinde*.[6] It is not merely his sense of decorum that leads Kierkegaard to insist that an adulterous affair with the daughter of one's friend is not the answer to the question torn open by the epistemological crises of his time. He contends that such an answer is self-delusive, the enjoyment merely temporary. As Pattison explains, in *Lucinde* Schlegel attempts to point a new way to "the primal garden," a way paved "simply [with] the freedom of sensuous innocence and delight," and Kierkegaard answers by naming the entire effort a ruse.[7] Kierkegaard's most extreme example of this problem is the young poet of *Repetition*, through whom Kierkegaard narrates the incapacity of such Romanticism to follow through. But in each of the pseudonymous texts we treat, we may perceive this problem with the supposed freedom of artistic endeavor: it cannot endure the test of time, on the lover or the beloved. Merely human creativity is incapable of sustaining an encounter with an actual other.

In answering poetic enervation, Kierkegaard does not lead us back, resolvedly, to William's resilient marriage.[8] We are left in the midst of the crises, finally incommensurate with both Kantian duty and Romantic play and incapable of either a truly "good" marriage or a truly satisfying tryst. Regardless of our choice, the margins remain unjustified, as do we. In the midst of actuality, we find ourselves perpetually indecipherable. The character "A" in *Either/Or* Part 1 gestures toward the matter by complaining:

When I consider its various epochs, my life is like the word *Schnur* in the dictionary, which first of all means a string, and second a daughter-in-law. All that is lacking is that in the third place the word *Schnur* means a camel, in the fourth a wisk broom. (E/O, 1:36)

In the texts we will consider, Kierkegaard suggests that the way into truth requires such an acknowledgment. To use Schlegel again as an example, he was right to recognize that a settled existence in bourgeois Germany was not the beautiful solution to life's illegible problem. But, Kierkegaard contends, he was wrong to think that his art (and play) could create a viable alternative. The self remains undefined, but not for the sake of the freedom Schlegel supposed. An individual is left with an

infinite multiplicity of possibilities, all of them incapable of summing up
his existence. What is required is a particular relation, a relation much
less comfortable than William's duty and considerably less enjoyable
than *Lucinde*.

For Kierkegaard, this vulnerable exposure must perdure. Winding
through all of the texts we read here is Kierkegaard's intricate summons
to bare vulnerability. And in this summons lies Kierkegaard's third relevant answer to philosophy. Hegel's systematic method sublates the very
fractures into which we must fall if we are to be saved. Both the task of
veritable love and the only route into that love require a humble receptivity that Hegel undermines, as do his presently confident, Christian,
interlocutors. Only by resisting the temptation to cloak ourselves in the
collective confidence of Christendom do we find ourselves exposed, and
thus capable of reception. Kierkegaard's fractured, irreligious, pseudonymous books are thus indispensable, for with them he pulls us into the
"strange language" of indebtedness described in *Works of Love*. Such is
the only language that approximates loving speech. Christians cannot
leave the confused, pseudonymous works behind as we attempt *Works
of Love*, because we learn the tongue of the latter text only inasmuch as
we know ourselves dumb, defined by a relation of perpetual need and
radical debt.[9] This does not mean that Kierkegaard is unconcerned with
truth, but that coherence becomes, through his texts, paradoxically defined by rupture. Many of the irreligious characters in the pseudonymous
texts stumble into an accidental realization of their own absurdity, but
Kierkegaard's Christian answer is not a hearty return to a crowded table.

These aspects of relationality and vulnerability increasingly emerge
as "the girl" reads the text. In deference to full disclosure, I must now
break the frame, so to speak, and acknowledge an alliance of sorts. My
interpretation of Kierkegaard's work is informed and emboldened by the
reading of other women who have found in the texts what Kierkegaard
continually endeavored to convey: that is, the girl exists. Feminism is a
conversation to which Kierkegaard was not privy but with which I am
involved, and I will note this debt explicitly in various places throughout
the chapters. But, to put the point more generally, female readers increasingly correct a tendency that Pia Søltoft, in her own text, perfectly
phrases thus:

Everything in the authorship purportedly consists in choosing, winning, finding, becoming or taking control of oneself. This book calls into question this
monomaniacal, monological interpretation of Kierkegaard.[10]

Søltoft herself reads Kierkegaard as describing and evoking a "svimmel-hedens etik," an "ethic of dizziness" that is necessarily off-kilter from the supposedly victorious, individual, self.[11] I also deem it not incidental that the American scholar most presently engaged with *Works of Love* is also in league with "the girl." M. Jamie Ferreira's book-length treatment of the text arrived as I was completing the final editing of my own, so it will be up to subsequent interpreters to negotiate our disagreements.[12] While Ferreira and I both find in Kierkegaard's work a call to relationality, she and Sylvia Walsh both concentrate on the hopeful possibilities therein. This book contrasts rather sharply, as I strive to preserve Kierkegaard's narration of the obscurity and danger inherent to proximity. The differ-ence is one of emphasis, although our emphases strongly diverge.

Feminism can, of course, become a sorority no more truthful than the "fraternity" of "*In Vino Veritas*" (to which we turn in Chapter 5). The epistemological privilege afforded due to our "otherness" goes only so far in interpreting Kierkegaard's textual aims. Here some feminists will believe that I betray the alliance by suggesting that Christ is the only an-swer to the conundrums posed by Kierkegaard's characters. Kierkegaard blocks women from the same options denied the men of these wayward tales. Even a life of wily seduction is increasingly accessible to women who would choose it, and we are ever more capable of living on William's side of his asymmetrical marriage. We cannot define ourselves, find our way out of confusion, or begin to love unless wed to the one who occasions our judgment and our salvation. While to do so may mitigate the universality of his indictment and call, I often employ singular male pronouns when referring to the reader or lover. I do this on the assumption that most men are less likely than most women to include themselves in a statement with a pronoun of the opposite gender, particularly when that statement is a call to humility. I will most often use first person plural pronouns, given that we are all at issue. By my reading, we must each comprehend not only abstractly but also with ardent hope that our worth is, as Gene Outka words it, "God-derived" and "conferred" through Christ.[13]

As we become involved in the misguided lives of Kierkegaard's char-acters and are pulled into his allegations against human love, we are to surmise that the possibility for true love depends on a factor beyond our own present capacities. This message runs as a refrain through each of Kierkegaard's books, and to this message we will repeatedly return. We begin in the first chapter by placing *Works of Love* within the critique in Kierkegaard's journals of Christian assumptions regarding the baptism of an entire culture in general and of marriage in particular. By reading through the rhetorical structure of the text, we may interpret *Works of Love* as Kierkegaard's attempt to retrieve the *theological* (or convicting) use of the law, which his contemporaries overlooked in favor of bolstering assurance. *Fear and Trembling* may be read as his more poetic effort to the same end, and in the second chapter I intertwine it with *Works of Love* in order to make this common aim more obvious. Through de Silentio's complex and perplexing text, the reader is opened to the possibilities of self-delusion and error, and, already here in this early pseudonymous text, Kierkegaard hints that new life involves our humble receptivity to God's grace. In *Repetition*, the text for the third chapter, Kierkegaard gives voice to the scrupulous "third party" against which he warns in *Works of Love*. Through this "fruitless" text, the reader is to be provoked to consult a "confidant" other than the cynical Constantin. By this point, the reader will be tempted to rest in Judge William's stalwart account of Christian marriage, but, in the fourth chapter, I argue that Kierkegaard means in *Either/Or* to preclude this as an alternative to the earnest repentance that eludes the previous characters – a repentance that is a key to faithful engagement in *Works of Love*. With *Stages on Life's Way* we have an opportunity to sit once more with several of the previous characters, to experience again Constantin's malevolence and the subtle threat William poses to Christian love. If Judge William's is not the way, then we may find ourselves, like the Diarist, despairing altogether of human engagement. In this, the fifth chapter, we contrast the Diarist's "high-flying" escape with the "humble and difficult flight along the ground" to which we are called (WL, 161, 84). It is in the final chapter that we look back upon each of the wrong routes tried and proven futile and describe for a final time Kierkegaard's effort to push us toward Christ.

It is up to my own dear reader to discern whether Kierkegaard's depiction of love was his own evasion – whether, due to fear of intimacy, he increased the requirement beyond his own and our possible reach. The evidence of his failed attempt to love not only seeps in around the edges, but overtly structures the questions he continually asks. Each reader must discern whether he may move beyond Kierkegaard's quandaries, into a realm to which their author had not access. For those who are currently assured, his texts and my book will fail to satisfy. But for those of us who continually find ourselves incapable of securely grasping belief, much less, as de Silentio puts it, "going further than faith," we now return, and return, to the task and to the text.

CHAPTER I

The call to confession in Kierkegaard's Works of Love

Christianity is not infrequently presented in a certain sentimental, almost soft, form of love. It is all love and love; spare yourself and your flesh and blood; have good days or happy days without self-concern, because God is Love and Love – nothing at all about rigorousness must be heard; it must all be the free language and nature of love. Understood in this way, however, God's love easily becomes a fabulous and childish conception, the figure of Christ too mild and sickly-sweet for it to be true that he was and is an offense . . . (WL, 376)

From Kierkegaard's conclusion to *Works of Love*, this passage reveals a salient feature of the text as a whole. Throughout the book Kierkegaard pushes the reader, in direct and subtle ways, to perceive Christianity as that which should cause precisely the "self-concern" that a falsely "soft" presentation of love seeks to palliate. He intends the text to evoke earnest self-examination. The sections incrementally build toward a confession of sin, and one reader at whom he aims his rhetorical power is the previously blithe Christian. In contrast to the "soft form of love," Kierkegaard's text is like a "strength-testing machine," a strenuous device whereby one discovers one's utter weakness (WL, 245). His complex prescriptions for and descriptions of faithful love place us before love's exacting test, revealing our inability to meet what faith requires.[1] With his unremittingly interrogative tone, Kierkegaard exposes talk about "the free language and nature of love" as a delusive distortion of the incriminating "rigorousness" that God's command entails. By homiletically explicating the gospels and epistles, he offers a scriptural antidote to the currently "sweet" description of the Christian life; discipleship becomes something other than a succession of merely "happy days" (WL, 376). He thus employs the very sources that Christians claim as their own, in order to expose their failure to meet the law therein. Faithful readers are to emerge from the text newly convicted and prepared humbly to request the radical grace requisite for any work of love.

A crucial emphasis in *Works of Love*, an emphasis on which Kierkegaard's constructive account of human intimacy depends, is one of humility before the law of love. The response that Kierkegaard intends is our recognition of epistemological and performative failure, a recognition that may enable our reception of grace and our humble approximation of God's command. This use of the law, what theologians call the theological or convicting use, evokes self-inspection, leading the individual toward confession. For Kierkegaard, this way of repentance must be the way of Christian love for the neighbor. In order for us truly to love our neighbor, we must first, and repeatedly, discover the ways we fall short of God's command. Only thus may we recognize the enormity of our debt before God and develop a profound sense of gratitude to God as our only help. This latter step of gratitude cannot come prior to the first step of repentance, nor can it be the terminus of the Christian life here on earth. God's extravagant offer of redemptive love for us is the underlying theme without which the reader would be thrown into despair, but Kierkegaard's understanding of our progress in grace involves our ever-deepening sense, before the law, of our infinite debt and dependence upon grace.

Because the faithful engagements to which Kierkegaard calls us in *Works of Love* depend upon this persistently self-conscious humility, a productive reading of the text must focus on the law that is to elicit our awareness of the fall and our falling. As Mark C. Taylor has put it, "For Kierkegaard as for Luther, in faith, the task is *semper incipere*."[2] The beginning, middle, and end of the Christian life involve a returning recognition of sin, debt, gratitude, sin, debt, and always a renewal of gratitude. The love to which God calls us requires our acknowledgment that, as lovers tested by God's law, we are always infinitely behind.

Kierkegaard's description of love's task is outrageously strenuous and intentionally discouraging. Some scholars have read his provocations and subsequently sought to soften the blow, so to speak. I wish to retrieve his intensity. Mine is a different reading of Kierkegaard's purpose in *Works of Love* than those which find there the law as a guide for discipleship (what some theologians call a third use of the law), readings which see in the text an account of Christian virtue, and interpretations which find continuity between our present desires and our graced love.[3] To state bluntly what will become clearer (and more interesting) in subsequent chapters: a didactic (or third) use of the law weakens the link Kierkegaard forges

between love and our sense of vast indebtedness. Moreover, to read love
as the cultivation of Christian virtue implies productive effort, stability,
and clarity, whereas Kierkegaard narrates love as requiring our being
thrown consistently off balance, in spite of ourselves. For Kierkegaard,
love depends on our abidingly repentant sense of potential and actual
transgression. Finally, Kierkegaard's stark contrast between merely human love and the love commanded, and his subsequent contrast between
our warped or feeble loves and Christ's fulfillment of the law are powerfully rhetorical, but they are not mere rhetoric. Kierkegaard intends a
full conversion from the way of sin and death, and he believes that such
a conversion requires a drastic change of perspective. To mitigate either
contrast is potentially to miss and undermine the meaning of his text.

Paul Müller and Bruce Kirmmse both find in *Works of Love* the freeing
gospel alongside the indicting law, and Müller in particular concentrates
on the warrant in the text for a love that is a fulfillment of "man's original
possibility." He writes that Kierkegaard "does not really discuss human
love vs. Christian love, which really would be unnatural in the deepest sense" but, rather, depicts love as "show[ing] forth the genuinely
human."[4] But, as David Gouwens notes, "the rhetorical force of *Works
of Love* is crucial for correctly understanding it; the dialectic of opposi-
tion is indeed offensive and it would be a serious misreading to make
this text inoffensive."[5] We are to be shocked and alienated by the text.
Kierkegaard intends to thwart our sense of progress and our presump-
tion of clarity with the radical discontinuity between our love and the love
commanded. *Works of Love* may be aptly read as Kierkegaard's sustained
attempt to reinsert the indicting use of the law into a conversation over-
confident in human effort and blithely reliant on God's corporate dispen-
sation of grace. We may interpret *Works of Love* as Kierkegaard's attempt
again to precipitate the awareness of sin indispensable for our repentance
and to evoke the confession necessary for our reception of grace.

Humility is crucial not only for the soldier, prostitute, spy, or hangman,
but also for the previously confident and secure husband. *Works of Love*
brings the corrective of law specifically to bear on those who find false
security in the performance of a familial role. Insisting that we cannot
know or perform our "Christian duty" nearly as well or as wisely as we
often assume, Kierkegaard brings the supposedly Christian home under
close scrutiny. The text prevents our hiding either from the rigorous
demands of God's law or from the confusion necessarily occasioned
by God's command to love. By exposing the occasions for ignorance
and error within intimate relations, Kierkegaard wishes to correct our

misuse of Luther's idea of vocation wherein the married state itself is cause for confidence.[6] In Kierkegaard's estimation, Luther's advocation of marriage is a historically particular statement against the secluded security of the monastery, a statement that has become an excuse to deem the home the site for blessed assurance. Kierkegaard well perceives the danger of this tendency to underestimate the sins inherent to desire, proximity, and familial comfort, and his drastic contrast between our default mode of loving (*Elskov*) and Christian love (*Kjerlighed*) is to effect in the reader an awareness of the considerable gap between, on the one hand, the affections normally internal to intimacy, and, on the other, the radical selflessness of *agape*.[7] Within *Works of Love*, Kierkegaard contests a generalized baptism of neighborhoods, marriages, and those who live within them in an effort to force us to reevaluate our own engagements. His depiction of humble, even wary, intimacy requires that we each find ourselves indicted by God's law, even while trusting in the grace that transforms guilt into hopeful repentance. In *Works of Love*, Kierkegaard thus employs Luther's theological use of the law in order to correct our self-serving misreading of Luther's praise of Christian marriage. The law is theologically applied to those relationships wherein we boldly suppose ourselves to be justifiably free.[8]

In this chapter, we will work through key entries in Kierkegaard's journals, turn to a structural analysis of *Works of Love*, focus on a particularly Lutheran section in the book, and then consider Kierkegaard's application of the law to familial and romantic intimacy. When focusing on Kierkegaard's theological use of the law, we should begin by considering his journals, because he most explicitly argues against the easy comfort of misinterpreted Lutheran grace in such entries. The journal entries help to provide a broader, theological backdrop as we interpret *Works of Love*. After attending to the journals, we will turn to *Works of Love* itself, reading the structure of both the first and second series as it builds toward our indictment and a summons for the reader to stand convicted and humbled before the command to love. Kierkegaard brings his charge against human love continually back to each of us, rhetorically prompting us to recognize our inability to reach or grasp the faithful state that we think ourselves already to have achieved. In order further to elucidate this Lutheran theme in *Works of Love*, we will then concentrate on a pivotal section, "Our Duty to Remain in Love's Debt," and its relation to Luther's depiction of graced love in *The Freedom of a Christian*. Our sense of indebtedness is crucial for Christian intimacy, and we will finally consider Kierkegaard's attempt to bring this Jesus, to whom we are indebted, into the previously comfortable Danish parlor. Kierkegaard's is a "contemporizing" of Jesus's work and parables, forcing the reader to reckon with the law's import for our personal lives.

There are, quite admittedly, other ways to read Kierkegaard's text on love than as a text to prompt humility. As many have observed, Kierkegaard's writing style is often self-superior in the extreme. If Kierkegaard intends for the discerning reader to take up this tone, then humility should not be the result. Particularly in his "edifying" discourses, Kierkegaard at times writes down from the pinnacle of philosophical wisdom, expressing disgust for the self-deluded reader and, perhaps, inspiring the insightful reader to climb up beside him. He further seems at points to include himself among the self-sacrificial saints, seeing himself as the one, persecuted truth-teller in an otherwise iniquitous world. Indeed, while I believe that Kierkegaard's intent in *Works of Love* is to humble the individual – to prepare us for the necessary reception of grace – there are several passages even in this lovely book wherein Kierkegaard seems to think himself above the fray he describes. Although it is tempting to ignore these (at times obnoxious) passages, it is important, before closing the first chapter, that we deal with this undercurrent of pride. These passages remind us that our beloved author knows well the necessity of love's law in part because he is himself sorely tempted toward self-defense and self-exaltation. Kierkegaard knows the contoured map of our unfaithful resistance to grace because he himself crawls along that path, even while writing a text on love. I am, as a much less faithful author than Kierkegaard, at least as susceptible to the same confusion. This first chapter thus ends by preparing us all for the next four chapters wherein we dwell humbly, in excruciating detail, on the ways we each evade God's command, resist confession, and eschew divine grace.

A word of encouragement to my own reader: we quickly cover a great deal of terrain here in Chapter 1, and the description is necessarily compressed. Those who know *Works of Love* well should rightly complain that there is much more there than we cover in this comparably blunt reading of Kierkegaard's textual aims. Those who do not know the book well *should* suspect that I give here merely a hasty run through an exquisite, lengthy text. To read through *Works of Love* in such a hurry is, inevitably, frustrating. This text, Kierkegaard's own work of love, requires our continual rereading, and the remainder of my book is an attempt to prompt exactly that. We will return again and again to this text that we only introduce here. The intricate details in Kierkegaard's depictions of sin and of love in *Works of Love* come alive as we read the book carefully alongside his other, pseudonymous, narratives. We begin that vivid, inter-textual interpretation in Chapter 2.

What Luther says is excellent, the one thing needful and the sole explanation – that this whole doctrine (of the Atonement and in the main all Christianity) must be traced back to the struggle of the anguished conscience. Remove the anguished conscience, and you may as well lock the churches and convert them into dance halls. (JP III 2461 [Pap. VII.1 A 192 n.d., 1846])

The relation of Kierkegaard's work to Luther's, in particular Kierkegaard's use of the law, is the subject of some debate.[9] David Gouwens reads Kierkegaard as improving Luther's focus on Christ's redemptive work by reintroducing Christ as a "prototype." In this reading, Christ "re-enters as a model for discipleship," toward "the end of imitation," subsequent to law and the confession of sin.[10] Gouwens perceives three related descriptions of Christ's work in Kierkegaard's writings: Christ acts as a "crushing" prototype, as a redeemer, and as a model for discipleship. Although Gouwens specifies that these three roles do not exist in "a completed dialectic," and that they exist perpetually in a "continuing three-stage" cycle, Kierkegaard's emphasis, by his reading, falls on Christ's role as a model for our emulation.[11] The difference between my reading and Gouwens's is perhaps a matter of accent, but the accent makes a difference. By my interpretation, if there is a "third" use of Christ as "model" in Kierkegaard's writing, this function depends precisely on Christ's ability to reduce us to repentance, and thus on the second, or convicting, use of the law. To move beyond the second use of the law to a new and distinguishable third use, is, in effect, to imperil the relation whereby we come to emulate Christ. (The difference is subtle, and it may be the slight variation between a Calvinist and Lutheran reading of the text.) By my reading, even Kierkegaard's frustration with Lutheranism illumines the extent to which he relies upon Luther's theological use of the law.

We may responsibly read in the journals and in *Works of Love* Kierkegaard's characteristically Lutheran reluctance to speak of *subsequent* imitation (even as part of an incomplete, cyclical dialectic) due to our perpetual need for and pathological resistance to repentance. The progress Kierkegaard most acutely describes is not a progress toward our more perfect imitation of Christ, but rather a progress toward our more perfect awareness of our imperfection. By this description, we best partake of Christ's modeling in our own humiliation, as we urgently accept Christ's work for us.[12] Because we are constantly tempted to separate our imitation and our humility, Kierkegaard, like Luther, binds the two together in Christ's person.[13] Although Kierkegaard's frustration with Luther himself becomes intense toward the end of his life, he most often views the problem facing his contemporaries as precisely the loss of an anguish Luther presupposed – as their too ready reliance on an empty construal of grace without recognizing their utter need. As we shall see, even while Kierkegaard wages battle with Lutheran*ism* in his journals, he has in mind a very Lutheran critique.

By Kierkegaard's estimation, those who become receptive to grace do so only after being prepared by revelation both to strive and to recognize the vanity of their efforts. In summarizing Luther's gloss on "the great draft of fish," Kierkegaard commends Luther's interpretation: "the apostles [caught the fish] not because of their toil and labor – no, on the contrary they [caught the fish] only after they had labored and toiled in vain" (JP III 2505 [Pap. x.2 A 162 n.d., 1849]). The "enormous danger" that Luther does not foresee is that his emphasis on grace "relates to and presupposes a first" condition with which Christians will be more than happy to dispense (JP III 2521 [Pap. x.3 A 217 n.d.,1850]). This presupposition, on which grace depends, is that we must struggle to fish in rough waters and come up empty after repeated attempts; Luther's antidote to our quest for merit assumes that one has heard the rigorous rule of God and that one is already seeking earnestly to discern and to meet God's demands. Gouwens reads this tendency in the journals as consistent with Kierkegaard's general contention that "becoming nothing before God" involves a "learned dependence arising specifically from striving."[14] Kierkegaard heartily agrees with Luther that grace requires the revelation of law to make the Christian yearn for righteousness, because "the anguished conscience is not a natural consequence like being hungry" (JP III 2461 [Pap. VII.1 A 192 n.d., 1846]). Our receptivity to grace is contingent upon our acknowledgment of our own ignorance and iniquity. A Christian who wishes to leap over the task of toiling in vain is like a mere "bricklayer's apprentice" who heartily eschews the hard work of learning, conveniently insisting that "scholarly achievement" ultimately amounts to nothing (JP III 2542 [Pap. x.4 A 451 n.d., 1852]). Seeking to meet God's command is a necessary step toward receiving the grace that Luther so rightly underscored.

Up until the very end of his life, Kierkegaard most often sees himself as retrieving the facet of Luther's theology that his own diluted Lutheran culture had distorted. When Kierkegaard begins to read Luther in earnest, he writes about his "relief" upon discovering in Luther someone who "can really stay by a person and preach him farther out instead of backwards" as do "contemporary pastors" who soothingly advise one to "take it easy" (JP III 2464 [Pap. VIII.1 A 541 n.d., 1848]). The time elapsed between Luther and the Lutheranism Kierkegaard observes in Denmark has led, in his estimation, to the church's simple-minded attempt to encourage those who, due to the dulling of the law's impact, no longer need the words of assurance. The obligatory mantra "Your sins are forgiven" is spread "just as a night watchman in a chain-series shouts out a watchword to the next one" without thought or notice, automatically and without interest (JP III 2466 [Pap. VIII.1 A 664 n.d., 1848]). The relation between Luther's early followers and Kierkegaard's own contemporaries is similar to the first grateful recipients of a canceled debt compared to those who, after many generations, have conveniently forgotten the gift. In this aptly extended metaphor, Kierkegaard tells a story of a radically generous landowner and indebted renters who "at the beginning knew very much had been canceled" but, through time, came to understand it "very sketchily." Eventually "in their lethargy people knew that [the debt] had been canceled, but how much nobody knew and nobody cared about it" (JP II 1499 [Pap. XI.2 A 286 n.d., 1853–4]). By Kierkegaard's time, Christians have forgotten the immense debt that their sins have incurred and continue to incur. The "faithful" instead take grace for granted, as if redemption is a trinket we receive "gratis, the way we get a pretty box or a decorated sack when we make a purchase" (JP II 1502 [Pap. XI.2 A 226 n.d., 1854]).

The one in whose person our sin is revealed and our debt cancelled – whose example shows our feeble attempts to be fruitless and whose sacrifice should render us speechlessly grateful – becomes, in this secure and comfortable context, a bland companion. Kierkegaard insists that "only sin can drive a human being to Christ," and thus Christ is "taken in vain" when presented as "a heavenly friend," as "the satisfaction of profound longings" or merely as presenting "gentle lessons about truth" (JP I 334 [Pap. X.1 A 279 n.d., 1849]). Because Christ's work as redeemer has been severed from the law that reveals the extent to which we were indigent, "the gospel and grace are taken in vain" (JP II 1484 [Pap. X.4 A 230 n.d., 1851]). Without my recognition of "the magnitude of my sins," I am easily persuaded to imagine away "the infinite distance between myself and God," thus falling for numbing accounts of God's work in Christ (JP II 1471 [Pap. X.2 A 189 n.d., 1849]).

Kierkegaard compels the reader to appreciate the vast distance between the created and fallen state by collapsing the temporal distance between Christ and the reader. Each Christian must be faced with the "contemporaneity" of Christ in order to accept the "tension of actuality" in the present life of faith (JP III 2500 [Pap. x.1 A 595 n.d., 1849]). Here Kierkegaard sees himself as going back to what has been lost since Luther, to retrieve Christ as first revealing the true rigor of the law (JP II 1484 [Pap. x.4 A 230, n.d., 1851]). He thus reveals the discrepancy between Christ and the would-be Christian. Insisting that one must consider Christ's words and deeds as well as the redemption he affords, Kierkegaard follows Luther in linking the Sermon on the Mount to the law on Mount Sinai (JP I 297 [Pap. II. A 473 July 7, 1839]).[15] By seeking to make Christ a new Moses, Kierkegaard, like Luther, homiletically joins our confession of sin and a faithful confession of Christ. We who would accept redemption must first see Christ, face to face, as the one who exposes the futility of our own attempts to meet God's law.

In making this move away from Christ as "gift" and toward Christ as the "pattern" whose life exposes ours as sinful, Kierkegaard understands himself to be making a friendly but necessary amendment to Luther's work.[16] In a long journal entry, Kierkegaard works out his relationship to Luther on this matter (JP III 2503 [Pap. x.2 A 30 n.d., 1849]). Kierkegaard considers Luther to have been "confronted by the exaggerated misuse of Christ as pattern" and thus to have shifted decisively the focus to Christ as gift. So many years after Luther, Christ's work as standard or "pattern" has been totally eclipsed by the easy acceptance of grace. What is needed presently is not a simple retrieval of the same use of Christ as pattern that prevailed in the Middle Ages and against which Luther reacted. Rather, "Christ as pattern ought to jack up the price so enormously that the prototype itself teaches men to resort to grace" (JP III 2503 [Pap. x.2 A 30 n.d., 1849]). What those against whom Luther fought did not grasp was our complete inability to meet Christ's demands. The example that Christ gives is to "humble us, teach us how infinitely far away we are to resembling the ideal" (JP I 334 [Pap. x.1 A 279 n.d., 1849]). This humility should not force the reader to give up the pattern, but instead elicit a dialectic between Christ as crushing "requirement" and Christ as "grace and compassion" (JP I 349 [Pap. x.2 A 170 n.d., 1849]). The Christian life, for Kierkegaard, remains caught in the tension between these two.

The law as revealed in Christ is not to become a guide subsequent to repentance. Rather, the law of Christ persistently confronts us, driving us to turn humbly to God's grace with each step. This theological or convicting use of the law is precisely the means by which a Christian is prepared perpetually to repent, to receive grace and, haltingly, approximate perfection:

> Either one believes he is achieving perfection by his striving, or one understands even more deeply how he stands in need of grace . . . If I were to define Christian perfection, I should not say that it is a perfection of striving but specifically that it is the deep recognition of the imperfection of one's striving, and precisely because of this a deeper and deeper consciousness of the need for grace, not grace for this or that, but the infinite need infinitely for grace . . . (JP II 1482 [Pap. x.3 A 784 n.d., 1851])

Take away the law, and Christianity forfeits the means by which we are prepared to receive the grace on which we depend. In this entry, Kierkegaard underscores a central theme in *Works of Love*. The law forms the link between our striving, our humiliation, our need for grace, and our love, and it is a key to Kierkegaard's homiletic method in *Works of Love*. Our recognition of our "infinite need infinitely for grace" is a necessarily recurrent step for those of us who hope even to approximate God's command.

Instead of struggling, confessing, and struggling again, Kierkegaard's Lutheran contemporaries have taken their redemption through Christ to be a cultural fact, as if icing on the happy cake they now eat. Into this scene, Kierkegaard's interjects Christ as "the sign of offense" in order that "everyone can be offended or believe" (JP 1 321 [Pap. IX A 57 n.d., 1848]). Remove the call to genuine obedience in the scriptures, Kierkegaard insists, and Luther's emphasis on grace alone becomes "permission to hang on to a thoroughgoing secularity, to arrange our lives so securely that it is a pleasure" (JP III 2521 [Pap. x.3 A 217 n.d., 1850]). In this sentence Kierkegaard characteristically indicts secularity (which becomes almost synonymous with bourgeois Denmark), security, and pleasure. The risen Christ who once testified to God's victory over evil becomes, by Kierkegaard's time, a mascot for the victory of commerce and polite society. In protest, Kierkegaard presents the offensive challenge that Christ poses to their collective and individual lives. Here Kierkegaard explicitly corrects a dangerous misuse of Luther's work on station and vocation, using a form of Luther's own critique of Christian triumphalism. Positing Christ as an offense, as the one whose ostracism, torture, and blood evince the infinite depth of our sin, Kierkegaard recasts the setting of Christian grace, graphically distinguishing faith from our mere compliance with society's orderly quest for comfort. Removing the call to suffering obedience, as "the dialectical element," from Luther's faith, Christianity becomes "a cloak for sheer paganism and epicureanism" (JP III 2484 [Pap. x.1 A 213 n.d., 1849]). Luther "marked out a simple secularity" in contrast to the "deluded inflation of asceticism," and Kierkegaard's contemporaries have written this corrective large, perceiving in Luther's theology an affirmation of the orderly, arranged pursuit of pleasure (JP III 2513 [Pap. x.2 A 558 n.d., 1850]). Kierkegaard disabuses us of the notion that Christ's suffering on the cross and our supposedly innocent enjoyment of life are compatible.

Kierkegaard's entries regarding intimate love and its relation to Christ's example are similarly pungent. The cross requires a critique of the assumption that marriage (and the self-satisfied, commercial domesticity that the institution of marriage supports) is the highest form of Christianity. Throughout his tirade against secularism, Kierkegaard complains that marriage itself has become the pinnacle of the Christian life, as "the highest and truest earnestness," (JP III 2600 [Pap. IX A 237 n.d., 1848]). From his perspective, Luther warned appropriately against undue asceticism, but did not foresee that others would self-servingly interpret marriage itself as the apex of Christian living. Luther aptly advised "against running to the monastery," but his followers came to see our running to the altar as a suitable substitute (JP III 2511 [Pap. x.2 A 364 n.d., 1850]). The result is that "getting married and not giving to the poor came to be regarded as a great step forward in religious life" (JP III 2522 [Pap. x.3 A 218 n.d.]). What was for an earnestly ascetic monk the right answer to God's call cannot be fashioned into an excuse to forgo the life of a "pilgrim here in this world" (JP III 2511 [Pap. x.2 A 364 n.d., 1850]).[17]

In these passages against easy domesticity Kierkegaard becomes most critical of Lutheranism. He sarcastically surmises that Protestantism took hold so well in part because "the Pope had become too expensive" and people found in Luther's words an excuse for not attempting the task of discipleship at all, for procuring "salvation a little cheaper, absolutely free" (JP III 2539 [Pap. x.4 A 371 n.d., 1851]). Kierkegaard further suggests that the "spiritual cost" of recognizing continually the debt paid by Christ on the cross is thus replaced by a ready acceptance that what fits best within polite society passes for faith.[18] Responding to this heresy, he retrieves Luther's original intent to make "the life of the spirit infinitely more strenuous than it was before" (JP III 2514 [Pap. x.2 A 559 n.d., 1850]). As an antidote to this sentimental distortion of Christianity,

Kierkegaard gives the bitter word of God's judgment on the most "lovely" of human endeavors.

We may read Kierkegaard's critique of secularism as intensifying precisely Luther's emphasis on grace, refusing Luther's followers any safe haven wherein we may remain assured of our worth, merits, and motives. By bringing Christ's pattern to bear on intimate relations, Kierkegaard startles his readers into an earnest recognition that, within our engagements, we require Christ's costly redemption and God's grace. Against an expedient reading of Luther's "swing away from the monastery," Kierkegaard provokes us to acknowledge that, "on closer inspection," there remain "huge conflicts" between "social morality" and true faith (JP III 2541 [Pap. x.4 A 394 n.d., 1851]). Luther did not mean for grace to be taken as something "settled and completed once and for all," and we who follow him unjustifiably use his theology to baptize an entire culture. What is called for is a continual reminder that "grace is needed in relation to grace" (JP II 1472 [Pap. x.2 A 198 n.d., 1849]).

Kierkegaard interprets his own writing as an effort to "contribute to our coming into a relationship with truth by means of confessions" (JP III 2543 [Pap. XI.2 A 301 n.d., 1853–54]). He intentionally provokes us to confess our sin, to acknowledge before ourselves and our God the manifold ways that we do not meet God's law. And he forces us to realize that the extreme debt paid is required not only for the egregious sins of the wicked. We are to confess that Christ must cover our private and seemingly minute transgressions. Kierkegaard prompts these "admissions about ourselves" in order to correct a "deficiency in fear and trembling," to awaken us to the ways we sin daily (JP III 2545 [Pap. XI.2 A 304 n.d., 1853–54], JP III 2544 [Pap. XI.2 A 303 n.d., 1853–54]). In a "sinful world" that "really does not suffer from an anguished conscience," the need is not for a renewed emphasis on grace, but on that use of the law that "arouses restlessness" and compels us to seek grace anew (JP III 2550 [Pap. XI. 1 A 193 n.d., 1854]). We thus turn to Kierkegaard's most sustained textual effort to arouse the individual reader, to prompt in each one of us a confession of sin, and of faith.

THE LAW OF LOVE

And now since people are so eager to be something, it is no wonder that however much they talk about God's love they are reluctant to become really involved with him, because his requirement and his criterion reduce them to nothing. (WL, 102)

Those who glibly speak of God's love and the Christian task, refusing to involve themselves with the weight of that calling, are like the second brother in Christ's parable from Matthew 21:28. In this story, a father commands two sons to go to work in his vineyard. The first son refuses to go, but then changes his mind. The second son agrees to go, but then does not. The supposedly religious people to whom Jesus told the story were to discover themselves in the second son's error. Kierkegaard's readers are similarly to identify with the brother who, in saying yes to his father's request, inadvertently trapped himself within a context of judgment. In his lengthy exposition of this parable, Kierkegaard explains that the son who eagerly promises but does not recognize the import of his promise is "facing the direction of the good," but "is moving backward further away from it," due to his continual inattention to the import of his promise (WL, 94). The better way is actually that of the first son, who interprets soberly the stark demands of an affirmative answer and thus says no: "The yes of the promise is sleep-inducing, but the no, spoken and therefore audible to oneself is awakening, and repentance is usually not far away" (WL, 93). We may read *Works of Love* as Kierkegaard's intricate attempt to convince us that we have indeed replied to God's commandment with a vacuous affirmative. In this text, he seeks to elicit our conscious, awake "no," so that repentance might follow. It is Kierkegaard's hope that love's law will appropriately reduce us to "nothing," but not so that the author and God can gloat. The brother who soberly denied his ability to meet his father's will is to become for us a guide in our attempts to love faithfully. By confessing the many ways that we repeatedly misinterpret and turn away from God's law, we become prepared to repent and receive grace, and thus to approximate more nearly the humble love to which we are called.

Those of us who have supposed ourselves to be meeting God's command to love our neighbor are persuaded throughout *Works of Love* to perceive the rigorous and multi-faceted law, and thus to understand ourselves as inadvertently or consciously breaking the very promise we believe ourselves to have made. Kierkegaard's textual methods are provocative, signaled by his subtitle to *Works of Love*: "Some Christian Deliberations in the Form of Discourses." In this subtitle, Kierkegaard distinguishes *Works of Love* from a more straightforward Christian discourse in that the latter "presupposes that people know essentially what love is and seeks to win them to it" (WL, 469). In contrast, a deliberation "must not so much move, mollify, reassure, persuade as awaken and provoke people and sharpen thought" seeking first to "fetch [the readers] up out of the cellar, call to them, turn their comfortable way of thinking topsy-turvy" (WL, 470, Supplement). The rhetorical momentum of *Works of Love* is indeed to disorient the reader. We are turned topsy-turvy in at least two related ways, one performative and the other epistemological. To the extent that we think we meet the law to love, we find that we fail. To the extent that we think we know the law to love, we find that we are ignorant. Simply put, we are both wicked and utterly confused, selfish and myopic. Kierkegaard at times presents love as unmitigatedly intricate, demanding of each individual Christian the disturbing acknowledgment that we do not in the least know how to love faithfully. He will then, as powerfully, present the command to love as inescapably blunt, demanding from us the confession that we know the law, but refuse to meet it. As an introduction to the later chapters wherein we dwell on Kierkegaard's depiction of our sin, we here consider the progression of *Works of Love* as conveying the complex and stark import of the law to love our neighbor. We will first read for the structural impetus of the book, building toward an indictment of the individual, then focus in on the means by which Kierkegaard brings Christ's pattern to bear on our intimate lives.

STRUCTURAL INTIMATIONS

Kierkegaard's entry and ending point, the prayer and the conclusion, frame his indictment in *Works of Love*, and the two together indicate the proper context both for assessing our inability to love and for finding the help required. In them, we read the tension between Christ as pattern and as redeemer. By considering these framing texts and the preface that punctuates the two series, we may interpret Kierkegaard as preparing his reader for the reception of God's grace. In the opening prayer, Christ is the standard and the savior, and as each he is the "witness" to our lives. By way of form and content, Kierkegaard thus creates the stage for our reading. We are to read precariously – in a prayerful and perilous setting. He brings this tone back, full circle, in the conclusion. Here, Kierkegaard's homiletic use of the "like for like" compels us to perceive that the context in which we choose to love is the context in which we will ourselves be loved. The twice-printed preface to each of the two series strongly suggests that love can only occur within such a relation of infinite inexhaustibility. Kierkegaard signals, in each of these ways, that his aim is not to convey a list of required deeds. His aim is to evoke a new, precarious, life.

In the Trinitarian prayer through which we enter the book, Kierkegaard calls upon God as the one whose love provides the supplicant with a "witness" for love, in two senses of the word (WL, 4). God's love both attests to an infinite standard to which the believer is held and reveals God as the only possible help should one choose to turn toward that standard. The prayer begins, "How could one speak properly about love if you were forgotten, you God of love, source of all love in heaven and on earth," and continues to call upon the "Savior and Redeemer" who "reveals" and also "saves," and the "Spirit" who "remind[s] the believer to love as he is loved" (WL, 4). From the onset, Kierkegaard literarily places love within faith; to forget God's love would be to forget the infinitude of the requirement and the infinitude of God's grace, and thus to misread the text. As David Gouwens observes: while "the Christological element is not at first glance structurally or formally central," the opening "sets the tone and mood of invocation and prayer."[19]

This prayer is thematically linked to Kierkegaard's conclusion, which charges that we choose carefully the proper context of our love. As we understand ourselves to be forgiven much and yet still loved, so are we to love the neighbor. The conclusion thus states more bluntly what Kierkegaard intimates at the beginning: love requires an alternative context. He begins with a prayer, and ends with a warning, a warning that one must always love in the midst of such a prayer. The "rigorous like for like" sternly advises that we attempt the task of loving with God's humbling and redeeming love in view, lest we find ourselves divinely judged by a measure we uncharitably apply to others (WL, 378). As the preparatory prayer exclaims, love is possible only if we remain explicitly cognizant of God as both our own stringent standard and as our salvation.

With the repeated preface Kierkegaard uses another rhetorical prompt toward this setting. At the beginning of the first and the second series, Kierkegaard suggests that the "curious" reader who interprets the book as if it were an elaborate list of necessary deeds will miss the author's aim (WL, 3, 207). We are thus told clearly, at the onset of both series, that the love described and evoked in the text is one which is "essentially inexhaustible" and "essentially indescribable" (WL, 3, 207). *Works of Love* is not a mere list of lovely works, but an evocation of an alternative stance, a particular relation to the one from whom all love flows:

[These deliberations] are about *works of love*, not as if hereby all its works were now added up and described, oh, far from it; not as if even the particular work described were described once and for all, far from it, God be praised! Something that in its total richness is *essentially* inexhaustible is also in its smallest work *essentially* indescribable. (WL, 3, his emphasis)

In his commentary on the preface to *Works of Love*, Kierkegaard imaginatively gives life to a character that embodies the way that we are decidedly *not* to read the text. This comical emperor leaves home determined to record all his deeds and thus brings with him "a large number of writers." Kierkegaard comments, "This might have succeeded if all of his many and great works had amounted to anything . . . But love is devoutly oblivious of its works."[20] We will ourselves be tempted to read Kierkegaard's book like a list, particularly as a confirmation of our own valor. But unlike the misled emperor who goes forth to "perform so many and so great exploits," we who hope to love properly must be, as the opening prayer suggests, prepared humbly to beseech the ineffable source of grace. The text is to propel us toward God's "inexhaustible" and "indescribable" work in Christ.

While the implicit subject of *Works of Love* is God's work in Christ, the explicit subject is the individual reader. A lengthy exposition of Luke 6:44 on "Love's Hidden Life and Its Recognizability by Its Fruits," Kierkegaard's first section addresses the individual who has taken up the text. If we have done so in order to discern the reliability of another's love, to become assured that our beloved is true or our neighbor Christian, we have come to the wrong text. If we are looking for an exquisite description of the most romantic lover, we are also in for disappointment. One cannot be certain of the motives of another, nor sure that another exemplifies the most beautiful of loves.[21] Using Jesus' metaphor from Luke 6:44, "every tree is known by its own fruit," Kierkegaard opens the first section by disabusing the reader of any assumptions regarding the perceivability of another's fruits; he turns the reader's inquisitive gaze toward himself and away from the other. When another's love is the object of our discernment, love is "hidden." We cannot find in another the one sign or set of actions that would assure us of the other's love (WL, 13):

The interpretation is that you who read these words of the Gospel, you are the tree . . . The divine authority of the Gospel does not speak to one person about another, does not speak to you, my listener, about me, or to me about you – no, when the Gospel speaks, it speaks to the single individual. (WL, 14)

Kierkegaard here uses the gospel to echo Nathan's words to David. The task of loving fruitfully belongs to the tree itself.

To the reader who would continue to search another for signs of love, Kierkegaard adds that the surest fruit of the reader's own love is his or her ability to see others as loving. In this way, he employs Nathan's tone in order to shift the reader's attention always back to his or her own reflection in the text. The book is always to serve as a mirror that reveals one's own love, not as a magnifying glass through which we view others. The chore is thus always my own, as I am called to turn my suspicion toward others into trust: "If mistrust can actually see something as less than it is, then love also can see something as greater than it is" (WL, 16). The "hidden spring" from which true love flows, God's love is to issue forth in the individual's ability to "abide" there and see others differently (WL, 9, 16). This requisite shift from mistrust to love, and the "abiding" that results, is a theme to which Kierkegaard returns again and again in the book. Here in the first section, Kierkegaard sets the tone of judgment, positioning the individual reader as the one to whom and about whom the text speaks. And to the extent that the reader is tempted instead to position the text between himself and another, as a tool for scrutinizing his neighbor, the reader is to discover, in such an act, his own incapacity to love. Here, so early in the text, Kierkegaard overtly and subtly prohibits the notion that love entails our evaluation of an other. The assignment is continually our own.[22]

In the next three sections on the love commandment (sections II.A, II.B, and II.C), Kierkegaard encircles the reader with the multiple implications of Jesus' words, intensifying the command's focus on the reader with each section, ending in section II.C with an explicit emphasis on the *You* to whom Jesus speaks. This three-part chain quite literally builds toward the individual reading the book, as we move from "You *Shall* Love" (II.A) to "You Shall Love *the Neighbor*" (II.B) to "*You* Shall Love the Neighbor" (II.C). We move from command, to the object of the command, to the subject of the command, the last being the reader himself. The call to love comes to us as an order, a shall, rather than as a mere description of existence, because it intrudes upon the individual's pervasive love of himself. Kierkegaard begins his discussion of the love commandment by likening Jesus' words to a "pick" that "wrenches open the lock of self-love and wrests it away from a person" (WL, 17). This "royal Law" of scripture, although repeated as if it were "a matter of course," finds indolent or intentional self-interest in every merely human endeavor, naming in particular those which are supposedly "spontaneous" or which are, conversely, self-protectively "sagacious" (WL, 24, 34). Here, Jesus' words become again a command precisely because they stand in glaring contrast to the reader's default interest in himself.

In the following section (II.B), Kierkegaard interprets *"the neighbor"* to be the term for the other that most confronts the reader with the other's distinctive identity, apart from any wishes, aims, or interest the reader has in the other (WL, 53–54). Whether the neighbor catches my eye or not, she is the one whom God calls me to love. The command thus corrects both my selfish interest in and my dismissive ignorance of each person I encounter. While I most often reckon the stranger, spouse, or lover only insofar as each one might fulfill some desire of my own, the love command places God as the "middle term," reminding me that the perceived is an other, equal before God (WL, 60).

Finally, in the third section on the commandment (II.C), Kierkegaard stresses that Jesus speaks to *"you,"* the reader. "Erotic love" (*Elskov*) is "defined by the object," and colludes with "worldly sagacity" to "take a careful look" before loving (WL, 66, 68). The command forces this meticulous speculation back on the lover himself, making him the object of his own scrutiny. Should we complain that the command seems too strident a gauge, Kierkegaard rejoins, "eternity" only continues to ask whether the reader has met the mark. He elaborates:

But when a person in the infinite transformation discovers the eternal itself so close to life that there is not the distance of one single claim, of one single evasion, of one single excuse, of one single moment of time from what *he* in this instant, in this second, in this holy moment *shall* do – then he is on the way to becoming a Christian. (WL, 90)

This describes well one of Kierkegaard's rhetorical aims throughout – he brings the command to bear right where we are – with no temporal or geographic space between Jesus' words and the command given to us. We are, unequivocally, to fulfill the law of love. It is with this realization, and all that it implies, that the reader turns to the longest section in the entire book.

Section III.A falls in the middle of the first series, and the lengthy exposition there gives the reader some clue as to the weight Kierkegaard places on law throughout the text. Linking inextricably law and love, Kierkegaard insists in "Love is the Fulfilling of the Law" (III.A.) that the apparent conflict between God's law and divine love is a result of the gap between our works and God's command. Kierkegaard argues against those who so dichotomize law and gospel as to free the Christian from the weight of God's requirement and powerfully retrieves the notion that Christ is the law's fulfillment. In his life and work, Christ "collides" not only with the "ungodly" but also with "the best and the most loving person" (WL, 110). Christians are tempted to lower the "requirement" of the law and put in its place some weaker version of love, so mitigating the infinite cost of sin paid by Christ. Against this, Kierkegaard insists that Christ's radical love remains the gauge that measures our sin (WL, 106).

Kierkegaard fully elaborates in this section on Christ's role as indicting example and the effect that it is to have on the reader. The emphasis builds from his story of the two brothers and the father's request to tend the vineyard (from Matthew 21, discussed above), to his explication of Paul's assertion that "love is the fulfilling of the law," to a detailed description of Christ's total and complete fulfillment of that law, and then to several paragraphs about the "earnestness" of "becoming nothing" through our comparison with God (WL, 91, 95, 96–102). Rather than allowing our curious, distanced, questioning – "But, what really *is* love?" – Kierkegaard follows Paul's answer by presenting Christ as the fulfillment. Christ is "sheer action"(WL, 98); Christ is "whole and collected" (WL, 99); for Christ, "everything in him was truth"(WL, 99); "his love made no distinction"(WL, 100); "in his love there was no bargaining," "no compromising"; and, this love consumed his life:

There was no moment, not a single one in his life, when love in him was merely the inactivity of a feeling that hunts for words while it lets time slip by, or a mood that is its own gratification . . . (WL, 99)

Summing up, "Christ was the fulfilling of the law," Kierkegaard moves to the effect of this comparison on us.

The "transfiguration" that is to take place involves our beginning to "learn humility in relation to God." Kierkegaard contrasts our efforts to compare ourselves to mere humans, whereby we will "in a very short time" be "advanced," to our comparison with the divine. There, you discover, even with the most exertion, that "you will still be as nothing, at an infinite distance from having achieved something, in infinite debt!" (WL, 102). The relation that is to occur in us is one that, in a certain sense, no words can effect, "because an entirely different revolution than any talking can produce must take place" (WL, 102). This "entirely different revolution" is one that we tenaciously avoid, for we know what will come of our present longings and expectations. Having brought Christ's fulfillment into our immediate setting, where we cannot evade one inch or one moment, Kierkegaard seeks to provoke our release. But before he moves on, Kierkegaard definitively closes a potentially remaining gap.

Kierkegaard explains how the law impinges on those relationships that we would mistakenly consider to be outside the law, insisting that "no love and no expression of love may merely humanly and in a worldly way be withdrawn from the relationship to God" (WL, 112). After leading the reader to the edge of the "revolution" of eternity, bringing us right up to the point where we must plummet into a relation to God, Kierkegaard provocatively reminds us that the Christian cannot merely give at the office or at the altar. This radically other relation brings with it drastic implications for the domestic sphere. Kierkegaard applies "those apostolic words" on which the section is based "to the daily situations of life, *precisely where the illusions are at home*" (WL, 124, my emphasis).[23] This corrective to our often subtle evasions and "self-deception" (WL, 113) leads into his next section, "Love is a Matter of Conscience" (III.B).

Kierkegaard endeavors in the next two sections (III.B and IV) to bring "the eternal itself so close to life" by making God's command to love a matter of individual conscience ("Love is a Matter of Conscience," III.B) and daily duty ("Our Duty to Love the People We See," IV). The import of the law permeates each interaction, making "every human relationship between person and person a relationship of conscience" (WL, 135). In his elaboration on this term, Kierkegaard reminds his readers that the priest, by asking each potential spouse, "Have you consulted with God and with your conscience?" transforms "an affair of the heart [into] a matter of conscience" (WL, 138). Conscience, we learn, is the marker for each individual's prior and perduring "God-relationship," and by means of it, Christianity "objects to the self-willfulness of drives and inclination" (WL, 140). We have, as the "eternal foundation" to every particular love, the crucial acknowledgment that the beloved is not our own, but God's.

Kierkegaard's subsequent contention that "Christianly, the entire distinction between the different kinds of love is essentially abolished" has seemed excessive to some, but his point is crucial for our reading (WL, 143). Kierkegaard intends with this affront to correct the tempting notion that some forms of love are private, appropriately hidden from God's vision, judgment, and redemption: "[I]t is God who by himself and by means of the middle term 'neighbor' checks on whether the love for wife and friend is conscientious" (WL, 142). To the Christian who continues to maintain that some forms of love involve unwilled attraction rather than chosen attention (and that the former is not a matter for God's judgment) Kierkegaard counters that the Christian has a duty, regardless of inclination, to see the other with faithful love.

Love is first a task, a task under God's own constant scrutiny. Section II.B ends, "Only then, when [love] is a matter of conscience, is love out of a pure heart and out of a sincere faith" (WL, 153). Faithful love is "purified" precisely as it is transformed from "a matter of drives and inclination, or a matter of feeling," to the sober, intentional setting of our relationship with God (WL, 143). With God as the consistently sobering third party to our relationships, we are no longer self-servingly to search for a beloved somehow "worthy" of our affection (WL, 161). Thus, in "Our Duty to Love the People We See," Kierkegaard asks, "Is this indeed love, to want to find it outside oneself?" and answers "I thought that this is love, to bring love along with oneself" (WL, 157).[24] Beginning with Christ as one who humanly sought companionship and closing with Christ's refusal to see Peter differently even after his denial, Kierkegaard in this section posits God's law as that which accuses the manifestations of our "natural" desire to love those who will meet our needs and expectations (WL, 154–74).[25] Again, this "shall," which has become intensely burdensome under Kierkegaard's multiple layers of explanation, is the reader's own task.[26]

The first series closes with Kierkegaard's section on debt, thematically linking the two halves of the book together. While we will consider this section at more length below, we should here note its placement in the structure of the text as a whole. With the strenuous and intricate depiction of love that has come before, Kierkegaard leads the reader to acknowledge the infinite distance between his own love and God's commands revealed through scripture. This acknowledgment prepares for the sense of indebtedness and gratitude necessary if we hope to approximate Paul's hortatory description in 1 Corinthians (the scriptural basis for much of the second series). Law, debt, and true love are strands often fused in this book, and Kierkegaard makes the relation of each to the other explicit in this pivotal section. Given that each of us is "in infinite debt" to God with regard to love's law, we must will to remain in that context if we are to love truthfully (WL, 187). To calculate and appraise others becomes, in this context of prayerful debt, nonsensical. To the extent that we cannot meet this requirement, we are yet again to acknowledge our debt. Thus to be in debt becomes "in the Christian sense, a new task," a new way of seeing ourselves in relation to God and thus to each person who is, *qua* human, the neighbor (WL, 188).

By living with the awareness that God "lovingly assumes God's [own] requirement," and that we continually live in and daily incur an incalculable debt, "there is no more mention of a festive mood and splendid achievements; love will no longer play" (WL, 189). We begin most clearly to hear in this section that the only real setting for love is the otherwise surreal context of infinite, inexhaustible, unrecoverable, indebtedness. We should recall Kierkegaard's prior contrast between the mighty emperor who wishes his deeds duly recorded and the humbled Christian. Kierkegaard begins the second series by reiterating the preface (to which the mighty emperor is a contrast) reminding the reader that works of love are not feats that one accomplishes amid fanfare but instead the result of a persistently humble relation to God as the "inexhaustible" source of love. The final section of the first series, on our debt before God, thus thematically leads into the now-repeated preface and into the second series describing the features of such an indebted love.

Words about love spoken frequently at sentimental occasions, even though scriptural, may become merely memorized aphorisms. So it is with the originally piquant words Paul wrote to the Corinthians. In the first four sections of the second series (I through IV), Kierkegaard attempts to "establish a new acquaintance with the old and familiar" by making it again "strange," so to speak – by rendering the "old and familiar" as a startling interloper in our midst (WL, 210). Starting with "Love Builds Up," Kierkegaard expands upon his assertion early on in the first series: that the task of love involves the "presupposition" that "love is in the other person's heart" (WL, 217). Given that reality itself comes up a draw "in the equilibrium of opposite possibilities," we are required first to decide whether we will exist in the context of love or mistrust, and then to will that choice continually (WL, 228). His contrast between love and mistrust is related to the section on debt and the "like for like" that punctuates his conclusion. Debt is love's element. And if we are to love well, we are to presume love within this setting. This section (II) wherein Kierkegaard poses the choice of "presupposition," entitled "Love Believes All Things – and Yet is Never Put to Shame," leads into the next section, wherein Kierkegaard explicates Paul's exhortation to hope.

In section III of the second series, Kierkegaard makes explicit that the possibility of "building up" and believing depends on a very particular hope: "Christianity's hope is eternity, and Christ is the Way; his debasement is the Way, but he was also the Way when he ascended into heaven" (WL, 248). In this, his only explicit reference to Christ's ascension in *Works of Love*, Kierkegaard joins Christ's humiliation, his resurrection, and our own hope. Christian hope, as he describes it here, is a work of love inasmuch as we refuse to leave the relation to which Christ ascended, that of "eternity" (WL, 248). But in order to enter and abide in that relation, we must join with Christ through a different debasement: the humiliation of self-discovery. By remaining within the "festival hall" of eternity, a place where "mirrors" reveal the truth about oneself, we discover the distinct difference between true love and "sagacity," "anger," "bitterness," "malice," and "a worldly, conceited mentality that would die of disgrace and shame if it were to experience making a mistake" (WL, 248, 257). The characteristic that distinguishes love from each of these vices is a vulnerable hope born of eternity. The "shame" we are to fear is not the shame of being unjustly deceived by another, but rather the shame of retreating to the context of comparison and self-protection. As Kierkegaard explains, "the world" commends a person who carefully avoids "injudicious miscalculation" in his or her distribution of expectation. But eternity negates the "sagacity" of such calculations and encourages instead the prodigal love of the father who welcomes the prodigal son (WL, 260, 263). By living in the cancellation of calculation, by courageously remaining where we may be, by the world's standards, fooled and cheated, the Christian is both humiliated and elevated in Christ.

The kind of love we are to choose, will, and cultivate has as its key the self-giving life of Christ, who did not "seek his own," the topic of the next section in this series. In order to hope in eternity in the way that Kierkegaard commends, we must cease counting up bits of love in a miserable attempt to determine whose love is greater or first or best, but instead "lose" ourselves in the assumption that the other's love is true (WL, 268–69).[27] Bringing in again what is a theme in the first series, Kierkegaard reiterates in this section that, in contrast to "erotic love and friendship," Christian love does not search for or insist upon what will meet the lover's needs but loves the other as another, distinct, self (WL, 269). The "pliability" that allows one truly to "comprehend others" (WL, 270) is a quality approximated only with a skepticism regarding one's own ability to see accurately, and with a generosity of spirit born of our gratitude for the debt Christ has paid.[28] The link to the last section of the first series is again clear: as we are loved generously by God, so are we to love our neighbor. Paul's description of love adumbrates the extent to which we do not currently meet the criterion of the Christian; I am to interpret my persistent mistrust and judgment of others as yet again a judgment of myself (WL, 233). Our accrual of debt thus continues into the second series.

As was the case with the first series, Kierkegaard places a key section for the second series in the middle. In "Love Hides a Multitude of

Sins" (v) the increasingly chastened reader is summoned to "discover nothing" that would implicate the other (WL, 283). If Christ's love is, as Kierkegaard suggests in the middle chapter of the first series, "the fulfilling of the law," then our love will be in response to that fulfillment. The ramifications of the previous sections prepare us for the conclusion that Kierkegaard's call to forgive is more than just, given that we who so feebly love had best hope and believe in the reality of forgiveness. In a world where everyone wishes to be remembered, the surest way to receive God's blessing is to forget our claim to worth by way of "comparison" and instead to "discover nothing" in the other that would incur blame (WL, 284). Kierkegaard offers us a continuum of response – from seeing no evil, to a "mitigating explanation," to forgiveness – but crucial to each response is Kierkegaard's contention that understanding itself is a choice for which the individual must be aware, responsible, and diligent.[29] The discussion of forgiveness thus becomes yet again a task for the reader, who is to collude with "goodness" by finding in the other what God graciously finds in us and, when necessary, forgiving the other as Christ forgives us all (WL, 285).

Kierkegaard warns that our "great inclination" is instead to "see [our] neighbor's faults," and he characterizes our search for sin in another as "a malignant curiosity" that inherently harbors an "understanding *with* evil" (WL, 286, 290).[30] We hunger for the knowledge of the sins of others in part because we believe that we can therefore find some "excuse" for our own (WL, 286). But such an effort only betrays the extent to which we are unable to love. We who either casually or purposefully cooperate with sin in this way not only reveal our own alliance with evil but make way for further "occasion for sin" by "provid[ing] the sin with sustenance" (WL, 298). We must live instead within the context of debt. As Gouwens describes it, "From the strictness of the law's demand [we are to be] led to the gentleness of forgiving one's neighbor."[31] The reader departs from this section desiring a reliable relation of love with which we can participate – seeking the "one environment that unconditionally does not give and is not occasion for sin" (WL, 298).

In the next two pages the reader catches again a passing glimpse of that source. As the next section (vi, "Love Abides") begins, Kierkegaard exclaims, "Yes, praise God, love abides! (WL, 300). He assures the reader, "if in any of your actions, in any of your words you truly have had love as your confidant, take comfort, because love abides" (WL, 300). Paraphrasing Paul's words to the Romans, Kierkegaard advises us to be confident in God's power to overcome both our greatest "despondency" and "the world's" inability to find even our most earnest striving admirable (WL, 301). This "very upbuilding thought" is of God's love itself, which "sustains all existence" and without which nothing Kierkegaard has prescribed would be even fleetingly possible (WL, 301).[32] Ever so quickly, Kierkegaard switches back to speak only of love's task, "But in this little work we are continually dealing only with the works of love, and therefore not with God's love but with human love" (WL, 301). The careful reader has nonetheless caught the significance of this self-purportedly extraneous passage.[33] The abiding love that Kierkegaard goes on to describe is only possible with God as the source of its endurance. The lover who would abide must acknowledge that true love involves God as well as the two individuals (WL, 304). God is the source, hope, guardian, and confidant without which the originally and perpetually fallen individual could not begin to remain committed to the fragile, flawed, difficult to forgive and easy to forget others with whom we are called to live.

The love that Kierkegaard has described not only collides in general with each individual, but clashes in particular with a society that counts large, public acts of beneficence, respectable acts of frugality, or reciprocated gestures of generosity as "earnestness" (WL, 320). In the next three sections (VII through IX), Kierkegaard writes small the victories of love, arguing that Christian charity is more about "mercifulness" than magnanimity ("Mercifulness, a Work of Love Even If It Can Give Nothing and Is Able to Do Nothing"), that love wins in a quiet way totally foreign to those who seek remarkable signs of achievement ("The Victory of the Conciliatory Spirit in Love, Which Wins the One Overcome"), and that loving those who can give back nothing is more akin to Christian love than receiving the approbation of others ("The Work of Love in Recollecting One Who is Dead"). After contrasting love's true currency with filthy lucre,[34] Kierkegaard writes that the "most difficult battle of all" for an individual is "with himself and God" (WL, 333). As "exactly the opposite of what the natural man most readily and naturally understands," the "conciliatory spirit" forgets himself, determinedly seeking "reconciliation" even when wronged and yet attributing any signs of accord as gifts from God (WL, 336). In all, we are to concern ourselves not with the other's ability to reciprocate our love, but rather with our own ability to love truly. In this sense, loving the dead can assist us in determining "whether love is entirely free" or instead depends on whatever we seek to gain from the beloved (WL, 351). His effort in this three-section sequence is "to make ashamed in a God-pleasing way the person capable of generosity and beneficence" (WL, 316). Lest the intractable reader still believe that he meets the exacting description prior to this section, Kierkegaard includes this grouping of short sections on the minute but intense characteristics of Christian love. As Kirmmse suggests of this section, "SK has been deliberately irritating to the social sensibilities of his reader in order to guarantee that the message, by its very abrasiveness, gets through."[35] A falsely confident reader is thus given one more chance to confess his present failure and alter his course.

After this lengthy, intricate explication of Christian love, Kierkegaard closes the second series with a section provoking the reader's recognition that, ultimately, "you are able to do nothing at all" (WL, 362). In this last numbered section (x) Kierkegaard offers his most blunt words on humility, "self-denial," and love, stating that the works of love described before depend most on one perpetually difficult movement: "I am to work together with [God], if not in any other way, then through the continual understanding that I am able to do nothing at all, something that is not understood once and for all" (WL, 363). Kierkegaard summons the reader to dwell only on "one thought" in a way that will lead him to "discover self-denial" and thus to perceive "that God is" (WL, 362). And here is the "blessedness and terror" of loving with God's grace; the reader must allow his "selfishness" to "be broken" in order to "hold fast to God" alone (WL, 362–64). By sitting still and determinately with the thought that "right where he is he is before God" the reader is to be humbled, to receive grace, and to live in a relation of profoundly unmerited love (WL, 365). All other methods for speaking about and acting truly in love are chimeras, traps out of which the self cannot escape without God's work. But, given human nature, the way of humility can itself become a pit. While the Christian may understand himself to be "nothing" before God, he may compare himself to his neighbor with some pride in his very ability to be humble (WL, 366). In this closing section, Kierkegaard admonishes the reader (and himself) to recover from this temptation. We must confess ceaselessly that God is the source of all good things, even of our ability to recognize our helplessness (WL, 374).

Kierkegaard concludes the book with an unambiguous call for us to practice living within the context of humility, forgiveness, and humility again. The preceding text is his attempt to place the reader underneath the "school-yoke" of the commandment, in order that we might see ourselves as novices rather than as veterans (WL, 376). In this effort to go forth heeding his call, we are to take with us "the Christian like for like" (WL, 376). Kierekgaard offers a powerful, final admonishment: should we at any point delude ourselves into thinking that we are less than "thieves" and therefore accuse another of criminality, we will be again in God's court with no leniency. He continues, "precisely when you come and inform on the other person, God begins to think about how you are involved" (WL, 382).[36] As we judge, so will we be judged. This temptation to remove others and thus ourselves from the language of absolute grace is perpetually before us, leading us to love in myopic and distorted ways: "the log in your own eye is neither more nor less than seeing and condemning the splinter in your brother's eye" (WL, 382). The reader is to return again and again to the law that convicts, knowing that when we speak humbly and graciously, God will be present as grace itself (WL, 386). In his conclusion, Kierkegaard thus loops the reader back to dwell again with the law that returns us to grace. He closes *Works of Love* by recommending the very book the reader is completing. The law's ability to convict, demonstrated throughout the text, is an essential and recurrent precursor for the kind of posture necessary for any and all works of love.[37]

THE BONDAGE OF A CHRISTIAN

Kierkegaard's construal of love is very much tied up with his reworked Lutheranism. In order more fully to understand this link, we must focus on Kierkegaard's section on "indebtedness" and its relation to Luther's articulation of love. This section of *Works of Love* is thematically and structurally pivotal, and we may interpret it as a dense commentary on Luther's theology of love, particularly in his treatise *The Freedom of a Christian*. In *The Freedom of a Christian*, the law sends us running, desperate, to the altar of marriage to Christ. Standing before the all-condemning law, we know we must turn to stand in reciprocal relation to a savior; in this marriage, Christ receives all our sin, and we receive all Christ's merits. Kierkegaard uses a different metaphor, one that conveys both the impetus for this relation and the relation itself: indebtedness. By describing this relation of indebtedness as love's only proper context, Kierkegaard retrieves Luther's theological use of the law and unites it, inextricably, with the relation occasioned by the law. Kierkegaard here in this section effectively reminds his readers that our relation to Christ is one necessitated by our own, incalculable, debt. Humility and love are one relation, rather than subsequent steps.

In *The Freedom of a Christian*, Luther links our release from damnable culpability to our graced capacity to love, exhorting that our liberation through Christ from the damning effect of the law issues forth in a life lived for others and not for ourselves. In "Our Duty to Remain in Love's Debt to One Another," Kierkegaard evokes and explicates Luther's link between faith in Christ alone and neighbor love. He begins by quoting the same text as does Luther at the onset of *Freedom of a Christian*: Romans 13:8 "Owe no one anything, except to love one another." Through faith we owe nothing, except to love one another – that is, through faith, we owe everything. The link Luther makes between faith and love, freedom and servitude, Kierkegaard explains as our duty to remain in the context of constant and "infinite debt." We are freed to love only as we know ourselves bound:

If you want to maintain your love, you must see to it that love, caught for freedom and life, continually remains in its element by means of the *infinitude of the debt*; otherwise it wastes away and dies. (WL, 180, emphasis in the original)

Seeking to reintroduce his readers to Luther's insight, Kierkegaard moves backward to link humility and joyful obedience to the context of confessed indebtedness. His correction is subtle, but significant. Whereas Luther employs the language of "surplus," "abundance," and "freedom," Kierkegaard consistently uses the metaphor of infinite debt. Our continual sense of indenture to God through Christ is requisite for faithful love, or else the "surplus" becomes mere license. Only by recognizing our utter need, and by becoming infinitely bound to Christ, are we truly freed for the neighbor. We are thus freed only inasmuch as we are also bound to Christ by his work. Kierkegaard retrieves this for readers who have blithely lost such urgency.

   In Luther's treatise, the sinner, discovering his culpability, does not merely flee once to the altar with Christ. The Christian must grab hold for dear life and not back away an inch or for a moment. Luther's marriage metaphor thus moves from wedding to consummation, as we are to live, "clinging to God's promise in such a way that Christ and the soul become one flesh"; this erocative imagery is unproductive unless we hear also his insistence that we remain perpetually with Christ, like a grateful newly wed who absolutely will not let go.[38] It is this relation, marked by our persistent humility and desperate gratitude, that Kierkegaard seeks to elicit in *Works of Love*, not only for the sake of faith, but so that we might love.

   This section, which is the fulcrum for the two halves of *Works of Love*, contains Kierkegaard's most explicit description of this persistently relational, indebted context for true love. He asks us first to consider what real love looks like: "Do not we usually think of a good lover as one who believes himself constantly in debt to the beloved?" If a lover instead seems to think of love as "an actual bookkeeping arrangement," do we not suppose that person to be involved in something other than love (WL, 176)? He here states a contrast between finite calculation and infinite love that defines the section. Kierkegaard moves the reader to see that a "distinctive characteristic of love" is that the lover remains in a relation of debt rather than carefully arranging things so as to remove himself from that relation of debt. One who would love well must choose to remain in a particular context, a relation of infinite debt, and eschew the alternate context of merit, desert, calculation, and comparison. Kierkegaard's aesthetic poetry ends as he quotes again Paul's letter to the Romans, "Owe no one anything, except to love one another." We are faced with a "duty to remain in love's debt," to remain resolutely in a relational context that will sustain true love.

Our task is to remain in debt, and the one thing we are to fear most is getting out of a relation of debt. The strange "inner coherence" of Kierkegaard's section requires that we undergo a "transformation," away from our usual tendency to think of our good works as "installment payments" on a debt. The change of "attitude and mind" must remove our love from the realm of finitude and place us within the realm of infinitude. The "odd difficulties that pile up," are so difficult because Kierkegaard backs the reader into a particular kind of relation with the infinite by way of the finite, quantifiable, temporal language of debt and repayment. We must seek a setting wherein "it is impossible to make an accounting," wherein the debt is infinite and thus all efforts at calculation impossible: "Ready, indescribably ready, as love's prompting is, he wants to do everything and fears only one thing, that he could do everything in such a way that he would get out of debt" (WL, 178). The only way to love truly is to remain resolutely in relation with the one to whom we are infinitely, eternally, indebted. If we begin to think about our love in terms of that which can be meted out, paid back, met in like terms, we lose the proper element for love. "Infinitude, inexhaustibility, immeasurability," these are the sources of sustenance for love; otherwise, our love "wastes away and dies" (WL, 180).

Kierkegaard describes what happens when we remove ourselves, even for an instant, from the relation of infinite debt. First, we begin to dwell on ourselves and, second, we begin to compare. "As soon as love dwells on itself, it is out of its element" (WL, 182). By "dwelling," Kierkegaard means something like our stepping outside of our relation of inexhaustible indebtedness in order to gauge our progress. When we do so, we effectively remove ourselves from the only relation wherein love exists. By "dwelling," we make our own love the object of observation, hoping there to find some worth, some quality, some measurable good – placing love in the context of finite, payable, accountable, debt. This leads to the disaster of "comparison." Dwelling on my own particular actions of love, determining their worth or lack of worth, I will soon begin to employ "comparison's sidelong glance," hoping to find there "a whole world of relationships and calculations," that may sustain my "selfish dwelling" (WL, 183). Kierkegaard insists that, if we begin to attempt to discern progress, we suffocate love by placing it in a context wherein it cannot breathe.

At the end of this section, Kierkegaard writes explicitly about this "infinite" with whom we are truly to dwell and to whom we are tellingly to compare ourselves:

Only the God-relationship is earnestness; the earnestness is that the task is pressed to its highest . . . God has truth's and infallibility's infinite conception of love; God is love. Therefore the individual must remain in the debt – as surely as God judges it, or as surely as he remains in God, because only in the infinitude of the debt can God remain in him. (WL, 190)

Here, in God, is the gauge by which we are to compare ourselves, and thus we are all in infinite, incalculable debt. Kierkegaard explains that if we are to love truly, we must make the "confession" of a "humble, loving soul," a confession that alone allows for love (WL, 191). By remaining in relation to Christ, as the one who binds us to God, we are able to approximate the love to which we are called.

In this way, Kierkegaard places the reader again in the context of infinite debt, in effect prompting a different facet of Luther's own marriage to Christ. We are to find ourselves again in the bridal chamber, and know ourselves beholden due to the infinite gift received there. For his readers, who increasingly take their relation to Christ for granted as their birthright in Christendom, Kierkegaard seeks to introduce through the language of debt the same altar and bridal chamber described by Luther. By stressing the debt, Kierkegaard focuses in on our necessary humility and receptivity. In doing so, Kierkegaard effectively employs Luther to correct complacent Lutheranism. He reasserts the God-relation, rather than our default national and familial relations, as the proper site for love.

CHRIST IN THE PARLOR

We pretend that only ungodliness had to collide with Christ. What a misunderstanding! No, the best and the most loving person, humanly speaking, who ever lived had to collide with him, had to misunderstand him, because this best person should first learn from him what love is, in the divine sense. (WL, 110)

We cannot flee to Christ unless we are startled awake by the contrast between his life and our own. One impetus driving Kierkegaard's protest in *Works of Love* is his disgust with domesticated Christianity. There are many ways Christians have glossed over that "everlasting chasmic abyss between the God-man and every person" in an attempt to get by with less than God's command (WL, 101).[39] The church for which he first wrote *Works of Love* evinced at least two errors that we cannot dismiss as historically particular. Christians attenuate the import of Christ on our lives by concentrating exclusively on his work for us – by seeing ourselves solely as the beneficiaries of rather than also the perpetrators of the cross. We deepen this error by considering the family to be a perpetually hallowed space, secluded from Christ's already diluted judgment. Romantic and familial engagements are often construed as either external to or, by default, blandly blessed by Christ. If we do perceive Christ as judge, we mistakenly think that he frowns only upon impolite behavior, excusing young love's exuberance and smiling upon the patterned comfort of staid love. When grace is a cultural commodity easily acquired and intimate love is cushioned from even the scant remaining cost, we are tempted to miscalculate our sin and overestimate the status of our soul. *Works of Love* is Kierkegaard's attempt to correct this tranquilizing heresy – to depict the individual as standing in desperate need of prayer in the parlor as much as in the prison. Kierkegaard interjects into the domestic sphere Christ's startling life and his parables, in order to remind us that Christ's love and our own supposedly apt love consistently and drastically collide.

We are challenged to encounter Christ's life itself as significantly dissimilar to our own. The pattern by which we are to judge ourselves, Christ is the only true fulfillment of the command he himself gave. Kierkegaard uses two stories that we are "now accustomed to praise" emptily, Christ's forgiveness of Peter and his forgiveness of the crowd, in order to uncover our hypocrisy (WL, 171, 287).[40] He brings into sharp relief the contrast between our seemingly perspicacious vision and Christ's own capacity to forgive. Playing on a theme that runs throughout the book, Kierkegaard focuses in on our incapacity to overlook another's sin. In this tendency to count splinters, we are to find the log in our own eye.[41] By contrasting Christ's vision and our own, Kierkegaard persuades us to count our vision as blindness.

In the first series, Kierkegaard compels the reader to "become contemporary with" Christ at the moment when simultaneously Peter denies Christ, the rooster crows, and Christ looks at Peter (WL, 171).[42] The reader is to imagine himself in the midst of "bloodthirstiness and savagery," desperate to find in the "wild crowd" someone familiar, and then to see Peter, a friend, who is at that moment denying that friendship to the authorities. It would be already "magnanimous" for us to turn away so as not to humiliate our friend, but Kierkegaard suggests that Christ looks "as when a mother sees a child in danger through its own carelessness," and "catches [the child] with her admittedly reproachful but also saving look" (WL, 170). Rather than thinking of himself when his friend most blatantly denies him, Christ "hastens to save Peter." This is in conspicuous comparison to our own tendency, in circumstances much less dire, to be disgusted with our loved one's "equivocation, double-mindedness, and evasion" (WL, 170). While "Christ's love for Peter was boundless," we continually appraise the other with an eye toward meting out our love accordingly (WL, 172).

Kierkegaard returns to this theme in the second series, where we are again to imagine "Christ at that moment when he was brought before the Council" (WL, 287). Even there, where his very enemies actively goaded him to see "mockery," "contempt," and "scorn," Christ "lovingly hid the multitude of sins" (WL, 287). If the very "prototype," the "perfect one" is able to love those so clearly imperfect beings who hated him, how much more are we, who are far from perfect, to forgive (as we have been forgiven) our admittedly imperfect loved ones (WL, 187, 173). Although "we human beings speak about finding the perfect person in order to love him," Christ speaks to us of "being the perfect person who boundlessly loves the person he sees" (WL, 174). With these two stories and others, Kierkegaard makes graphic the distance between our own love for those with whom we are engaged and Christ's love for even those who hated him.

As the details of Christ's life can become blurred by an exclusive focus on grace and/or dulled by frequent recitation, so can we miss the accusatory quality of Christ's parables by reading them merely as assurance of our salvation. Kierkegaard retrieves Christ's intent to force the inquisitive one to discover in Christ's parabolic answer much about himself:

The questioner did indeed always receive an answer, but in addition to the answer he in one sense learned too much. He received an imprisoning answer that did not ingeniously become prolixly involved in the question but with divine authority grasped the questioner and placed him under the obligation to do accordingly . . . (WL, 96)

The man who would be righteous, for example, is forced to compare himself to the one who truly treated a stranger as a neighbor. Kierkegaard explains that "Christ does not speak about knowing the neighbor but about becoming a neighbor oneself" (WL, 22). In his parables, Christ sought not only to depict God's love for Israel, but also to implicate the hearers in a comparison between the love narrated and their own. Kierkegaard employs and thus heightens this rhetorical technique by reviving Christ himself, by bringing his words alive to the reader's present.

Although readers often interpret the parable of the prodigal son as assurance of God's love for us, Kierkegaard recovers another facet to the story: "the prodigal son's father was perhaps the only one who did not know that he had a prodigal son, because the father's love hoped all things" (WL, 221). This hope is the inverse of our desire to evaluate before trusting and to determine the conclusion before investing our hope in those we supposedly love. Kierkegaard also retrieves a less obvious angle to Christ's parable of the wedding banquet, finding here a judgment on those whose love is contingent upon the caliber of the potential recipient. If this parable is read as an indictment, it is most often interpreted as admonishing those who were too preoccupied to respond to the host's invitation. Yet, at Kierkegaard's prompting, we are to compare our present parsimony with our own dinner-partner to that seemingly "ludicrous" host who happily invited the "poor and crippled" to his lavish celebration (WL, 83). In both of these parables of Christ, which the reader can most likely recite by heart, Kierkegaard seeks to elicit the inherent conflict between Christ's love and conditional affection.

Through these and other means, Kierkegaard endeavors to explain that God's word in Christ, whether in narrative, parable, or command, bares the real basis from which we most often love. He redefines romantic love and familial relations, sheltered like much of what is assumed by his contemporaries to be harmlessly secular culture, to render every moment one of conscience, retrieving what is Luther's lesser emphasis on the occasions for sin within intimacy. Here Kierkegaard describes a crucial tool for self-inspection. When I love another, more than likely

I am loving myself in the beloved, rather than the neighbor in the form of the beloved:

It will now be shown that passionate preferential love is another form of self-love, also that self-denial's love, in contrast, loves the neighbor, whom one shall love. (WL, 53)

Even when I proclaim that I love another dearly, what I am likely cherishing is some aspect of the other that relates to my own self-centered hopes and dreams. Kierkegaard calls this preferential form of affection loving the other as the "other-I" or the "other self" (WL, 54).

The term "neighbor" exposes this otherwise camouflaged self-centeredness in that if one were to place "neighbor" as a limiting block between myself and my beloved, I would balk. Kierkegaard explains this denial of my beloved's status as neighbor in at least three related ways. First, I neglect to love my beloved when, due to the other's change, temporary annoyance, time's tedium, or my fickleness, he does not meet my needs or desires (WL, 173). Second, I effectively steal from the beloved with whom I am currently involved, not acknowledging that she is an entity unto herself (WL, 55). Third, when devoted to another, I will hear nothing of her request that I distance myself from her (WL, 21). Rather, I insist that my love manifest itself in proximity, where I can most easily acquire whatever property of hers I want or presume myself to need. This "redoubling" of the self that is manifest in the term "neighbor" is to disclose to the reader the extent to which I am, in my love, actually loving myself. As Kierkegaard concludes:

One really does not need to be any great judge of human nature in order with the help of this clue [i.e., the term neighbor] to make discoveries about erotic love and friendship that are alarming to others and humiliating to oneself . . . (WL, 54)

The command of God embodied in and spoken by Christ is to bring into sharp focus the surreptitious motives with which we "love" in the privacy of our own intimate relations.

This humiliation in the home, where we think ourselves decent, or at least concealed, is central to the effect Kierkegaard wishes to have on the reader. An overly sanguine construal of Luther's marital vocation and a cultural eclipse of the convicting use of the law collude to provide a safe domestic haven for sin. Even youthful, reckless, and overtly uncommitted love can be excused as a somewhat unseemly but necessary precursor to the mutually beneficial bliss of marriage. Kierkegaard throws a significant wrench into this cultural machinery by forcing each of us to acknowledge that there are no safe spaces wherein we can, with impunity, serve ourselves by use of another.

David Gouwens aptly suggests that Kierkegaard recurrently throws one back to Luther's question "How is one to stand before God?"[43] In his journal notes on the "Conclusion" to *Works of Love*, Kierkegaard retells a story of a clergyman who sought for a location where he could be with "a woman of dubious reputation" safe from observation (WL, 465, Supplement). Finally the woman found a spot and (mischievously) said to the clergyman, "Here you can be absolutely safe, here no one ever comes, and under this arch no one can see us except God." Kierkegaard intends textually, thematically, and rhetorically to remind the reader that there are no locations, relations, or moments hidden from God.[44] Standing before God we are to be humiliated, humbled, and prepared to love in another way, with resonant gratitude but also with a sense of imminent transgression. Kierkegaard does not wish for the reader to be humiliated for humiliation's sake, but for the sake of the self-denying love to which we are called. We are to revisit the text, not only to be repeatedly indicted but also to be renewed in our determination better to approximate with grace what we cannot do alone: love those persons to whom and with whom we are ourselves intimately engaged.

A PENULTIMATE NOTE

If humility before the law is a response Kierkegaard desires in his reader, there is another strain in the text that threatens to undermine that aim. Before closing this chapter on law, humility, and repentance, it is important that we face this potentially problematic aspect of the text. At the end of the First Series, Kierkegaard warns the reader "in good time . . . if you do this [love faithfully] or at least strive to act accordingly, you will fare badly" (WL, 191). We are to read this in two ways. First, one fares badly in that we are unable to meet the demands before us; our own sin originally and continually hinders our efforts to meet God's law. We will have reason to turn back continually to this first aspect of Kierkegaard's warning as we consider our resemblance to the numerous ill-faring lovers of his authorship.

There is a second way that we are to read this warning. One may fare badly due to the ignorance and sin of others. Kierkegaard repeatedly contends that, wherever you find true love as he describes it in *Works of Love*, "you will find it hated and persecuted by the world" (WL, 122). Given how sinful and self-centered we all are, an example of truthful love comes to us as a threatening offense to which we respond, at best, with mockery and, at worst, with violence. Most often Kierkegaard includes himself among the fallen, hateful and persecuting, warning himself and us that we must avoid the temptation to despise true love. But when speaking of this danger, Kierkegaard's narrative voice at times shifts to become that of a knowledgeable, self-righteous informant. He drops his dominant literary voice to offer private advice to a comrade in his struggle against the misguided masses:

If, then, you in any way, even in human frailty, will aspire to carry out the words of the apostle, that love is the fulfilling of the Law, then take care with people! Take care lest they trick you out of the highest because you can't bear to be called self-loving! (WL, 129)

In this passage in particular Kierkegaard rhetorically aligns himself with Socrates, who refused to be "corrupted by relatives and friends" (WL, 128). Implied in these passages is the notion that Kierkegaard and the most faithful reader of the text are the misunderstood lovers who may be held up as paradigms by which the world is to be judged.[45] His public "collision" with the one to whom he was engaged becomes, during unguarded moments, evidence of his righteous suffering and a statement against his dull-witted neighbors.[46]

These passages are problematic on at least two levels. First, it is not always clear, even to Kierkegaard himself, that his own suffering is a result of his unappreciated efforts to be selfless in his loving. While Kierkegaard maintains in these passages a consistent message that the Christian must be a servant for the truth, he makes clear elsewhere that one is called to suffer for others, that truthfulness and love work together for the good of the neighbor. We follow Christ to the extent that we empty ourselves in an effort better to love others. Given that Kierkegaard speaks of sin as most often manifesting itself in prideful self-centeredness, a call for one tenaciously to interpret one's afflictions as caused by the sin of others is potentially a call to self-delusion. And second, for one who has advocated a trusting presupposition of good on the part of others, Kierkegaard's bitter pessimism regarding his neighbors is troubling and may distort the forgiving vision with which we are to perceive others. Kierkegaard's lack of humility here is troubling and may allow a textual escape route for the persistently proud reader. In his critique of the stultified banality of society, Kierkegaard at times misses that some may evade his call to love by imagining themselves as apart from and independent of his more general indictment – by seeing themselves as approximating Christ without the recurring prerequisite of penance.[47]

Such would be a misreading of *Works of Love*. In the section at the end of the book, on the praise of love, Kierkegaard again powerfully compares himself to Socrates, but this time as a confession. Kierkegaard explains that it was courageous for Socrates to praise beauty, given that he himself was not beautiful. Socrates' defense of beauty effectively made him appear all the more ugly in the light of truth. So has Kierkegaard, as the "most self-loving among a people whom loving speakers call the people of love," effected in the text a brutal distinction between his own and true Christian love (WL, 373). And then he adds, "so much for the speaker." We should note here that Kierkegaard prepared, but then decided not to include, an extensive "Self-Defense" in which he claims "If anyone is hard working, I am more so . . . if anyone is sacrificing himself for a cause, I do it more" (WL, 456, Supplement). This defense was, initially, to run right alongside his confession. What remains is the confession.

Kierkegaard does not merely tell us that he is also the subject of this text, in these sections; he performatively demonstrates it. With this complex book, Kierkegaard has given the reader a gift of sorts, in that it includes the strands of his own confused attempt to determine when suffering and self-defense are commands of God, and when they are evidence of self-deluding pride. This is a knotted issue that Kierkegaard seeks to solve throughout his life, attempting narratively, poetically, and discursively to unravel the truth or falsehood of his own love for and disgust with his beloved and others with whom he becomes engaged. In *Works of Love*, Kierkegaard's description of humble, giving love exists interwoven with the traces of his own struggle to move beyond his tendency to see himself as the only truly suffering, loving, and righteous man in Denmark. With his determination to counteract our obsequious or selfish concern with the crowd's approval and thus to place himself and the reader before God alone, he at times shifts his rhetorical tone to position himself and us against the deluded masses. But, as he ends his section on the love commandment itself, Kierkegaard insists, "O my listener, it is not *you* to whom *I* am speaking; it is *I* to whom eternity says: You shall" (WL, 90, emphasis in the original). The fact that the "speaker" himself aids in his own indictment grants a way for this scholar humbly to proceed, by involving myself not merely as narrator but also as subject, and by recognizing the possibility that my description of vice reveals as much about myself as anyone else.

DWELLING WITH SIN

Wherever the purely human wants to storm forth, the commandment
constrains; wherever the purely human loses courage, the commandment
strengthens; wherever the purely human becomes tired and sagacious, the commandment inflames and gives wisdom. (WL, 43)

One who is to love rightly must frequently sit still and self-consciously
with God's commandment to love, with the thought that "right where
he is, he is before God" (WL, 365). If we are to approximate the law
of love revealed in scripture, we must allow ourselves to face the many
ways that we currently live, before God, in sin rather than love. The
love Kierkegaard describes in *Works of Love* depends upon this continual
movement of repentance, and thus the theological use of the law is intrinsic to the path of true discipleship. Dwelling on the extent to which we
remain in sin is not to be merely an exercise in self-abasement for its own
sake, but a preparation for penitent and grateful hearts. In the passage
above, Kierkegaard characterizes the commandment's power in three
ways, each one intrinsically linked to our humble turn to grace alone.
First, we who wish truly to love are, through the commandment, made
aware of our sinful tendency perpetually to transgress the boundary between another and ourselves. The theological use of the law should effect
a sense of limitation, even caution, in the Christian who would otherwise
"storm forth" (WL, 43). God's requirement demands that we "manage
love" that would otherwise run like a "snorting steed" intentionally or
inadvertently trampling those in our path (WL, 189). Second, with the
knowledge of our transgression and our gratitude for the immense deficit
paid, we are to live a life free from comparison with others – devoid of the
world's "tired and sagacious" tendency to calculate and measure prior
to our commitment to one another (WL, 43). Without first weighing the
possibility of love on the part of the other, faithful love gives courageously,
consciously living within the "infinitude of the debt" that Christ has paid
for us (WL, 180). Kierkegaard describes less fully the third facet of the
Christian life, hopeful vision, perhaps in part because he himself found
this attentive manner of seeing difficult and perilous. But Kierkegaard
also gives an account in this text of God's transformation of the Christian, from one who obediently regards the other as a neighbor from a
distance to one who is actually able to love the other "despite *and with* his
weaknesses and defects and imperfections" (WL, 158).[48] The fact that
we quite often slip when in such proximity, either to consume the other
or to retreat protectively into a mode of calculated security, is to return

us again to the command, to our need for repentance, and to the source of our hope.[49] When, not if, we fail to recognize limits, give without calculation, and forgive the other, we are to return, again and again, to God's grace.

But before we may hear Kierkegaard's positive account of graced love, we must dwell considerably on the effects of the fall. Years before Kierkegaard wrote *Works of Love* he attempted to discern and depict through intricate poetics and narrative the multiple ways that our love goes awry. While Kierkegaard wishes it to be difficult for us to see ourselves reflected in the true love he describes in *Works of Love*, we are easily to find our own vices mirrored in the gnarled, misguided, and maddeningly confused characters of his pseudonymous, more narrative texts. Interwoven into *Works of Love* are perceptive sketches of the other side of human involvement wherein love begins or becomes something muddled or menacing. By reading *Works of Love* alongside four other texts wherein Kierkegaard narratively inhabits these missteps, we may fill in the sketches of vice in *Works of Love*, resulting in a fuller account of our predicament. And by tracing each pseudonymous character's failed attempt to escape his particular impasse, we may hear Kierkegaard's stylistic attempt to persuade us that we stand in desperate need of grace. Kierkegaard's pseudonyms portray different distorted characters with a "once upon a time" sort of quality, but we are to find ourselves described and implicated in the narrative world created.

Those who skim past Kierkegaard's poetic authorship to the more explicitly Christian prose of *Works of Love* are given in the pseudonymous authorship (in particular *Fear and Trembling, Repetition, Either / Or*, and *Stages on Life's Way*) a necessarily confusing and humbling precursor. Both confusion and humility are important for the work before us. To read *Works of Love* without our narrative entanglement in the authorship might lead us to commit one of two errors. We might over-estimate either our capacity to love or our capacity to repent. By my intensified interpretation of *Works of Love* in this chapter, we are clearly to repent of our self-centered intentions, but we must not do so without also confessing our utter confusion. Given the complexity of existence, our repentance itself requires time and meticulous self-inspection. To resist the confession of sin would be to err, but to repent all at once, succumbing under the unendurable weight of *Works of Love*, would also be to mistake Kierkegaard's aim. A univocal confession of sin, however heart-felt, may too easily lead into the situation Kierkegaard sought to correct: we confess our sins, we accept our forgiveness, we confess our Christ, and our lives become simpler, more comprehensible, in the process. Reading *Works of Love* with the authorship helps to amplify Kierkegaard's call to discomfiture.

In the remainder of this book, we will become slowly entangled in and sobered by the musings, machinations, and slightly askew protestations of Kierkegaard's characters in order that we might know the failure of our own knowledge and perceive our fallen perception. As he explains regarding the purpose of a "deliberation" like *Works of Love*, one cannot "presuppose that people know essentially what love is"; the writer must first "turn their comfortable way of thinking topsy-turvy" (WL, 470, Supplement). To become aware that our own thinking is comfortably awry requires that we experience for some time the considerable discomfort of an epistemological melt-down. The pseudonyms write to precisely that effect. What Frederick Sontag suggests about one book in the authorship applies as well to the other works we will encounter: each pseudonymous text "appears not to be an advance, yet, without its chastening effect, no real advance is possible."[50] With this in mind, we turn to Kierkegaard's most notoriously confusing text, *Fear and Trembling*.

CHAPTER 2

Provoking the question: deceiving ourselves in Fear and Trembling

I could easily write a whole book if I were to expound on the various misunderstandings, the awkward positions, the botched up movements I have encountered in just my own little experience.

(FT, 46)

It takes no time at all to be deceived; one can be deceived immediately and remain so for a long time – but to become aware of the deception takes time . . . No earnest person, therefore, wearies of tracking down the illusions.

(WL, 124)

INTRODUCTION

It may seem odd to read *Fear and Trembling* as related to *Works of Love*. In *Works of Love*, Kierkegaard describes God's command to love the other, while Johannes de Silentio, the character/narrator of *Fear and Trembling*, meditates on Abraham's absolute faith. There is an obvious Other in *Fear and Trembling* with whom the reader must grapple, but that Other is, most obviously, God. Indeed, it may appear at first glance as if de Silentio focuses solely on the individual's relationship to the Almighty. Yet Abraham is not alone with God on Mount Moriah. Isaac is there. And the very human other whom de Silentio can neither marry nor receive back with joy is significantly present in *Fear and Trembling*. Or, we should say, the girl's absence is saliently conspicuous, for the circumstance on which de Silentio bases his admiration and poetic description of Abraham is the girl's dismissal, or murder, or sacrifice. We may therefore interpret de Silentio as referring, in the quote above, to the very book he authors. *Fear and Trembling* is Kierkegaard's poetic exposition on the "various misunderstandings, the awkward positions, and the botched up movements" that make up a collision between the poet, God, and the girl; by way of this text, we are to question whether said girl has been

banished due to divine command, fear, lack of faith, or dearth of imagination. Through de Silentio's convoluted musings on his own multiple
possibilities, Kierkegaard prompts our own work of self-critical discernment. To employ the quote above from *Works of Love*, two assumptions in
de Silentio's text are (1) that we are deceived, and (2) that we must "take
the time to become aware of the deception." By way of his pseudonym,
Kierkegaard textually pesters us, at length, to be sufficiently "earnest"
and "track down" our own illusions.[1]

De Silentio's poetic work thus depicts literarily the theme of self-
delusion in *Works of Love*. In order for us to read *Works of Love* well,
we must be pried open to the possibility that what we think to be the
case about ourselves and our purposes toward others is a knot of faulty
suppositions. It is helpful to read *Fear and Trembling* first in our treatment
of the pseudonymous works, where he repeatedly sorts through a character's surreptitious role in a girl's eviction, as well as the reader's own
conflicting motives toward the beloved. One of Kierkegaard's textual
purposes in *Fear and Trembling* is to initiate this question of cloaked causes,
to evoke in the reader the strong sense of self-skepticism necessary if we
are to read *Works of Love* effectively – as more than merely a detailed
description of the idea of love. The law of love, as Kierkegaard describes
it in *Works of Love*, "prevent[s] love from coming to a standstill in any self-
deception or from gratifying itself in any illusion" (WL, 126). We may
read the call, in *Fear and Trembling*, for us to stand shuddering and baffled
before Mount Moriah as in service to the larger, more explicit summons
to undeceived repentance in *Works of Love*. Kierkegaard intends for us
to involve ourselves with de Silentio, Abraham, and each of his other
conjured characters in order that we might liken and distinguish our
predicament from Abraham's and acknowledge our veiled and distorted
aims with respect to our beloved. To read *Fear and Trembling* with *Works of
Love* heightens Kierkegaard's call in *Works of Love* for us to acknowledge
the resilience, complexity, and ambiguity of illicit aims and, ultimately,
the treachery of our love.[2]

The quote from Hamann, through which the reader enters *Fear and
Trembling*, implies that the message of the text is itself deceptive: "What
Tarquinius Superbus said in the garden by means of the poppies, the
son understood but the messenger did not" (FT, 3).[3] In this opening
reference, Kierkegaard indirectly suggests that the sender of the message
does not trust the messenger, and that the meaning of the text is in some
way encoded. The writer prompts us, at the beginning of the text, to
suspect both that our messenger, de Silentio, is unreliable, and that he is

incapable of grasping the meaning of the text he writes. The meaning we are to receive from the book is hidden, encoded in a form that our narrator cannot perceive.

The reader's task is thus comparable to excavation, and the merman discourse of Problem III is a clue to the text's meaning, buried as it is deep in the last of de Silentio's quandaries. Perhaps because this section comes at the end of a labyrinthine text, some commentators have overlooked its potential significance for our reading of the book as a whole. The conundrum we are prompted to consider in the merman passage is that, while those around Abraham could not understand his act because Abraham had received a private command from God, one who similarly acts outside the ethical, by breaking an engagement for instance, may be acting out of sin (FT, 88). We are introduced to the debauched merman, who must go back to the ocean without his chosen prey (Agnes), because, disarmed by her innocence, he is unable to complete his act of seduction (FT, 92–94). That is, the merman turns back from the act not because of his own virtue, but through the accident of Agnes's. Kierkegaard prods the reader to consider the possibility that our hidden and obscure actions may not be laudable in any sense, but may rather be a matter of self-deception, malice, or cowardice.[4] For those living in the aftermath of the fall, the encoded message may be a summons to discover, disclose, and confess what otherwise remains hidden to us and to the world. As C. Stephen Evans sums it up, "For some people, the possibility that ethics is not the final word is very important, for if ethics is the final word, then their lives are hopeless."[5] If we are more often like the duplicitous merman than the divinely sanctioned Abraham, then our hope lies in finding another way to God, another way to make "a movement by virtue of the absurd" – a way that Kierkegaard charts through repentance and the humble reception of a gift.

With this reading of *Fear and Trembling*, another hero emerges, or rather an alternative heroine, again from Problem III: Tobit's Sarah, whose courage humbly and graciously to receive Tobias's self-sacrificial gift of love may prefigure our own reception of grace through Christ. Here again, a prominent strain from *Works of Love* resonates with de Silentio's meandering reflections. According to Kierkegaard's description of faithful intimacy in *Works of Love*, true love is contingent upon our recognition that we are dependent upon God's work in Christ; we love best within a relation of gratefully acknowledged indebtedness.[6] De Silentio moves, in this section of *Fear and Trembling*, from the merman, to a call to judge oneself honestly, to a consideration of Sarah's willingness to receive love, even though she is "a damaged specimen of a human being" (FT, 104). One moves with de Silentio in order textually to glimpse the possibility of sin and guilt, to consider the likelihood that one is, oneself, a "damaged specimen," and to be introduced to this other biblical mentor, Sarah, who humbly wills to be beholden. Kierkegaard's homiletic aim is more implicit than explicit in this pseudonymous text; we are narratively prepared to keep stumbling toward repentance. Although de Silentio is, as one who lives in infinite resignation, unable ultimately to make the final movement toward repentance and grateful reception, the reader is given a hint as to Kierkegaard's cryptically Christian message delivered by the poet. By analogy with Kierkegaard's opening epigraph: what Kierkegaard says in the text by means of the poet's musing, the careful reader may understand but the poet does not.

Abraham is not thereby excluded as a guide. While *Fear and Trembling* is about sin, duplicity, and our need for graced forgiveness, it may return to the reader as a text about ethics, the untranslatable obligation of the individual before God alone, and God's judgment against an idolatry that fuses self and other. As Ronald M. Green argues against Gene Outka in "Enough IS Enough! *Fear and Trembling* is NOT about Ethics," the text speaks of "divine conduct" and even "the classical Pauline–Lutheran theme of justification by faith," but this is also a text about "human conduct" in the midst of faith.[7] Although the latter theme is necessarily dependent on the former, as faithful love depends upon repentance, ethics is not as "radically secondary" as Green contends.[8] On the other side of our recognition of "persistent human failure," and "God's redeeming grace" lies our "direct relationship to God" and all the terror that such a relationship ethically entails.[9] The text supports both Green's and Gene Outka's readings because Kierkegaard intends for the reader to experience in *Fear and Trembling* the perils of truly Christian ethics. Both scholars are correct but mistaken in that neither a strictly soteriological nor an exclusively ethical reading is in itself sufficiently troubling. This tension will be clearer as we proceed.

Our soteriological reading of the text should not eclipse Abraham as a focal point for our imaginations. Instead, Problem III disorients and repositions our relationship to de Silentio's defense of Abraham in Problems I and II. While we who live in sin are not able to walk along confidently with Abraham up Mount Moriah, we must be startled and instructed by his story; his example is indeed to have "normative force," but of a strange kind.[10] The chastened and humbled individual who completes *Fear and Trembling* must perpetually reread (and relive)

Problems I and II, reconsidering Abraham as a disquieting reminder to love our beloved from a self-critical and reverent distance. And here again *Works of Love* instructively intersects with *Fear and Trembling*. Kierkegaard makes clear in *Works of Love* that those who would live faithfully and love truly must face God's demand that each of us relate to God as individuals. The most fundamental and thus prior relationship for which I exist and for which my beloved exists is the God-relationship.[11] My recognition of conscience requires of me a distance from my beloved, both for the sake of my own and his own life before God. Abraham, Isaac, and their incomprehensible climb up Mount Moriah must function as a recurring, disconcerting motif, as we attempt to love knowing that Isaac does not belong to Abraham. My beloved is not my own, and I am not his.

We who are fallen must be baffled and hindered by this motif, rather than stalwartly encouraged by Abraham's story. Abraham's faithful resolve to kill Isaac remains in irresolvable tension both with the merman's duplicity and with Sarah's humble reception of Tobias's love. Given that we, like de Silentio and the merman, continue to live in sin as well as grace, we are unable to map the trajectory of our own climb up Mount Moriah. We rarely discern our motivations honestly when distancing ourselves from our beloved. And even when we do glimpse truthfully our broken aims, we too often resort to a self-protective cloak of silence. Abraham was the father of faith, but we are the children of deception. Those who live in the midst of the fall cannot well discern whether our wariness in love and our refusal to speak are due to deceit and/or cowardice or to holy caution and apt reserve. The note of peril must return in that we can neither "fully anticipate what God commands us to do" nor accurately assess whether the voice calling us to leave the beloved is of God or of self.[12] The task of loving both God and neighbor faithfully is thus one undertaken not with blessed assurance, but rather with fear and trembling. To the extent that we repeatedly scrutinize our motives, Sarah's story of confession and receptivity returns to inform our response.

In this chapter, we will tread closely behind de Silentio as he muses on Abraham and the other conjured or borrowed characters, in order to note these significant facets of *Fear and Trembling*. My method will be to read Kierkegaard's pseudonymous work with an eye toward its textual and thematic intersections with *Works of Love*. *Fear and Trembling* provides a preliminary occasion to till the ground, so to speak, for our receptive reading of *Works of Love*. Before we meet and struggle with Kierkegaard's other characters, we should first allow this riddling poet to instruct and prod us

in our love, and de Silentio more effectively provokes if we read his text
knowing that we must also read *Works of Love*. We will first move through
the introductory sections of the book, wherein we are separated from
Abraham and are ourselves called into question; consider Kierkegaard's
radical position in Problems I and II; proceed to the passages from Problem III in which de Silentio introduces sin, repentance, and gratitude;
and then return to consider Abraham as a stark reminder that we each
belong to God. Through this means of interpretation, we may attend to
the suggestive but underdeveloped religious and ethical intimations of
Fear and Trembling. In her trenchant reading of *Fear and Trembling*, Louise
Carroll Keeley persuades that "despite the poetics of their presentation
and theme, a point of religious instruction is at stake."[13] De Silentio's
instruction is incomplete, but instructively so. The reader is prompted
by *Fear and Trembling* to seek a more religiously reliable messenger than
this poet. We must read on.

CONSIDERING ABRAHAM AND DOUBTING OURSELVES

While many who teach *Fear and Trembling* skip over the first four sections to
dwell on Problems I and II as the heart of the matter, we must give careful
attention to the discussion that precedes de Silentio's first quandary.[14]
Before explicitly beginning his philosophical argument on Abraham's
case against Hegel and Kant, de Silentio moves from a Preface to an
Exordium to a Eulogy to a Preliminary Expectoration. Through these
multiple beginnings, de Silentio distinguishes himself and the reader from
the righteous Abraham before finally discussing Problem I, "Is There a
Teleological Suspension of the Ethical." These complex, preliminary sections disconcert and distinguish us from the scriptural story of Abraham
and Isaac, in a way not dissimilar from Kierkegaard's attempt in *Works
of Love* to make strange again the biblical command to love. Before we
consider the possibility that God calls us to sacrifice someone on Mount
Moriah, we must trudge slowly through de Silentio's extensive qualifi-
cations of our relationship to the one who was so called. By the time we
move to de Silentio's more straightforwardly philosophical discussion in
Problems I and II, Kierkegaard has trained the reader to view Abraham
as one whose faith and action "no thought can grasp" (FT, 53). Through
de Silentio's complex confusion in these initial sections, Kierkegaard
compels the reader to perceive Abraham's case as beyond our moral
comprehension. Abraham's narrative, through de Silentio's rendering,
calls into question the comprehensibility of morality itself. But if we are,

as de Silentio suggests, qualitatively different from the father of faith, and yet we are in a whirl of moral cacophony, then we must seek an alternative explanation for our disorientation. Kierkegaard thus leads us to consider why our own lives, loves, and actions are not readily demarcated as obedient or rebellious. It is not until Problem III that de Silentio stumbles on sin as the circumvented answer to this question.

Allowing de Silentio the poet to be our guide as we begin to consider Abraham is a risky business. As Kierkegaard explains in *Works of Love*,

the poet can understand everything, in riddles, and wonderfully explain everything, in riddles, but he cannot understand himself or understand that he himself is a riddle. (WL, 30)

By this definition, the poet exists in the middle of a conundrum that he may only interpret through the multiplication of puzzles. This form is crucial to the matter at hand; both the explicit and implicit subjects of *Fear and Trembling* require unease. Kierkegaard has taken up this riddling and perplexed poet for his voice precisely because de Silentio can achieve the dizzying effect requisite for a text on faith and morality. Looking into the many facets of Abraham's case and our own relation to it, de Silentio further fractures an already fracturing narrative, creating an intricate kaleidoscope of insight and misinterpretation. This is the case particularly in his four prefatory sections. Even with considerable mental effort, the reader cannot distinguish definitively which colorful sliver is the result of de Silentio's keen perception and which is warped by his poetic vision. To extend and enlarge this metaphor, one reads these sections of *Fear and Trembling* as if walking through an excellently wrought maze of mirrors, a kind of life-size kaleidoscope, wandering through doors that seemed to be mirrors and smashing into what otherwise seemed an exit.

In this way, the task of self-discernment becomes both impossible and inescapable. Through the poet's riddled method, Kierkegaard complicates Abraham's work beyond our comprehension and goads the reader to acknowledge that we exist in a carnival house of fractured truth and error. In Ed Mooney's close reading of the text, he suggests that the poet's method "not only preserves a complex truth from oversimplification, it also puts responsibility for grasping the truth where it belongs, with the reading, listening self."[15] One significant temptation is to discount the disorder as solely de Silentio's own, but to pull de Silentio before the grand inquisitor of accuracy and condemn his missteps would be to miss the point altogether. Although we must be suspicious of our (often maddening) guide, we must also allow the text to do its work on us as readers and listeners. While we are to want more about the moral life than de Silentio can give, we are also to suspect ourselves and our own ability to perceive. While involving ourselves in the text, we must not forget that, as Kierkegaard puts it, "the most dangerous traitor of all is the one every person has within himself" (WL, 23). Our mistaken narrator does not pose the greatest danger. What Kierkegaard says about the hypocrite is true also of the poet: "[no poet] has ever deceived anyone who in fear and trembling before God was afraid of himself" (WL, 15). It is Kierkegaard's purpose, through de Silentio, to evoke in us such fear.

De Silentio begins *Fear and Trembling* with a preface, stating that he must drive up the price of true understanding. While some suppose themselves to have made a "preliminary movement" of doubt and to have "gone further" than faith, de Silentio, as he states later in Problem III, wishes to "chastise many a man in our day who believes he has already attained the highest" (FT, 5, 100). We enter the book under a memorial to René Descartes, that "venerable, humble, [and] honest thinker" who spent much time attempting to doubt sufficiently (FT, 5). De Silentio seeks to evoke "proficiency in doubting" in order to reacquaint the assured reader with "the anxiety and trembling that disciplined the youth" (FT, 6,7). This text on Abraham, Isaac, and God's command to the individual thus begins with de Silentio's suggestion that we imagine ourselves as Descartes, who "found [him]self embarrassed with so many doubts and errors that it seemed to [him] that the effort to instruct [him]self had no effect other than the increasing discovery of [his] own ignorance" (FT, 6). From the outset, de Silentio links the possibility of faith with the prerequisite of self-doubt. As Louis Mackey so well phrases it, Kierkegaard wishes, through de Silentio, to "deceive this generation out of its self-deception."[16] To those who cheerfully hope to ride "the system" in order to arrive at faith (like one boards the new omnibus in order to reach the market) de Silentio suggests that we become sufficiently addled by Abraham's story to be, like Descartes, convinced of our own ignorance (FT, 8).[17] We are duly forewarned that the form and the content of the ensuing text are intended to disconcert.

We are eventually to confess ourselves at the very least ignorant and even willfully self-deceptive in our attempts to determine what is definitively ethical. In both *Works of Love* and *Fear and Trembling*, one's hidden and obscure intentions are at issue. We are warned in *Works of Love*, that "there is no work, not one single one, not even the best, about which we unconditionally dare to say: The one who does this unconditionally demonstrates love by it." Everything "depends on how the work is done"

(WL, 13). This obscurity applies, in *Works of Love*, to our discernment both of our own and the other's motives; one's own intentions are often at a basic level selfish, and our perception of another's work is most often clouded by our desire to judge others to our own advantage. Given the resilience of our selfish aims and the hiddeness of our motives, no act in itself discloses either devotion or transgression. Even an act so supposedly selfless as donating everything to the poor may be done with an intention that renders the giver self-loving rather than truly charitable (WL, 13).

In the Exordium, we walk along with de Silentio as he follows Abraham up the mountain, doubting the possibility of insight into Abraham's action. How was Abraham able to walk resolutely "with sorrow before him and Isaac beside him" (FT, 9)? Anticipated grief and companionship seem mutually exclusive. If Abraham must obey God and thus distance himself violently from Isaac, then how is he to keep Isaac truly in view? We are to "understand the story less and less" (FT, 9) as we read four possible interpretations of the scene. If Isaac had pleaded for his life, desperate to delay his father's act, surely Abraham would have been tempted to shield Isaac from the truth and present himself as an idolater (FT, 10–11). If Abraham had been determined to meet God's requirement, how could he have gratefully received back his son from the hand of the one who had threatened to destroy Isaac? Surely Abraham's eyes would have been "darkened" and his joy extinguished after such a radical encounter with God's power over life and death (FT, 12). How could Abraham help but doubt his reception of God's command? How could he fail to understand himself as a terrible sinner rather than as the father of faith (FT, 13)? What effect would such irresolution have had on Isaac, who had to return to live alongside a father who doubted God's goodness yet also went up the mountain toward death (FT, 14)?

Kierkegaard next has de Silentio bring Abraham's conundrum into the nursery. Following each possible interpretation of Abraham, de Silentio ponders the many methods of weaning a child, considering the ambiguity of the process and a mother's ambivalence as she separates from her child (FT, 11–14). This under-treated portion of the Exordium is telling, for in it, Kierkegaard moves us from the scriptural setting of Mount Moriah to scenes of supposedly ordinary domesticity. The extraordinary sacrifice of Isaac is somehow akin to this, one of the most commonplace of tasks. Kierkegaard will continue this method as we move abruptly from mountaintop to prosaic parish, from commendable sacrifice to a broken engagement. Our mundane lives are strangely related and radically dissimilar to the work of the father of faith. How is a mother to remain loving and confident that her child will survive even while she very physically distinguishes herself from the infant as a dependent other? Each installment of the Exordium asks a similar question, moving from mountain to household. Ed Mooney is one of the few interpreters who neither rushes (with eyes averted) past these nursing/weaning passages nor considers them "an outcropping of anomalous imagery." He suggests that "these vignettes describe an ordeal of love and separation, of anxiety and hope."[18] Our lives, and our daily loves, are somehow implicated through Abraham's singular task. At this point in the text, we have no way even to begin an interpretation of the connection or the disjuncture. De Silentio concludes his Exordium asking, who indeed can understand the work of Abraham? Kierkegaard wishes for us already to intimate that our own work will become, through the work of the text, equally bewildering.

We who would be ethical must therefore spend much time and effort determining our intentions toward another. But, as de Silentio implies already here at the beginning of the text, such work is fraught with occasions for self-delusion; it is a task as treacherous as our escape from de Silentio's kaleidoscope. Discernment requires, from the onset, a confession of one's consistent tendency toward self-deception. De Silentio's attempt, in the preliminary sections of *Fear and Trembling*, alternatively to fracture and simplify the motives and actions of Abraham gives the reader a model for the manner of searching necessary as de Silentio proceeds with his discussion of sin and as Kierkegaard proceeds, in *Works of Love*, with his portrayal of truthful love. What if Abraham had not traveled up the mountain, knife in hand, due to and together with an absolute faith in God? What if Abraham had not loved Isaac, but instead wished, on some almost indiscernible level, to be rid of him? By considering the alternatives to Abraham's unsearchable faith, de Silentio gives us an instructive opportunity to become morally befuddled.

The transition from Exordium to de Silentio's Eulogy is jarring; we are no longer in the nursery because not one of these four takes on the scene describes accurately Abraham's climb up the mountain. In the next two sections, de Silentio focuses our attention on two features of the story that make it particularly inexplicable within his and our moral universe: Abraham is certain that the command to kill his son is from God, and Abraham unquestionably loves Isaac even while unsheathing the knife.

First, Abraham's act defies each of the Exordium's imagined scenarios because Abraham is absolutely certain and unwaveringly resolute in his adherence to God's command. Abraham is neither bewildered nor torn; he is faithfully single-minded. In his Eulogy on Abraham, de Silentio thus begins his book a third time, underlining Abraham's lack of doubt: "He knew that it was God the Almighty who was testing him" and thus had no moment of indecision (FT, 22). Using Paul's refrain from Hebrews 11:8–19 as his own, de Silentio relates Abraham's enduring confidence, from the onset of his summons, that the voice is God's own. Abraham becomes the father of Israel "by faith," and, for de Silentio, the crux of the matter is Abraham's capacity to trust, hear, and obey God's call (FT, 19–20). This, de Silentio surmises, we can neither understand nor approximate. Given that we call out to the mountains, "Hide me" when overwhelmed by mere "vicissitudes," and, even when obedient, remain unable to carry out God's command with confidence, we can scarcely understand Abraham's work (FT, 21). And this difference is a line between faith and unfaith:

If Abraham had doubted as he stood there on Mount Moriah, if irresolute he had looked around, if he had happened to spot the ram before drawing the knife . . . he would have kept Isaac, and yet how changed! For his return would have been a flight, his deliverance an accident, his reward disgrace, his future perhaps perdition. (FT, 21)

Abraham's ascent is disgrace, unless his assent to the truth of the command is unequivocal. De Silentio insists that "anyone who looks upon this scene is blinded" (FT, 22). Abraham's ability to go up the mountain and then return to sit "happily together at the dinner table" with Isaac,[19] trusting that he has heard and obeyed God, is more than de Silentio or we may comprehend.

Although he should be struck blind and dumb by Abraham's certainty, de Silentio goes on to consider Abraham's inscrutable love. Beginning the text for a fourth time, with a Preliminary Expectoration, de Silentio explains that one necessary cause of Abraham's holy anxiety is that he was called by God to go against his deeply held love for and commitment to Isaac (FT, 30). It is key that Abraham was asked to give up not "the best" as some "vague" symbol of that from which we may all comfortably part, but rather the son whom he was called to, and indeed did, love more than himself (FT, 28). The fact that Abraham was truly called also to love Isaac, and that he met this divine command even while sacrificing Isaac, is as crucial as Abraham's lack of doubt. Imaginatively placing himself in that moment on Mount Moriah, de Silentio insists, "that I loved [Isaac] with my whole soul is the presupposition without which the whole thing becomes a misdeed" (FT, 35). If God's command to give up Isaac had come as anything other than a terrifying collision of two commitments met, Abraham would not be the father of faith but instead a monstrous opportunist. The clash between the "ethical expression for what Abraham did" and "the religious expression" is to "render" us "sleepless." If we are to begin to comprehend Abraham, we must be "willing to work and be burdened" by the fact that God definitely called Abraham to go against God's own command that Abraham love Isaac (FT, 28).[20] As de Silentio describes him, Abraham was "great by the love that is hatred to oneself" (FT, 17). It would be horrifying rather than holy if Abraham were great by a love of self that is a lack of love for Isaac.[21]

In a blink, we are back down the mountain and in the local parish, with de Silentio pondering how a pastor should bring Mount Moriah to the average Christian. De Silentio's chosen homiletic method would be to preach as he writes – that is, initially to spend much time (whether successive Sundays or multiple, preliminary sections of the book) distinguishing Abraham from those listening comfortably in the pew. Abraham was "worthy of being called God's chosen one" whereas "who [here] is such a person?" (FT, 31). Who can claim Abraham's certainty regarding his required task? De Silentio suggests further that the preacher should spend several Sundays intensifying the effect of Abraham's love for Isaac: "I hope to describe [Abraham's love] in such a way that there would not be many a father in the realms and lands of the king who would dare to maintain that he loved in this way" (FT, 31). If the homily is to work, the preacher must dumbfound the hearer by the collision of command with command. Otherwise, the sermon will be a description of divinely justified murder. He continues, "If it were done properly, the result would be that some of the fathers would by no means demand to hear more but for the time being would be pleased if they actually succeeded in loving as Abraham loved" (FT, 32).

These two methods by which the preacher should introduce and then remove the listener from Abraham correspond to de Silentio's efforts in his Eulogy and Preliminary Expectoration. Due to his capacity to hear clearly God's command to kill, and his unwavering love for Isaac, Abraham must be portrayed in contrast to the listener. Having begun with a Preface calling us to acquire a "proficiency in doubting," de Silentio then marvels at Abraham's certitude and divine justification (FT, 6). By "speaking humanly about [Abraham's greatness], as if it happened yesterday," de Silentio intends to "let the greatness itself be the distance that either elevates or judges" (FT, 34). The link between our requisite doubt and our necessary awe is forged somehow in this "elevating" or "condemning" "distance." The remainder of the Preliminary Expectoration is de Silentio's confused and confusing attempt to bring us to the edge of that distance.

Next, de Silentio explicitly imagines himself at the foot of Mount Moriah, trying both to sort out the distinction between willingness to obey and undue alacrity and to describe what it would mean to hear the voice of God. This latter description is, he decides, impossible. We are decidedly not Abraham because "in the world of time God and [we] cannot talk with each other, we have no language in common" (FT, 35). Even if he were capable of hearing and heeding such a command from God, de Silentio would not have been able to receive Isaac again as a gift from God. By his estimation, we could not endure the collision. We could not hear the command to kill and the command to love, one in either ear; we would hold an ear shut and run to the task. De Silentio muses that he would not have "dragged and drifted" or "caused a delay" but instead would have "arrived too early in order to get it over sooner" (FT, 35). He could not have possibly walked "with sorrow before him and Isaac beside him" (as he has previously described Abraham's walk, FT, 9) but rather would have resolutely resigned himself to leave Isaac behind on the mountain (FT, 35). This, "the infinite movement of resignation," which he calls a "substitute for faith," stands in conspicuous contrast to Abraham's movement up the mountain both heeding God and loving Isaac (FT, 35). Abraham "needed no time to rally to finitude and its joy" upon receiving back Isaac, thus revealing the truth of faithful love; Abraham never relinquished Isaac in a way that impoverished either his obedience or his love for his son. Although there may be a person genuinely called by God and enabled to continue like Abraham up, and back down, Mount Moriah, de Silentio stops: "Abraham I cannot understand; in a certain sense I can learn nothing from him except to be amazed" (FT, 37).

MOUNTING A WINGED HORSE

To further draw out the difference between himself and Abraham, de Silentio posits three knights, the happy knight of faith, the knight of resignation, and the knight who moves from resignation to faith. Studying his descriptions of these knights, the reader begins to surmise that our narrator is intimately at odds with his subject: faith. Our narrator's own confessed inability to "make" the "movements of faith" colors the supposedly accurate way that he "describe[s] the movements of faith," in that even his faithful knight does not receive "the finite whole and intact" (FT, 37). As de Silentio understands faith, one does not receive the *other*; indeed, one does not *receive* at all, but rather one "gains" (FT, 37). The form of de Silentio's discourse reflects two facets of de Silentio's error: first, in his account of our resignation prior to faith, the beloved, whether in the form of Isaac or a previously betrothed girl, is lost, and, second, the movements of each knight are of his own making. Our poetic narrator attempts to depict Abraham's singular predicament so close to life that we might be appropriately "elevated or judged" (FT, 34). But in so doing, the scene on Mount Moriah becomes refracted through de Silentio's own confusion. We do, in the process, discover ourselves judged, but in a way that de Silentio does not foresee.

In his refracted depiction of resignation and faith, de Silentio reveals his own inability to receive the beloved back from God, in life or in the text. By the time de Silentio describes the knight of resignation, whose work he knows personally and with whom he identifies himself, Kierkegaard grants the reader a clue to de Silentio's particular distortion of faith. The movement of resignation de Silentio makes is one that he wills, as he puts it, "all by myself" (FT, 48). By "starving [him]self into submission," de Silentio hopes to hurry the process along, renounce the girl and the world, and prepare himself for the absurd (FT, 48). His impatience betrays him as one who, like his contemporaries, wants to hurry past the real work of faith: "We mount a winged horse, and in the same instant we are on Mount Moriah, in the same instant we see the ram. We forget that Abraham only rode an ass, which trudges along the road" (FT, 52). By the end of de Silentio's Expectoration, Kierkegaard leaves us in anticipation of an alternative way to bring Abraham's story near, so near as to allow for our distinguishing between his and our predicament.

According to de Silentio's account, a true movement of faith "must continually be made by virtue of the absurd," but in such a way "that one does not lose the finite but gains it" (FT, 37). De Silentio confesses that, although he has tried to follow and detect the precise choreography of this absurd dance, he has not himself "found a single authentic existence" (FT, 38). The first refraction appears as he tries to imagine a faithful person on the other side of such a gain. This knight of faith does not show himself as a clear marvel but rather as one whose life is akin to "bourgeois philistinism" (FT, 38). As we watch this man on his walk to and from work (in which he visits "for a moment" with a passerby and looks forward to dinner) we discover that he is "solid all the way through," and has no "poetic incommensurability" about him (FT, 39). In his brief description of this life, de Silentio grasps a thread that Kierkegaard takes up later in his insistence that a faithful person is often "impossible to distinguish" from the "rest of the crowd" (FT, 39), but the way that de Silentio draws out that thread reveals his mistake. The absence of "poetic incommensurability" in this, de Silentio's first description of a knight, comes at a price, and he is particularly awry on the matter of receiving back the finite. First, the most significant object of love for which this knight is hopeful is a "roast lamb's head with vegetables" (FT, 39). In de Silentio's short narrative of the happy knight of faith, the knight does not receive back an invested attention for a beloved with whom he is to sup and live, but rather wills for himself a bumbling and "reckless" "freedom from care" (FT, 40). His movement of supposed "faith" after resignation is about his own resilient amusement. This knight's "movement of infinity by virtue of the absurd" manifests itself most clearly in his "passion" for food and his "keen appetite," but we get no clue here about how such a knight relates to the beloved waiting at home (other than that she will cook the meal). De Silentio's report of faith's return to the finite is marked by one's "finding pleasure in everything," note, without "attachment" (FT, 39). Secondly, this knight does not *receive* back finitude but, rather, "*grasps* it by virtue of the absurd" (FT, 40, my emphasis). There is no real other or Other in this refraction of Abraham's tale. What de Silentio apparently does not realize is that Isaac is surely not akin to a good meal, and God's gift is not to be seized.

It is almost as if de Silentio knows that this tale does not quite work, and we move briskly on to our narrator's next attempt to bring Abraham close – "to express the sublime in the pedestrian" (FT, 41). Conceding that the happy knight of faith, as he has described him, may "easily deceive," he creates another knight, to "illuminate" faith's "relation to actuality" (FT, 41). In this section, de Silentio attempts to parse out and inspect the movement from love to resignation and the shift from resignation to faith. His second knight falls in love with a princess but, after "examining the conditions of his life," decides that his love "cannot possibly be translated from ideality into reality" (FT, 41). While the young man "feels a blissful delight in letting love palpitate in every nerve," he determines that the girl, the occasion for that blissful love, is herself an impossibility (FT, 42). As de Silentio speaks of this knight's love, he once again loses all sense of the other.

According to his account of this "love," the knight becomes "totally absorbed" with his own experience of loving the girl and quickly moves beyond the tediously mundane matter of the girl herself (FT, 42). De Silentio explains that this knight concentrates on the love itself in an attempt to "transfigure [it] into a love of the eternal being," for otherwise his love might dissipate. The latter possibility would be embarrassing, and he "is too proud to be willing to let the whole substance of his life turn out to have been an affair of the fleeting moment" (FT, 44). So the young man wills himself above her. At this point, de Silentio concedes, "From the moment he has made [this] movement, the princess is lost" (FT, 44). The young knight is decidedly above reality and the girl who lives within the finite. He is left clutching "the deep secret that even in loving another person one ought to be sufficient to oneself" (FT, 44). By disconnecting himself from "the lower natures," the young lover is able, according to de Silentio's calculation, to move beyond what he also calls the "baser natures" and to prepare himself for faith (FT, 44–45).

De Silentio attempts then to move from the knight of resignation, so described, to a new depiction of a third knight of faith who receives back what the second knight has resigned. But here, in his final attempt to distinguish and depict Abraham's faith in its "relation to actuality," de Silentio involves the reader in a treacherous, exhausting labyrinth of misunderstanding. The description of faith's precursor reveals much about our narrator's mistake. First, the girl, the other, is lost, whirled poetically into the knight's idea of his love for her. She is banished from his life and from this poetic text due to her apparent participation in prosaic finitude. Only if she "has the courage to enroll herself" in this alternative realm does she become again a viable (and decidedly ethereal) option (FT, 45). Second, according to de Silentio, the movement of faith that follows true resignation should occasion a change in the finite, external possibilities. Faith does not hold direct implication for this self who has determined the finite to be impossible. As with his first, happy knight, this knight loses both God and the girl.

As de Silentio shifts from the third to the first person, we surmise that our narrator is the personification of his own refraction. The willfully "courageous" manner of de Silentio's resignation of the finite (not, we note, of self) promotes a stance that cannot prepare for the receptivity of faith. Something is clearly amiss when de Silentio revels in his own power "through resignation" to "renounce everything" and "make a movement all by [him]self" (FT, 48). To his credit, de Silentio seems to have some perception of his plight, for he explains that, through this mustering of strength, he exhausts himself beyond "getting" the princess back (FT, 49). Nonetheless, our pitiable narrator does not grasp that love cannot be about grasping. While de Silentio may, in his courageous act of resignation, "gain" his "eternal consciousness in blessed harmony with [his] love for the eternal being," he is left alone (FT, 49). Although he has moved beyond what he has, mistakenly, relegated to the "lower" or "baser natures" – who, tellingly, "forget themselves" and thereby "become something new" – he has done so without the girl and without the God to whom he must humbly turn for new life (FT, 43). Forgetting the girl rather than forgetting himself, refusing to become something new, de Silentio tricks himself out of love.

The formidable work of appropriately releasing the beloved while also sustaining a hope of receiving her back is also a motif in *Works of Love*, but in a different "key" than in *Fear and Trembling*.[22] In his "Preliminary Expectoration," de Silentio describes faith as an effort to transcend and distinguish oneself from "the baser natures," a refrain throughout this section. For de Silentio, the movements toward faithful love ascend from the prosaic girl and her impossibility, "upward" to the idea of loving her, on to the love itself, to love for "the eternal being," and then back to the idea of loving, without a corresponding return "below" to the girl in her actuality (FT, 44). Through this supposedly upward progression, de Silentio hopes to protect his love from the fluctuating nature of what is possible and impossible. By contrast, Kierkegaard insists forcefully in *Works of Love* that the first and recurrent movement of faithful love entails a movement of self not upward from finite reality, but inward toward one's relation to "duty's shall," the only means whereby "love is eternally and happily secured against despair" (WL, 40). Whereas the young man described by de Silentio aspires to "examine the conditions of his life," and evaluate externally the probability of "translating ideality into reality" (FT, 41–42), the imperative made explicit in *Works of Love* is to turn "duty's shall" inward in order to examine the currently implicit conditions of one's love. The first movement toward veritable love is thus self-inspection in the face of God's command that we continue to love regardless of external circumstances.

Kierkegaard does suggest that such self-inspection requires distance from the beloved, but the sort of distance recommended in *Works of Love* contrasts decisively with the distance achieved by de Silentio's young knight. In *Works of Love*, the call to relinquish the other acts as a wedge between the lover and his parasitical and/or deluded dependence on another. Error ensues precisely when one attempts, as does de Silentio, to progress from "relating oneself with infinite passion to a particular something" to love for the eternal (WL, 40). One message *of Works of Love* is that one must wrest oneself away from the illusory state wherein the beloved becomes a "possession" by means of which the lover climbs to eternity; one must turn toward God as the sole definition and source of one's love (WL, 38). Whereas de Silentio asserts that his resigned distance from the girl establishes that he is "one who is sufficient unto oneself" (FT, 44), Kierkegaard represents resignation as the necessary condition of turning to God as the sole source and test of love's possibility. The movement from love of the beloved to love of God is thus not a willed upward progression, as de Silentio suggests; on the contrary, it involves a humiliating break of self from the other and a full turn toward God. Only then may one attempt, with God's law and grace in view, to love within the uncertain realm of finitude: "The love that has undergone eternity's change by becoming duty is not exempted from misfortune, but is saved from despair" (WL, 42). As Kierkegaard describes it in *Works of Love*, the command to love distances the lover from the beloved in order to place God between the lover and the object of his possession. Only then can the chastened young man receive back the one with whom he is daily to sup.

As we shall see when we move to *Repetition* in the next chapter, Kierkegaard's characters and pseudonyms are often revealingly mistaken in their use of scripture. While de Silentio rightly seeks to distance the reader from Abraham and rightly undertakes to precipitate in the reader the disorientation such a story affords, he also, by his own admission, wishes "like a leech [to] suck all the anxiety and distress and torment out of [Abraham's] suffering" (FT, 53). In his narrative construal of his predicament, de Silentio closes the gap between himself and the "father of faith" by likening his dismissal of the girl to Abraham's obedience to God's call that he sacrifice Isaac.[23] De Silentio's resignation comes after he "examines" the situation and "convenes" his own thoughts to conclude that he cannot marry the girl; even as he describes it, it is evident that he has not heard a command from God that she be sacrificed (FT, 42). De Silentio reveals, in this section, the danger of bringing Abraham's story so close. The juxtaposition of existence and scriptural narrative may judge, but it may also provide the means for false elevation. The "tears" with which he has spun his yarn and sewn his protective shirt are not his own but Abraham's (FT, 45).[24] The security and "protection," the "peace and rest" this borrowed story of righteous suffering provides are potentially delusive.

Through de Silentio's delusion, Kierkegaard warns the reader of a double danger. Under and through de Silentio's earnest discourse on faith and resignation, Kierkegaard manages subtly to suggest that we should suspect the counsel of our self-appointed guide up Mount Moriah. As one who is, by his own confession, in a state of perpetual resignation, de Silentio cannot himself understand the import of his tale. But Kierkegaard's further warning involves the reader himself. Kierkegaard's purpose is not simply to inspire us to censure de Silentio, for in that case, these sections would indeed be dispensable. On the contrary, it is Kierkegaard's purpose that we should find, in de Silentio's misunderstanding, evidence of our own. We are to proceed up Mount Moriah, and through the Problems, suspicious of ourselves.

Before de Silentio returns to questions that will similarly probe his own situation, he embarks on a much more directly philosophical consideration of Abraham's paradox. By "drawing out in the form of problemata the dialectical aspects implicit in the story of Abraham," de Silentio takes up Abraham's own case before the tribunal of current human understanding (FT, 53). We will move with de Silentio through this two-part defense and then return to Problem III, wherein the situation again becomes more self-implicating than defensive.[25] It is within this third section that the reader is given a corrective lens through which to read the first two problems, lest Problems I and II similarly invite self-delusion. We who are mired in sin must take care not to follow uncritically de Silentio's false lead, creating our own crises of possibility and resignation, thus precluding the other preparatory movement toward faith: repentant confession.

LIFE UNDER DIVINE CONFISCATION

As we move from the prefatory comments in *Fear and Trembling* to Problems I and II, the literary tone of the text shifts from poetic to philosophical, and the argument becomes more straightforward, even though its conclusions are radical. Although we should read these two short passages with de Silentio's prefatory meanderings and subsequent discussion of sin in view, Gene Outka is correct to say that, for Kierkegaard, these two problems propose the possibility upon which the remaining text is built: the individual stands before God alone.[26] While we should reread de Silentio's defense of Abraham from a self-critical distance, and readjust our vision of our own predicament after sin is introduced in Problem III, these two sections are crucial. We cannot proceed without accepting what Kierkegaard wishes very forcefully to bring home to us in these first two problems: any theory of ethics that reduces the individual's moral calling to a clearly articulated understanding of "social morality"

(Hegel) or some rationally grasped universal proposition (Kant) reduces God to an "invisible vanishing point" and belies the radical individuality and potential obscurity of each person's duty before God (FT, 55, 68). Abraham, like each one of us, lives a life that is "like a book under divine confiscation" (FT, 77). His and our responsibility before God is ultimately not "public property" whether the notion of public be socially complex or derived from some reasonably distilled version of the collective *nous*. If Abraham's story, or Mary's, or Christ's, is to have significance for those who profess to have faith, the faithful must not succumb to the explanatory power of Kant's or Hegel's moral system. Kierkegaard intends to interject Abraham's story into the felicitous conversation between philosophical ethics and faith, positing it as a quandary out of which we cannot reason ourselves.

It is too simple, though, to presume that these two problems in themselves affirm Abraham's situation as a trope for our own. I will return to the "normative force" of Abraham's obedience below, but first we must note another important strand of argument in Problem II: de Silentio intimates that Abraham's faith and our own faith require a confession of ethical "ignorance," and have as a consequence a sobering sense of moral peril. Abandoning his prior, poetic description of "infinite resignation," in which the individual rises above the finite in order courageously to grasp the infinite, de Silentio tries out the possibility that infinite resignation occurs "only when the individual has emptied himself in the infinite," and he links this to the individual's recognition of ignorance (FT, 69). De Silentio's rectifying shift in this section is a subtle one: the would-be knight of faith is first to resign *himself* rather than resigning *the finite*. In relating himself "absolutely to the absolute," the person of faith acknowledges that there is no intermediary source of assurance that he is in the right (FT, 71); vindication is hidden with and utterly dependent upon God. The only measure by which one's act is, in fact, justified is the same measure by which the act is condemned: Abraham "must love Isaac with his whole soul," else the act is murder, but the law of parental love to which he thereby conforms condemns his action as heinous (FT, 74). The "absolute contradiction" must be complete in that his love for Isaac may at no point wane, but his very love for Isaac bespeaks his moral obligation to Isaac. In this way the knight of faith "creeps along slowly" (FT, 77). It is in this untenable situation of extreme incongruity, justified before God yet morally damned, that the faithful individual must proceed at a crawl. The surest indication that one recognizes one's position before God is in one's consequent stance of "fear and trembling" in full knowledge of "the terrors, " "the distress and anxiety" of faith (FT, 75). Only in this precarious state may one call out, saying, "'You' to God in heaven" (FT, 77). All else is illegitimate familiarity.

FOR CAIN AND ABRAHAM ARE NOT IDENTICAL

De Silentio warns us that Abraham "must love Isaac with his whole soul," else Abraham's witness would be as blasphemous as the witness of Cain (FT, 74). If Abraham's love of Isaac had been diminished in any way, if his willingness to kill had approximated Cain's stance for even a moment, he would have walked up the mountain a murderer. De Silentio's at times agonized and at times detached consideration of Abraham's plight, his struggle to draw up a complete and secure depiction of this collision, is, in part, his attempt to clarify and redeem the knight's sudden break with the princess. If, in even the smallest way, his or our actions differ from Abraham's holy work, then we each share in Cain's, not Abraham's, condition. True discernment of our status thus requires a brutal self-honesty and unflinching self-appraisal. We must be willing to send out "well-trained doves" of a very different sort than does the knight of resignation, who sends out inquisitors to test the finite (FT, 42). The source of our scrutiny must instead be our own self; we must live "under [our own] surveillance" (FT, 75). This theme in *Fear and Trembling* parallels Kierkegaard's more explicit text on honest self-examination. Much of *Works of Love* is Kierkegaard's effort "to penetrate into the innermost hiding place" where a person seeks to evade the law of love, and thus to deny to us "the least little way of escape" (WL, 18). God's requirement is like a hall of mirrors wherein one is refused "even the most unnoticed crevice to hide in if you would be put to shame there" (WL, 248). In his chapter on the law in *Works of Love*, Kierkegaard emphasizes that the command to love our neighbor as ourselves forces us out of "any self-deception or illusion" as to the quality of our love (WL, 113, 126). By considering, with de Silentio, alternative explanations for the young man's broken engagement, we detect the possibility that we are, in our own situation, more like Cain than Abraham.

De Silentio posits that, for Abraham, moral speech is precluded due to God's inexplicable command. The sinner hides from moral inquiry for a very different reason. The subtle difference between Abraham and the sinner is, as de Silentio suggests, "a subject for a poet who [knows] how to pry secrets out of people" (FT, 93). In Problem III, in an effort to pry open his own secrets (and ours), de Silentio brings up two possible scenarios involving action that is enigmatic because it is outside what is understandably ethical. Yet the open disclosure of secrets, to which we are called in this section, does not lead one inexorably toward a happy coincidence with the universal. There exists for the merman and for Abraham an "interiority that is incommensurable with exteriority" (FT, 69), and Kierkegaard assigns de Silentio the task of correcting philosophy's confidence in appearances. Like the merman, we are called to confess that we are unable immediately or ultimately to do what is commanded. Sinner and saint are both related as "the single individual in relation to the absolute" (FT, 93), the saint through extreme obedience and the sinner through rebellion, whether original or commonplace. What is "concealed" from "Sarah, from Eliezer, and from Isaac," is a paradox that may be either "divine or demonic" (FT, 82, 88), and Kierkegaard prompts us to determine for ourselves what we conceal, to allow this poet to uncover the "esthetic *illusion* of magnanimity" in our own narratives (FT, 93, my emphasis). We are, like Queen Elizabeth I, to sit still and ponder, biting our finger, suspecting the motivation behind our willingness to sign Essex's death decree. If we signed the decree even in part because we were angry for lack of a ring from him, we must pray lest we meet Elizabeth's fate.[27]

In this section, de Silentio first has us consider (yet again) the plight of a young man who must call off his marriage to his beloved, this time due to a private, definitively divine pronouncement. If the young man hears from the gods that his marriage will end in tragedy, then he has several possibilities before him (FT, 91). The true mess would be if the man heard not a "pronouncement" from the publicly recognized augurs but instead an encoded and "purely private" revelation regarding his fate (FT, 93). This would place the young man "in an absolute relation to the absolute" and render his predicament completely untranslatable to his beloved and his peers (FT, 93). As far as de Silentio can perceive it, such a young man "would not enjoy his silence but would suffer the agony," and in this way prove himself genuinely "justified" (FT, 93). There are two necessary features of his justification. First, the young man hears the pronouncement privately, in a way that does not allow him any recourse to explanation. Second, and this is crucial, the young man suffers from "having been placed" in the predicament rather than "wanting to place himself" outside the ethical. If the young man's "noble silence" were due to his own movement away from the "universal," he would be duly "disturbed by the demands of the ethical" (FT, 93). This nuance whereby the young man is, in de Silentio's estimation, either "justified" or hiding in the "illusion of magnanimity," is writ large as we move to one who clearly exists, of his own accord, apart from the ethical (FT, 93).

In contrast to the righteously justified young man, de Silentio has us consider the merman, a "demonic" seducer (FT, 94). In this story, the merman's "natural element is disloyal to him" (as de Silentio politely puts it) when he sees that trustful Agnes is "willing to go with him" (FT, 94). The chase is over before it is begun, and thus the merman "cannot seduce Agnes." Given that the merman is, after all, "only a merman," he must return to the sea without Agnes (FT, 95). In this version of "boy loses (or sacrifices, or abandons) girl," the merman's silence on the matter is due to his determination to deceive Agnes; if he speaks in order to explain his separation from Agnes, he will disclose to her his menacing motives. But before narrating the merman's next move, de Silentio considers a possible twist on the story: perhaps Agnes is not so very innocent. Perhaps she is instead "a woman who demands the interesting" (FT, 95). De Silentio is tempted to dwell on this comforting thought, that "Agnes is not entirely without guilt," but instead returns to consider the merman's impasse and the ways in which he might resolve it (FT, 95). The merman may choose to "surrender to this demonic element" that takes hold as he "becomes even more unhappy, for he loved Agnes with a complexity of passions and in addition [has] a new guilt to bear" (FT, 96). If he were to follow this possible trajectory, the merman would revel in his torment and would thereby begin outwardly to resemble the justified young man. However, this would be a "similarity that can be misleading"; "all the anguish the merman suffers in silence seems proof that his silence is justified," but the merman's silence would be due to his determination to mislead and to cloak his original deception (FT, 96). Rather than moving from repentance to disclosure, the merman instead would rupture Agnes's love for him by "endeavor[ing] to incite all the dark passions in her, to belittle her, [and] to ridicule her . . ." (FT, 96). Through this movement, the merman's motive "remains hidden," and he rids himself of (or, as de Silentio tellingly puts it "saves") Agnes (FT, 96).

As de Silentio sees it, there are two other options open to one who is, like the merman, aware of his own guilt. First, he may "remain in hiding," give up his beloved and his responsibility to her, relinquish his hold over her to "the divine," and enter a monastery (FT, 98). The only other option is to "become disclosed" by accepting "refuge in the paradox" (FT, 98):

In other words, when the single individual *by his guilt* has come outside the universal, he can return only by virtue of having come as the single individual into an *absolute relation to the absolute.* (FT, 98, my emphasis)

Here, Kierkegaard gives the reader his most direct textual prompt regarding the crux of *Fear and Trembling* as a whole: "I would like to make a comment that says more than has been said at any point previously" (FT, 98). This ponderous subject that de Silentio admits he has heretofore "assiduously avoided" is sin. Given that the merman's retreat from the girl is due to sin, only by making an *alternate* movement by virtue of the absurd could he have avoided total isolation.[28] The anguished merman is not saved by his anguish; on the contrary, justification requires repentance, followed by self-disclosure. The merman may receive Agnes back only if he arrives at a condition of hopeful repentance; the girl may return to the merman and to the text only through God's grace.[29]

According to Louise Carroll Keeley, Kierkegaard is recommending, in Problem III, that "guilt learn to recognize itself as absolute," thus exposing the "bankruptcy of the ethical view."[30] The absolute relation to which we sinners are called is outside the ethical, but in a way that differs from Abraham's untranslatable obedience. Both Abraham and the merman exist outside the universal, but the merman is outside the ethical because he "lacks the *conditio sine qua non* [indispensable condition]" (FT, 98). As Keeley aptly words it: the merman (like us) suffers from "residual guilt," that, "like sediment at the bottom of the self, is absolute."[31] More pedantically to map this scene: Abraham is qualitatively outside the ethical because he exists in a saintly realm above it, and the merman, due to sin, is qualitatively outside the ethical because he is in a realm absolutely below it. Both Abraham's life and the merman's life must stand under "divine confiscation." The plight of both holy Abraham and the guilty merman is relevant to God alone, and each is to find his source of aid in God alone. But their lives are incommensurable due to starkly different conditions, and they must therefore call out to God with differently anguished voices. And if my *own* inability to meet the universal is due not to a private, divine pronouncement but to duplicitous aims and dastardly motives, then I must make a movement toward God by disclosing myself and coming into a totally different relation to the absolute, by way of the absurd. Louis Mackey puts the point well when he explains, "The man originally flawed by sin is beyond the end of his ethical rope and beyond the reach of the universal imperative."[32] For those of us who live in the reality of sin – that carefully circumvented subject – the text points to the ridiculous hope that moves from repentance to disclosure.

Fear and Trembling is thus, in part, a call for de Silentio's readers to "judge themselves honestly" (FT, 100); by means of the pseudonymous text, Kierkegaard prompts us to be sufficiently forthright, to "know what [we] are able to do and what [we] are unable to do" (FT, 101). De Silentio explains that, for those of us who resemble the merman or Cain more than Abraham, the first task is to "take the time to scrutinize in sleepless vigilance every single secret thought," to allow ourselves "in anxiety and horror [to] discover . . . the dark emotions hiding in every human life" (FT, 100). Whereas most of us, in the hustle and bustle of the modern life, "so easily forget" to be "conscientious about time" and so happily provide one another with comforting "evasions," de Silentio wonders what would occur if each of us sat, individually, before the thought that the merman is literally sodden with guilt, powerless to return to the world (FT, 99–100). Such meditation, de Silentio asserts, would "chastise many a man in our day who believes that he has already attained the highest" (FT, 100). Through de Silentio, Kierkegaard invokes both Abraham's and the merman's anguish – the one religious and the other demonic – to call into question our present confidence in our individual and collective progress. There is a method to the ethical muddling that has brought us to this point: we are to seek a way of justification that differs radically from the route of moral certitude.

THAT THE LORD MAY HAVE MERCY UPON US

After making "the infinite movement of repentance," one "cannot possibly come back under his own power and grasp actuality again" (FT, 99). The absurd reality to which we are subsequently called involves something akin to bared receptivity. De Silentio surmises that, perhaps, what we most need is a story wherein "love is made ludicrous," but not so that we will laugh. Rather, such an "inspired character would remind [us] of what has been forgotten" (FT, 102). Confident of our progress, few of us are prompted to acknowledge our debt, nor do we respond to the call to grateful wonder. We must be reminded of what we have forgotten. We who resemble the merman are, therefore, to go on with de Silentio to read about Tobit's Sarah:

She is the one I want to approach as I have never approached any girl or been tempted in thought to approach anyone of whom I have read. For what love of

God it takes to be willing to let oneself be healed when from the very beginning one in all innocence has been botched, from the very beginning has been a damaged specimen of a human being! (FT, 104)

Sarah, a girl living under a demonic curse that endangers anyone who dares to love her, accepts Tobias's selfless love for her. Sarah's "ethical maturity" manifests itself precisely in being willing "in humility" to accept self-giving love from another. Tobias's prayer for Sarah, "that the Lord may have mercy," is also a call for Sarah to be willing openly to receive that mercy from the hand of God (FT, 103).

While de Silentio the poet may not grasp the soteriological implication here, the one seeking faith may recall what we too often forget. Sarah is to become for the reader an alternative heroine, a model for the humility necessary if we are to accept God's grace in Christ. De Silentio does not dwell here for long, moving restlessly on to another riddle, but the reader catches sight of someone whose relation to the universal more nearly approximates our own after repentance. Subsequent to moral bewilderment and an acknowledgment of guilt, we should seek to embody Sarah's humble and hopeful receptivity to the loving work of another.[33] As de Silentio closes this chapter, he reminds the reader that, "unless the single individual as the single individual stands in an absolute relation to the absolute," Abraham himself is "lost" (FT, 120). In Sarah, even more than in Abraham, we glimpse what that "absolute relation" might entail. What the reader may surmise but the poet cannot yet grasp is that, without such a relation, we are all not only lost, but unredeemable.

We must turn to *Works of Love* and away from the poet's riddles for a fuller account of redeemed love. De Silentio attests early in *Fear and Trembling* that he is "convinced that God is love," but his knowledge of such love is purely poetic: "for me this thought has a primal lyrical validity." Given this limited view of God, he himself acknowledges that he does not have faith (FT, 34). He does not have the "humility" sufficient to ask for more than a "left-handed marriage in this life"; he is incapable of the kind of love for God and reception of love from God that brings all of one's supposedly "little troubles" before the Almighty (FT, 34). C. Stephen Evans notes that as de Silentio's voice shifts into Kierkegaard's own in *Works of Love*, we have "morality in a new key, for its motivational propeller is not autonomous striving" but rather "grateful expression" for the life that we have "received as a gift."[34] When Kierkegaard shifts from a pseudonymous, poetic voice to a more directly religious one in

Works of Love, he clearly calls the individual to remember Sarah's sense of humble gratitude: "in relation to God, every person begins with an infinite debt, even if we forget what the debt amounts to daily after the beginning" (WL, 102). With God's work for us so in view, one may exceed de Silentio's merely poetic appreciation for the divine and approach this "morality in a new key."

In his section on "Our Duty to Remain in Love's Debt to One Another," Kierkegaard calls the individual lover to acknowledge daily the accumulated and original deficit he has incurred, the "infinite debt that cannot possibly be repaid" (WL, 177). As Kierkegaard describes our condition, it is before God that we both realize the infinitude of our debt and find our sole source of redemption. We discover before God that we are, like Sarah, "botched," that our attempts at intimacy precipitate treachery, yet we also discover that there is one who has and will mercifully love us even though we are "damaged" and dangerous "specimens." This "strange way of speaking" requires "a certain transformation of attitude and mind" in order that the lover remain constantly aware of his indebtedness to God (WL, 178). The "freedom and life" (WL, 180), the sense of import, gratitude and hope involved in this context is quite different from the poet's insufficiently "lyrical" perspective on and description of God's love.

We may also, with Kierkegaard's help, contrast the merman's fearful flight from Agnes to Sarah's vulnerable willingness to accept Tobias's love. De Silentio's merman is entangled in at least two, integrally related errors: first, he searches Agnes in order to distinguish purity from guile, and second, refusing "to make the movement by virtue of the absurd," he can neither repent of nor disclose to Agnes the fact that he is a rapacious merman. De Silentio colludes in the merman's plight by turning Agnes round and round to inspect whether she is "utterly, utterly, utterly innocent." He decides that he must narratively reconstruct her; he must refine Agnes into someone who can "save" the merman through her naiveté (FT, 95). But even with an innocent Agnes before them, the merman and de Silentio stop at a confession of guilt, unable to open themselves to receive love and forgiveness from an Agnes who is innocent and willing. De Silentio condemns as ineffective his construction of an Agnes who has even a trace of guilt but knows that the merman will flee from an Agnes who is guiltless. At de Silentio's prompting, we leave the merman in the sea, alone, reveling demonically in his own guilt. Incapable of repentance and disclosure, the merman's errors are formed in the context of unfaith. Whether utterly innocent or a smidgen guilty, Agnes cannot redeem the merman. She cannot effect in him the relation "by virtue of the absurd" that, alone, will allow him to return to her.

Whereas de Silentio creates an Agnes who is both irreproachable and unapproachable, leaving the merman both to compare his own guilt with her sheer innocence and despair in his own contrasting culpability, Sarah does not look closely at Tobias to determine whether she will accept his love. Even knowing herself a liability, Sarah "ludicrously" accepts Tobias's love for her. Reading *Works of Love* here heightens the difference between the two routes. With his emphasis on indebtedness in *Works of Love*, Kierkegaard clarifies that the beloved's innocence or guilt should not be a factor in determining our own love. The lover must submit himself to scrutiny, and he must resist the temptation to inspect the potential object of his affections. With his subsequent findings, the lover is to discover his own debt, turn to God's mercy, and eschew "comparison's sidelong glance" whereby he "too easily discovers a whole world of relationships and calculations" (WL, 183). Like a person who suddenly becomes aware that she is walking on ice, one who begins to compare herself with her beloved will inadvertently slip into despair of love's possibility (WL, 186). We are like arrows who fall to the ground if we turn to compare our flight with another's (WL, 182). Kierkegaard explains that the lover who would be true looks only to God's requirement and God's grace. But this depends upon our entering that particularly "absurd" relation of indebtedness, an absurd relation which de Silentio, who does not have faith, cannot specify but only intimate. The hope to which we are summoned in *Fear and Trembling*, albeit by a misguiding and riddling poet, requires redemption.

RETURNING TO MOUNT MORIAH

After introducing the issue of repentance, de Silentio gives the reader a clue to Abraham's relation to those who live within a context of guilt:

> The analogy to Abraham will not become apparent until after the single individual has been brought to a position where he is capable of fulfilling the universal, and now the paradox repeats itself. (FT, 99)

Once inside the context of Sarah's humble reception of grace, we may receive Abraham as an ethical guide. Living with grateful receptivity to the grace that alone restores the "*conditio sine qua non*" of the ethical (FT, 98), we may return to Mount Moriah. Abraham may come back to redeemed mermen and mermaids as a mentor for love. In Problems I and II, de Silentio is at pains to prove philosophically that the individual stands before God alone as the judge and justifier for Abraham's and our work. Because, due to sin, our situation is significantly different from Abraham's holy predicament, we are to find ourselves challenged and inspired by his singular relationship to the Almighty. His untranslatable obligation to God alone must return to the justified sinner as a stark reminder (1) that we must understand each person as ultimately, individually, accountable to God alone and (2) that we are to place our hope solely in God's ability to enable our beloved to return. As those whose lives and loves are, through Christ, "under divine confiscation," Christians may again heed Abraham's example of reverence toward God alone.[35]

Abraham's willingness to separate himself, in faith, from his beloved child is the most salient and urgent message of Problems I and II. *Fear and Trembling* and *Works of Love* intersect very clearly on this aspect of faithful love. Kierkegaard insists in *Works of Love* that intimacy goes awry when we tie ourselves inextricably to our beloved, whether through worship or another form of idolatry. This false kind of union may take two forms, both of which are challenged by Abraham's stark example. First, in our self-deception, we often disguise self-love as adoration of our beloved; we assume ourselves to be worshiping the beloved when we actually esteem the beloved only as she relates to ourselves (WL, 19–21). For this reason, each of us must distinguish self from other and resist the "intoxicating" forms of adoration whereby we seek to fuse ourselves to our beloved (WL, 38). When joined to our beloved in this way, we are seldom willing to acknowledge that she may be called by God to separate herself from us. God's command to love faithfully thus entails some form of sacrifice, in that we must be willing to let go of the beloved if she deems that God requires that of her and of us. Some of us are also tempted to another form of idolatrous fusion whereby we lose ourselves in another, allowing the beloved to define who we are. Through this other type of "self-willfulness" and false "devotion," the lover loses the only self through which she relates to God, who is the rightful claimant on her life (WL, 55). Kierkegaard calls such self-abasement an "abomination" whereby the individual "refuses to know anything higher" (WL, 125). God's word prohibits our complete subordination to any human being or project and thus demands that we be capable of envisioning ourselves alone before God.

We are called to be ready and able to discern God's will and to follow it even when it would bring us and/or our beloved to grief. This requires that we be able to distinguish ourselves from another and confess our lives as confiscated by God (WL, 130). In his conclusion to *Works of Love*, Kierkegaard gives a more direct form to what is left oblique in the pseudonymous musings on Abraham in *Fear and Trembling*:

In the Christian sense, a person ultimately and essentially has only God to deal with in everything, although he still must remain in the world and in the earthly circumstances assigned to him. (WL, 377)

The only relational calling that can be clearly defined for each of us is to love the beloved as, first, God's own. Thus our deepest concern for the other must be that our love for her not hinder her relationship with God (WL, 130). For our own sake and for the sake of those we love, we must recall continually that we "ultimately and essentially" have to do with God, not one another. For those of us who seek to love properly in the midst of grace, Abraham's willingness to sacrifice Isaac may serve as an extreme reminder that truly we do not belong to one another, but to God.

We must not only walk up Mount Moriah but also descend again, with Isaac beside us. Thus, truly faithful engagements require hope as well as deferential distance. De Silentio can only marvel at Abraham's ability to receive Isaac back from God with gratitude. Both de Silentio and the merman fail in love partly because they do not trust that, on the other side of either resolute release or repentance, the beloved will return. De Silentio's young man examines the "conditions of possibility" before sealing his engagement and cannot bend his imagination to accept in hope the absurd reality whereby his engagement would be plausible. As de Silentio describes the situation, in order for the merman to receive Agnes again, he must trust in an absurd possibility that she will accept his confession of malice aforethought. We must, as Kierkegaard explains in *Works of Love*, sufficiently "presuppose that love is in the other person's heart" to enable our courageous confession of ulterior and inferior motives (WL, 217). The love to which Kierkegaard directly calls us in *Works of Love* requires our tenacious determination to place our hope in the possibility of invested yet reverent engagement and in the reality of forgiveness when (not if) we inadvertently or intentionally forget that our beloved is not our own. Against "hateful expectancy" that deems true engagement, forgiveness, and reconciliation as unrealistic possibilities, Kierkegaard encourages our ridiculous trust in God's goodness and in our beloved's willingness to forgive (WL, 263). He contrasts a "temporal expectancy" that may end in disappointment to an "eternal expectancy" that corresponds to radical Christian hope (WL, 249). We must cease our careful calculations of love's potential and, like Abraham, trust solely in God's ability to return to us our beloved.

Even with this hope, however, we are to return with de Silentio to be morally baffled by Abraham's work. Reading *Works of Love* and *Fear and Trembling* together, we face the disturbing notions that the truth of our own actions toward our beloved is very seldom clear even to us and that God's will hardly ever comes as a thunderbolt. It is rare that we walk together with our child, spouse, or parent with a lucid sense of God's immediate call. Mooney characterizes Abraham's import this way: "The journey [toward Mount Moriah] stands for a way of dialectical reflection, of threading through one's intentions, of clarifying one's soul, of checking the purity of its motivations."[36] If we do not experience fear and trembling before such an examination, we are morally obtuse. At any given moment we may appropriately be distancing ourselves from another or, instead, retreating out of fear or frustration. Abraham's act is holy only if his love for Isaac is sufficient to make the act absurd. How is one to behold the beloved lightly enough to hear God's call while also caring and attending as God also commands? Who among us is willing to let go of our beloved while also investing sufficiently to love her with our "whole soul" as Abraham loves Isaac? Returning to de Silentio's initial musings, who can both wean and love the child well, walking with loss before us and Isaac beside us? As Ed Mooney gracefully phrases it, this task of "giving up the temporal and getting back is then a test of selflessness, a test of care."[37] It is a task for which few of us, if any, are well prepared.

Most of us could, with de Silentio, write a whole text about our own "botched movements" in our relations with our own beloveds. *Fear and Trembling* thus returns again as a summons, calling for the reader to ask humbly for God's aid in each engagement. We can and should combine Green's and Outka's readings of the text: we must indeed "cleave to God as the subject of unique veneration" precisely because we are befuddled and irresolute sinners. As we continue reading through Kierkegaard's authorship, we will carry with us this tone of peril and perplexity in the midst of faith and hope.[38] The poet who writes *Fear and Trembling* should effect in us a sense of apt bewilderment even as we look forward to Kierkegaard's direct description of faithful intimacy in *Works of Love*. In the closing paragraph of *Fear and Trembling*, de Silentio recounts the story of "Heraclitus the obscure" who insisted that one "cannot walk through the same river twice" (FT, 123). A disciple refused to "remain standing there" and objected that "One cannot do it even once!" De Silentio's convoluted text pushes us to acknowledge that, although we daily come to that river, we have not even begun to cross it. Kierkegaard insists that "the struggle of faith" is one "in which you can have occasion to be tried and tested everyday" (WL 380). With fear and trembling before such a trial and test, we are to hope in the grace that allows us to keep slogging through.

We now move from Mount Moriah to the parlor of a poet who is, temporarily, in love. Published with *Fear and Trembling*, *Repetition* is another of Kierkegaard's puzzling, poetic texts. Again, our narrator is himself intertwined with the narrative. The pseudonymous author of the book, Constantin Constantius, is at least as questionable as the dear poet, de Silentio, whom we now leave behind. Or, perhaps we should consider the possibility that we do not leave de Silentio behind at all. Rather, perhaps the poetic world we will now enter describes the route by which de Silentio came to resign himself and leave the girl. Either way, Constantin Constantius's influence on his young charge describes, in colorful detail, the perspective that causes us to scrutinize, despair, and flee those whom God calls us to love.

CHAPTER 3

The poet, the vampire, and the girl in Repetition *with* Works of Love

> When we speak this way, we are speaking of the love that sustains all existence, of God's love. If for one moment, one single moment, it were to be absent, everything would be confused.
>
> (WL, 301)

> Underneath it all, there must be a misunderstanding.
>
> (R, 136)

INTRODUCTION

As the reader moves from de Silentio's question of crossing the river even once to the enigmatic exchange between the cynic and the poet of *Repetition*, the conundrum of "the girl" becomes explicit. While one might (albeit mistakenly) speak as if Abraham and God were alone on Mount Moriah, the problematic presence of the other is precisely at issue in *Repetition*. In this story, the beloved on whom the young man focuses his gaze and esteem quickly becomes an encumbrance from which the cynic must rescue him, and the ensuing narrative reveals several facets of love's demise. Kierkegaard's sobering rendition of the love commandment in *Works of Love*, wherein the beloved is more than merely the beholder's vision of her, exposes that there is indeed an other in the story, imperiled by two characters who would idolize, trick, or banish her. In *Works of Love*, Kierkegaard distinguishes true love from the poetic perspective, which distorts the other to fit the lover's ideal; from the vampiric gaze, which devours her; and from the sage's inspection, which deems her blameworthy and disposable, and he skillfully depicts each of these three distortions in *Repetition*. By reading the two texts together, we learn that love, when unguarded by God's command, endangers the beheld as well as the overlooked. Using *Works of Love* as the lens through which we interpret *Repetition* allows us to consider false love's perfidious perception of and parasitic relation to the (here female) other.

Through this reading, Kierkegaard reveals not only the danger of mistaken love, he also narrates its instability. *Repetition*'s poetic young man embarks on an informatively futile endeavor by choosing Constantin, rather than God, as the "third party" for his own engagement, and the warped, unsteady perspective which he consequently adopts stands in instructive contrast to the vision of *Works of Love*. The book records the decomposition of merely human love, and, as Joakim Garff notes, the summons emerges precisely through "the absence of result."[1] The failure of this earlier, pseudonymous text to cohere, Constantin's failure to achieve his attempted repetition, and the young man's failure to sustain his commitment to the girl are all carefully constructed to be, as Louis Mackey phrases it, "an invitation to an indefinitely postponed atonement," goading the reader toward God as the only confidant for true love.[2] The poetry, cynicism and thievery in *Repetition* help narratively to depict the perils of human interaction, and the reader again surmises that the possibility of crossing the river, of meeting God's command and loving the other, lies outside the skewed purview of *Repetition*.

TEXTUAL INTENTIONS

By noting the interplay between *Repetition* and *Works of Love*, we may more accurately interpret the common textual momentum toward our necessary sense of peril, otherwise less obvious when either text is read alone. This intertextual reading thwarts the efforts of those who seek, either in the epistemological pandemonium of *Fear and Trembling* or in the aesthetic acquiescence of *Repetition*, a call to liberated play rather than to confession. While Kierkegaard does endeavor, in both pseudonymous texts, continually to dismantle our easy use of language, as well as our coherent configuration of beauty, for him, the most fitting stance subsequent to demolition is decidedly not the freed exploration of possibility. Reading Constantin's *Repetition* by way of Kierkegaard's *Works of Love*, we learn that to take liberty with the breakdown of moral and epistemological certainty is, in an ultimate sense, irresponsible. We begin, with *Repetition*, to hear Kierkegaard's warning against playful misprision. The manner of our gaze and interpretation matters, for the one gazing as well as for the one on whom our gaze falls. The stakes facing the neighbor warrant close, contrite, attention.[3]

The Christian reader should also experience the textual confusion in Repetition as a reproving prerequisite to Kierkegaard's description of engagement in *Works of Love*. Postmodern interpretations of Kierkegaard's texts rightly deny that the pseudonymous authorship leads the reader resolutely from leap to leap, on through the stages of beauty, duty, and the holy. All three categories must be poetically dismantled in order for us to perceive accurately our plight and our redemption. Christians who would skim with doctrinal hubris through *Fear and Trembling* and *Repetition*, toward the more straightforward, seemingly reliable, prose of *Works of Love* are forced, through this interpretation, to submit to the fissured and fissuring tale about resilient error and vice. By way of the pseudonymous texts, the task of faith becomes disconcertingly less reliable. Revealing to us our exposure, Kierkegaard denies the faithful any comfortable "leafage of language by which [we] can conceal [our] misery" (FT, 61). Those seeking to find, in *Works of Love*, a defense for their own life and love are given in *Repetition* a necessarily humbling precursor. To quote again Frederick Sontag, *Repetition* "appears not to be an advance, yet, without its chastening effect, no real advance is possible."[4]

The poet, cynic, and thief are manifestations of iniquity out of which one cannot even falteringly emerge without an active decision to live in debt before God. Neither the young poet nor his cynical mentor, Constantin, takes that route. The young man comes to depend on Constantin as the one in whose presence he will "talk aloud to himself," thus sealing the fate of his idolizing and evaluative love (R, 135). Constantin becomes a mentor that the young man cannot shake; his presence pervades and infects his perception. Kierkegaard uses this metaphor for perception and relationality in *Repetition* and in *Works of Love*: each of us ineluctably adopts a "third party" to be our "confidant" in matters of love (WL, 165, 416). Apprehension is, itself, relational. The question put in these two texts is: in which relational context will you apprehend and love? If we are to behold the other lovingly, we must enter an alternative context – we must be, ourselves, beholden – and he describes in detail the deluded manner with which we encompass and then test the other when we remain within "merely human" love. Our judgment of *Repetition*'s lovers prepares us to acknowledge the distorted vision with which we view and through which we judge the worth of our own loved ones, and provokes us to choose differently.

Repetition begins with an epigraph: "On wild trees the flowers are fragrant, on cultivated trees, the fruits," and was originally to end, "but the fruits of the spirit are love" (R, 127, 276). On the title page of his final manuscript, Kierkegaard also wrote, then crossed out, wrote again, and deleted, a further subtitle, explicitly labeling *Repetition* "A Fruitless Venture" (R, 276). While these two, deleted, clues might have been overly directive, they might have prevented one misreading of the text as describing an individual's progress from one stage of existence (the melancholy aesthetic) to another (Religiousness A). Such readings fail to note that this text is decidedly relational; the "other" is, precisely, at issue, and thus the matter of love is crucial to the text. And, further, such readings miss what Kierkegaard wishes us to note: the young man's supposed advance is hardly that. The young man's collusion with Constantin, and poetry's collusion with cynicism, reveals an insurmountable rift between the world of *Repetition* and the world of *Works of Love*. Reading Constantin Constantius's text with Kierkegaard's *Works of Love* (rather than with Johannes Climacus's *Concluding Unscientific Postscript*), we are able better to note the other clues remaining within *Repetition*. Kierkegaard meant the culminating sterility of this "fruitless" text to elicit nothing less than our quest for the one, true source for love.[5]

This intertextual interpretation allows us, therefore, to retrieve the girl. Although the focused gaze brings with it perpetual occasion for sin, one cannot, according to Kierkegaard, best love either humanity in general or the beloved from a distance. While God's guardianship does require of us a respectful distance, we may instructively distinguish between the young man's escape from the (no longer) beloved at the end of *Repetition* and the engagement to which Kierkegaard calls us in *Works of Love*. At the conclusion of the young man's correspondence, he is flung "above the stars," distanced indeed from his actual betrothed (R, 222). No longer will her faults vex him, because she marries another, saving him from love's tedium. This false resolution does save the girl from the poet's distorting gaze, but it also spares the poet from the difficult task of loving faithfully the one whose perfection or frailty tempts him to theft or irony. We have in *Works of Love* an alternative account of humbled, attentive love wherein I acknowledge my beloved as truly other, but seek in the midst of my own infinite debt to God to see through the forgiving, charitable, attentive eyes of faith. Whether saved from the temptation and frustration of intimacy through death, thunderstorm, or severed betrothal, the one who loves safely from a distance misses half of what God's presence requires – a true engagement with the beloved as other. A close reading of the two texts may further humble and inspire us to take up Kierkegaard's perilous charge.

LOVING AS THE POETS DO

Poetic love, deluded by a mixture of fear and self-indulgence, misses the intricate reality of the beloved. As Kierkegaard characterizes him in *Works of Love*, the poet writes large one or another pleasing quality he has found in the beloved, loving that portrait rather than the complicated reality of his lover. The beloved becomes a projection of the lover's "passionate preference" (WL, 53). Within this delusion, the lover indulges in "the beautiful dizziness of infinity," becoming "intoxicated" by his own manifestation of the beloved (WL, 19). Kierkegaard strongly implies that all erotic love (*Elskov*) involves this poetic leap over the complex, actual beloved in order to love instead one or several specifically pleasing facets (WL, 19). Merely human love has, at its core, the acquisitive self, a self who fashions, whenever circumstances permit, an accommodating chimera. As Kierkegaard diagnoses us, we often do not love the other herself, but instead use her as an opportunity for our own self-defined purposes or desires.

As *Repetition* opens, the young man comes to Constantin at the height of his infatuation with his beloved. Constantin Constantius (the book's author and himself a character in the narrative) likens the young man to one who "is praying with his whole soul" (R, 134). Such love appears initially to Constantin as "wholesome, pure, and sound," as it might to us (R, 135). Because the poetic lover seems to lose himself in the other, first love may, at first glance, appear quite beautiful. The "purity" with which the poet seems to focus his will, in order to concentrate his attention on his construction of the beloved, can be misleadingly appealing. But what Kierkegaard (in *Works of Love*) and Constantin know is that young love most often escapes actuality by way of a self-interested fantasy, rather than by real attention to the multifaceted other herself, and both Constantin and Kierkegaard attempt to disabuse young love of its illusion. The corrective procedure for Kierkegaard, in *Works of Love*, is the term "neighbor," which interrupts the lover's gaze with the truth that my beloved is other-than-me and distinct from my wishes (WL, 55). As *Repetition* unfolds, we discover that Constantin's prescription for the poet's fantastic love is a discriminating inspection of the girl herself. Both elders (Kierkegaard and Constantin) determine to correct young love's intoxication, but the sobering techniques differ from one another in a fundamental way.

This state of poetic love is unstable (by both Constantin's and Kierkegaard's count) in part because it cannot be sustained in proximity with the other. At some point the beloved punctures the poet's constructed image, either simply by varying from that image or by refusing to conform to the lover's aims. As Kierkegaard describes it, the poet thinks he "loves the person even more than himself," but his love cannot bear (and thus he will not tolerate) the beloved's distinguishing herself from his purposes for or images of her (WL, 21). This distorted form of love is, literally, self-absorbed, and it cannot endure the impinging existence of the other. It is no surprise that, under Constantin's expert tutelage, the young man wavers in his appreciation of the girl herself. He begins to see her in a new, seemingly perspicacious light, without the haze of his false adoration. Within two weeks "the adored young girl was already almost a vexation to him," Constantin reports (R, 137). Pacing back and forth, the young man resorts to poetry itself, repeating verses about longing for a love past (R, 136). Propelling her poetically into the past, as again a decidedly abstract ideal to be loved and recollected from afar, the young man saves himself from the actual girl. At this point Constantin's and Kierkegaard's perspectives join to acknowledge that "the young girl was not his beloved: she was the occasion that awakened the poetic in him and made him a poet" (R, 138). Constantin concludes that the young man "does not know the girl at all," but instead sees her through a poetic, melancholy haze, by this method saving his self-serving, atemporal, construal of her (R, 185).

One clue as to why the young man so quickly retreats from his love involves his relationship to the passage of time. Even if one can maintain his illusion about his beloved at this moment, time will eventually challenge that mirage. We must distance ourselves from the "occasion" of our poetry in order not to see the effects of the passing years. It is, in part, his fear of change that leads the young man to distance himself from his beloved in the recitation of poetry:

Then, to my easy chair, Comes a dream from my youth. To my easy chair. A heartfelt longing comes over me for you, Thou sun of woman. (R, 136)

The young man "leap[s] over life" straight to the loss of his love, scarcely after it has begun, because, "in the very first moment he [becomes] an old man in regard to the entire relationship" (R, 136). As Constantin suggests, this "recollecting" allows the young man to be "safe and secure" in that, because he "*begins* with the loss," he actually has "nothing to lose" (R, 136, my emphasis). Constantin here remarks that the young man does not have the "elasticity of irony" that would enable him to look the inevitable in the face, to determine that loss is par for the course, and to shift his gaze at will toward the most malleable candidate (R, 145). As we shall see, this response to temporality and consequent change leads Constantin also to an "easy chair," but one from which he can observe, scoff, and indulge. When a lover sees rightly that the other, as a temporal being herself and not merely an illusion, will change over time, he may attempt to save himself through various methods. In contrast to both the young man's beautiful melancholy and Constantin's ironic resilience, Kierkegaard, in *Works of Love*, commends the commandment as that which alone can "secure" temporal love (WL, 40). It is only within the context of God's command that the lover may view time and the beloved as transformed by eternity, and thus resist the temptation to flee.

But the girl continues to exist in this narrative of fruitless repetition. The young man eventually comes to "curse life, his love, the girl he loved" (R, 139). Trapped in a closed circle of recollection, the young man wishes to but cannot escape the girl herself. Within this context, the young man has two choices. Either he may heed Constantin's call cleverly to trick the beloved (who Constantin will "demonstrate" is beneath the young man's concern) by pretending that he is an irresolute seducer, or he may find an alternative route back to the fantasy from whence his love came. If the latter is to be a possibility, the young man has to make some sort of movement out of his current quagmire. And because the perpetuation of his ideal cannot succeed without considerable distance from the actual girl, the young man must rid himself of her.[6] But this must be done in such a way that neither the poet nor the one poeticized is deeply implicated, lest his saving ideal be tarnished. We will return to this pristine escape route, which the young man eventually takes, after considering with Constantin the alternative. Constantin's cynical option colludes with the ethereal movement above in that he convinces his young charge that loving the girl in proximity is not an option. The clever, self-protective, detection to which Constantin introduces the young man deems the *other* to be the selfish one, and Constantin vows to "give [himself] the pleasure of letting her incur revenge or laughter" (R, 143). It is not until God enters the relationship, with *Works of Love*, that the poetic lover is called to turn Constantin's scrupulous perspective inward – finding himself culpably deluded – thus allowing a third way out of the ordeal.

THE TOUGH SLIME OF SAGACITY

Constantin embodies what, in *Works of Love*, Kierkegaard warns against as the "third party" that corrects youthful enthusiasm with a critical, all-encompassing eye for the beloved (WL, 165). With this perspective, the lover is constantly "testing, searching, criticizing" the other, although the

lover knows such a view will ruin his love and would "upset the beloved
if [she] knew that this third [were] present" (WL, 165). As Kierkegaard
describes the influence of the cynic, even when the two lovers are seemingly alone, his detecting vision intrudes and informs the way the lover
perceives his beloved (WL, 165). In this tale, after the young man reaches
the point of cursing himself and the girl, he swears that he will no longer
associate with Constantin and his circumspect observation of her. To
Constantin's amusement, this resolution does not last long, and the young
man begins to meet with him again "in out-of-the-way places" away from
the unsuspecting girl (R, 140). He keeps his collusion hidden from her,
but, whenever they are together, the young man interprets the girl, and
their love, under the cynic's direction.

The perspective with which the young man has begun to see his beloved becomes more explicit and insidious as Constantin seeks to assure
the young man that marriage to the girl is an impossibility. The young
man becomes increasingly mired in Constantin's view, unable to commit
to his beloved, but still unwilling to break from the ideal to which he has
poetically secured himself. He cannot bear to alter the "purely poetic
relationship" he has with the girl, but neither can his commitment with-
stand his increasingly critical vision of her (R, 143). Kierkegaard puts
the young man's plight metaphorically in *Works of Love*: with this bifocal
vision, the lover seeks to secure himself against the potential worthless-
ness of his current obsession (WL, 166). In this case, the young man
seems at war with himself, increasingly "disgusted with himself and his
love because of being fastidious," as Kierkegaard words it in *Works of Love*,
but is nonetheless unable to break his ties to Constantin or to the girl
(WL, 165).

As we become acquainted with our narrator, Constantin Constantius,
we learn that he understands himself as a "secret agent" who can "expose
what is hidden" (R, 135). With a "critic's screen that tests every sound and
every word," Constantin intends to inspire one "calmly [to] put one's
eye to the microscope" (R, 134). He admits that this perspicacious vision
may cause one initially to "suffer exceedingly," but argues that, eventually, through much training and effort, one gains "an investigative rapport
with actuality" (R, 146). Kierkegaard describes Constantin's malevolent
effect on love throughout *Works of Love*, wherein we are admonished
to turn this discriminating eye inward to detect instead our own questionable aims. The one who becomes privy to Constantin's art is like
"one who is jaundiced," in that everything begins to look discolored;
our eyes become "sharpened" in such a way as to see "the depravity

of others," rather than our own (WL, 286). From the first section forward, Kierkegaard warns of the "conceited sagacity" that seeks to see accurately but instead becomes more and more mired in deceit (WL, 5). Should one turn this vision toward the beloved, the result, Kierkegaard predicts, will be a tendency toward appraising leeriness; the lover seeks to assess the value of the actual beloved and judge her compliance with his ideal. Kierkegaard personifies the influence of this perspective, writing it as a relation that tempts us out of love:

Beware of comparison! Comparison is the most disastrous association that love can enter into; comparison is the most dangerous acquaintance love can make; comparison is the worst of all seductions. (WL, 186)

The tragedy is, Kierkegaard insists, that such a vision will find precisely what it has set out to find (WL, 157). Kierkegaard thus describes non-pseudonymously the effect of our pseudonym on the lover and his love. By "looking askance at [the young man's] beloved," Constantin does in fact deem *the girl* to be the culprit of the affair. By his "jaundiced" view, she is manipulating the poor, young man, and he thereby justifies, to himself and to his apprentice, the deceptive scheme by which they may break the engagement (R, 143).

The poet's evasive love is infected with the cynic's suspicion and informed by the thief's cant. Before we learn of the young man's decision between trickery and higher poetry, we learn about the thievery that inspires cynicism. The narrative hits a break in sequence as Constantin flashes the reader back to his own predatory search for renewal in the actual. In the traveler's diary ending the first half of *Repetition*, we have an account of Constantin's attempt to survey the terrain of possibility. Constantin explains at the close of this description of his trip to Berlin: "That was how far I had come before I learned to know that young man" (R, 174). It is this trip to Berlin – the robbery, voyeurism, pleasure, and disgust – that comes to bear on the young man as he attempts to love the girl. Constantin returns home resiliently incapable of love. He is ready to render any aspect of reality appropriate for amused derision: "no sigh is so deep that [one] does not have the laughter that corresponds to it in his jargon" (R, 145). Detached cynicism appears as the "triumph" over his frustrated thievery in Berlin, after which he deems all to be folly:

Farewell! Farewell! You exuberant hope of youth, what is your hurry? After all, what you are hunting for does not exist, and the same goes for you yourself! (R, 175)

Kierkegaard describes precisely this argot in *Works of Love*. When in the presence of youthful enthusiasm, "experience speaks deprecatingly about hope"; and as such "experience" personified, Constantin comes to influence the young man (WL, 250).[7] In the absence of the eternal, one is subject to a "variously tough slime that is called practical sagacity," (WL, 251) and we find here a clue as to the young man's flight, away from the complexity of reality, into the safer world of idealistic poetry.

THE VAMPIRE VISITS BERLIN

Kierkegaard makes clear in *Works of Love* that one who seeks renewal must first recognize, through self-renunciation, his own responsibility for being unable to love another; the command to love is spoken as an indictment and task for the beholder, not the beheld (WL, 4, 90). A journey wherein one searches for something worthy of love is not only wrongheaded, but also leads to the suspicious inspection and disdain described above. Yet Kierkegaard explains that merely human love is most often precisely about this parasitic pursuit of valuable particulars:

Purely human love is continually in the process of flying away after, so to speak, or flying away with, the beloved's perfections. We say of a seducer that he steals a girl's heart, but of all purely human love, even when it is the most beautiful, we must say that it has something thievish about it, that it really steals the beloved's perfections . . . (WL, 173)

While most readers note that Constantin's attempt to find renewable pleasure in Berlin fails, we too quickly distance ourselves from the "comedic" theft therein.[8] Kierkegaard's insistence that our default mode of loving is akin to thievery should prompt us to pay attention even to Constantin. By my interpretation, to dismiss Constantin as an ethical aberration is to dodge Kierkegaard's moral blow. The narrative in Berlin not only reveals the origins of the young man's poetry but writes thievery large enough to make our own, perhaps more subtle, occasions of theft more apparent. As Constantin luridly focuses in on his various, unsuspecting victims, so do we, in less obvious ways, attend to the other with appropriation in mind. The vice involved in this section is severe and warrants our close reading of the text as it stands, largely without *Works of Love*'s intervening correctives. In Constantin's intensely selfish and cowardly attempt at satisfaction, we are to recognize our own forms of illegal acquisition.

Constantin introduces his "investigative journey" to Berlin with a lecture on renewal through repetition. He links here repetition, the interesting, and the shame or innocence of "young girls" (R, 147). The story of his previous encounter with a "beautiful young girl," who trusted him on her way to Copenhagen, is framed by conclusions regarding girls in general: the girl who seeks the interesting "becomes a trap in which she herself is caught," whereas the one who does not so seek is honorable (R, 148). Young people who are on the verge of discovery (or at least young females) are foolish if they do not realize that "the interesting can never be repeated" (R, 147). Rather than turning this critical vision inward (a turn that might better align him with the true lover in *Works of Love*), Constantin begins his investigation of repetition by admonishing the most decidedly other: the young female. He embarks by distinguishing himself from the category deserving of scorn. With this judgment and condemnation, of those from whom he most often pilfers, Constantin travels to Berlin, seeking to find again some satisfaction, a renewal through vampirism and disposal.

A bandit like Constantin requires distance adequate for cover but proximity sufficient to appraise the potential goods. Recollecting what he once had, Constantin travels from Stralsund to Berlin by stagecoach. To be fair, even Kierkegaard's most faithful seeker would find some difficulty traveling for thirty-six hours jostling limb to limb with his neighbor in a rumbling coach. Constantin is most definitely not up to that assignment and begins immediately to dread the entire enterprise, wondering if he will be "able to disengage [himself] in the singleness of isolation," rather than (horror of horrors) "carry a memory of being a limb on a larger body" (R, 151). He hurries to his lodgings, hoping that, protected there, he may separate himself and salvage his mission. Constantin wistfully recalls his sitting, previously, by the same window, as a sort of stage phantom, caped and creeping "along the wall with a searching gaze" (R, 152). He remembers that, in this dim lighting, he cannot be seen by others but can observe them as they pass, unsuspecting, by the opening to his lair.

Constantin approaches his apartment anticipating the enjoyment of this felicitous setting but first is forced to visit with his landlord, who has married in the interim. To make matters worse, Constantin arrives in Berlin on the "Universal Day of Penance and Prayer" (R, 153). While he insists that "this is of little concern" for his own project, his mood is soured for the search. As with the disturbing interlude on the crowded stagecoach, Constantin dismisses this potentially instructive facet of his trip in favor of self-satisfied isolation. Instead of recalling the fate he has in common with his neighbors, he "settle[s] himself cosily and comfortably in his quarters," where he may have a solitary space "from which he can rush out, a secure hiding place to which he can retreat." This is essential because, "like certain beasts of prey," Constantin cannot enjoy his spoils unless safe from the returned, implicating, gaze of another (R, 153).

In the next section, Constantin attempts to pass off his desire to be hidden as instead originality of mind and appropriate disregard for approval. If one wishes to attend the theater without a concomitantly required response, he should attend a farce. Here, Constantin informs us, "every general esthetic category runs aground," and there is no "uniformity of mood" (R, 159). The effect of the presentation "depends largely on self-activity and the viewer's improvisation," and thus the individual must be willing to "risk" (R, 159, 160). This is the perfect setting for Constantin, who fancies himself to possess "sufficient self-confidence to think for himself without consulting others" (R, 160). In this section, Constantin conflates self-confidence with self-absorption. His unwillingness to expose himself to scrutiny, he tries to pass off as aesthetic courage. The limits that a populated theater might place on a viewer do not apply to Constantin, because he determinedly resists any memory of "being part of a larger body" (as on the stagecoach). He finds "infinite possibilities" at the farce (R, 161) because he is able to sequester himself mentally (and physically) from the other's returned and thus limiting scrutiny. His hiddenness is carefully constructed so that he is never himself the recipient of another's gaze, but always the observer. "Risk," the prerequisite of farce, is precisely what Constantin seeks to avoid.

The interplay between the farcical actors and the public for which they perform provides a revealing contrast to Constantin's secluded voyeurism. Those who come to watch do not laugh from a distance but rather *with* the actors, those "dancers of whimsey" who, "plunged into the abyss of laughter," are able to impart their hilarity to others (R, 161). The shared unselfconsciousness of the farce is to and with others, who are quite aware of their being in the presence of others.[9] Constantin himself sits where he may "be quite sure of getting a box all to [himself]" (R, 165). Here he may "sit as comfortably and well, almost as well, as in [his] own living room," from which he has previously watched unsuspecting others. Here in the theater, he is resolutely unaware of the presence of others, seeing in the place of the audience "mainly emptiness" as if he were in "the belly of the whale in which Jonah sat" (R, 166). Unlike Jonah, who reconsidered his own singularity after being spat upon shore by a much larger beast, Constantin lies "stretched out by the stream of laughter and unrestraint and applause" (R, 166). Constantin seeks not so much to be a unique individual among others, as to be left alone to enjoy his masturbatory consumption.

But this is not enough. Viewing the actors, who know that they are being viewed, is not sufficient to bring Constantin's theater visit to a climax. Integral to his whole project is Constantin's desire to construe the other as merely an object for his own pleasure. Common to the thief and the poet is their refusal to grant an other her separate existence apart from their own aims and interests. In the thief's case, he can best take from an other while imagining her solely as an amalgam of available characteristics – as a smorgasbord for the viewer. The hallmark of the thief, Kierkegaard contends, is his unwillingness to recognize what is "yours" in the distinction between what is his and what belongs to another (WL, 267). While some thieves physically grapple with another in order to procure their quarry, Constantin does not even give his victim that chance. Rather, he keeps himself from the risk such an encounter would pose. Furtively seeking what he lacks, Constantin catches sight of a "young girl," who, he notes, "had hardly come to the theater to be seen" (R, 167). Unlike the actors or other "odious" females, the girl is the *unwitting* object of Constantin's vampiric gaze. Only while watching her watch the performance is Constantin fully able to "yield" to the "greater pathos" of the farce. It is her "unawareness" that delights him, as he explains, "If she had even suspected my mute, half-infatuated delight, everything would have been spoiled beyond repair" (R, 167). Returning again and again to the theater to view her, Constantin finds in Berlin what he has previously found at home: a place from which he can hide (behind a tree, no less) to take in the unselfconscious activity of a young female.[10]

Kierkegaard notes, in *Works of Love*, that the pirate who knows no "yours" neither truly has a "mine," in the sense that he forfeits himself in the stealing. He explains, "the richer the criminal becomes by the stolen *yours*, the less *mine* he has" (WL, 267). Constantin's satisfaction is unstable because parasitic. We are warned that when love is "thought of as admiration's wide-open eye," one will eventually "complain that the search is futile" (WL, 161). If the lover's focus on another is a means merely for taking from another what the lover needs, love cannot be sustained. Increasingly stuck in his pattern of sneaky filching, Constantin is dependent upon others, while also irritated by their shifting and thus untrustworthy forms.[11] Unable to participate in the farce, dependent on the unsuspecting girl for his satisfaction, Constantin is thwarted on his return to the theater. His secure lair is occupied, so he must sit with others. He cannot see the girl, because she is mixed in with the larger body of people. Exposed, knee to knee with his neighbor, Constantin determines, "there is no repetition at all" (R, 169). Becoming desperate, Constantin searches, at the coffee shop, again at the theater, in the restaurant, he "pluck[s] a hair from every head, even the bald ones," but is unable to find what he wants (R, 170). The section concludes with his declaration that "all is vanity" (R, 173). Given that even a "speck of something" lodged in one's eye can ruin one's vision of "the highest of all," there is no reason uniformly to seek satisfaction (R, 173).[12] If one is to resist the captivating consistency of death, one must hope only in the sporadic occasion for theft – for fleeting, voyeuristic joy – and learn to be satisfied primarily in the knowledge that one is wiser than those who continue to hope for more.

THE HIGHER POET OF REPETITION II

Some have found in the second half of this narrative a hint as to how the individual is to receive the beloved back from God.[13] In his later "Little Contribution" on *Repetition*, Constantin explains that one should particularly heed the second half of his text. There one will find "everything crucial that is said about repetition," whereas what comes before is "either a jest or only relatively true" (Supplement to R, 304; Pap. IV B 117 n.d., 1843–44). As we read the culmination of the young man's distress and its resolution, we do well to suspect this, Constantin's advice.[14] Constantin's predatory and cynical perspective as heretofore narrated has much to do with the form of the young man's renewal. In hearing the young man's own voice through his letters, we begin to sense the extent to which the young poet has internalized the sage's cynical detachment from the girl, an objectivity cultivated in conjunction with Constantin's clandestine thievery. Through his struggle with guilt or innocence, to his passionate meditation on the righteous sufferer, to his exultation above the stars, the young man's repetition reveals Constantin's work as a "midwife." (R, 230) The supposed rebirth of the young man is one Constantin himself contrives. We discover that, indeed, "underneath it all" there is a serious "misunderstanding" and the poet's renewal is born of that mistake (R, 136). As we assess the young man's repetition, using

Works of Love as contrast, we will resist Constantin's misleading appraisals of the young man's blissful escape.

The second half of the story begins as the young man has fled from Constantin and the girl; he escapes from the pernicious influence of his confidant as well as from the person he has come to behold under this influence. Constantin reports that the young man has deemed him "mad," and that he wishes to keep hidden (even from himself) his relationship to Constantin (R, 183). Given that the young man has determined (under Constantin's advisement) that "humanly speaking, his love cannot be realized," and given that he lacks the "resiliency" to put into place Constantin's plan to trick the girl, the young man has, by Constantin's estimation, two options. Either he may expect the "absurd" or, if he has "hidden" something from his confidant and thus truly loves the girl, he can "murder" the confidant once and for all (R, 186). The reader is left wondering as to the poet's decision, but not for long.

The poet cannot extricate himself from his relationship to this thieving cynic. He continues as the voice with which the young man converses; his most secret prayers are to this, his vicious confidant. Even from a distance, even cursing Constantin to silence, the young man continues to hear Constantin's voice, taking it up as his own in the first letter (R, 193). He is able to realize that Constantin is cruel, cold, in effect dead to the world, and protests that Constantin would balk if, in the middle of the plan to deceive the girl, he magically switched places with the injured and discarded one (R, 192).[15] But, while defending the girl's innocence and implicating himself, the young man cannot ultimately escape Constantin's sneaking suspicion that, really, she is the one at fault. The passage wherein the young man addresses Constantin, attempting to extricate his own from his mentor's perspective, is worth quoting at length:

And thus she was in fact guilty of everything, although innocent [due to her naivité]. Would this not be too rigorous toward her! . . . No! No! No! I could not, I cannot, I will not, I will not do it for anything. No! No! No! I could despair over these written symbols, standing there alongside each other cold and like idle street-loafers, and the one "no" says no more than the next. You should hear how my passion inflects them. Would that I stood beside you, that I could tear myself from you with the last "no" . . . And yet, if I stood face to face with you, I would hardly say more than one "no," because before I got any further you no doubt would interrupt me with the cold response: Yes, yes. (R, 183)

Exclaiming "No! No! No!" to Constantin's persistent "yes," the young man moves from imagined vehemence to an incapable "no" followed again by his confidant's "yes" (R, 193). In this passage, and in what follows of the text, the young man not only fails to "murder" his confidant. He ultimately allows Constantin the last word.

Suspecting his beloved and justifying himself, the young man strengthens his resolve, in the letters that follow, to see himself as innocent. Refusing to accept explicitly Constantin's explanation – that the girl is guilty – and unwilling to consider the deep error of his own ways, the young man comes up with an alternative explanation and solution. By commandeering the story of righteously suffering Job, the young man determines ("just as one becomes ill with the sickness one reads about") that he too has "lost" his beloved through no fault of his own (R, 206, 198). He decides that "the secret" in Job – that Job, "despite everything, is in the right" – is also the enigmatic explanation for his own loss (R, 207). The young man turns to this wretched and inculpable character as one who can give "voice to [his] suffering" (R, 197). After struggling to determine fault and weigh guilt, in an effort to judge himself, his beloved and their situation, the young man relies on Job, "appropriating everything" to deem his circumstance similarly "an ordeal" (R, 209).[16]

The young man evades the import of his predicament by taking himself out of the moral equation, and this is a critical juncture in the text. He briefly, but notably, considers the possibility that his break with the girl is due to "something darkly hidden in [his] soul," but he decides, instead, that his "loss" is understandable only as part of "the whole weighty defense plea on man's behalf in the great case between God and man" (R, 201, 210). Mistaking, in Louis Mackey's words, "nervous apoplexy as divine intervention," the young man becomes ever more confused.[17] This blundering poet, who has broken his promise and left his betrothed (note, with neither apology nor explanation) unquestionably likens his suffering to a man whose entire household died, distinguishing himself from Job only in that he has "lost" only one beloved, whereas Job lost several (R, 198).

The "absurd" possibility on which the young man then places all his hopes is the return of the beloved who has, supposedly, slipped out of the text and his life through no fault of his own. Rather than first recognizing his guilt and subsequently relinquishing *himself* in prayerful repentance before God, hoping in the possibility of his own forgiveness and transformation, the young man imagines himself as, in all innocence, religiously relinquishing *the world*, of which his beloved is a part. The young man's chosen answer thus lies too in a "thunderstorm," wherein he will, like Job, receive back from the hand of God what has been "lost"

(R, 212). By missing this opportunity to acknowledge his crooked ways, by likening himself to Job rather than to Cain, the young man remains within this vicious text.

And the girl does not return. For all that Job received back, he did not receive his children a second time. As the young man explains, "here only repetition of the spirit is possible" (R, 221). And this is the repetition for which the young man has carefully "clipped" himself under Constantin's tutelage: "I sit and clip myself, take away everything that is incommensurable in order to become commensurable" (R, 214). His incommensurability, he interprets as religious. As he sees it, a divine gift of resolution is the next step in his relation to the one who also allowed Job's affliction. He seeks to sit still enough to receive back the beloved, as well as "his clean hands," without the requisite step of repentance. (We must wait until Chapter 5, in *Stages on Life's Way*, to hear again from the poet and discover the result of his efforts.)

This "repetition of the spirit" wherein the poet receives back the very same ideal that he has created is tragically convenient. Earlier, we hear from him what Constantin has throughout contended: that his love for the girl "cannot find expression in a marriage," in part because, "the moment it becomes a matter of actuality, all is lost." The young man describes himself as "split," only capable of loving the girl as if "grabbing at a shadow." And it is merely a shadow that he ultimately receives (R, 201). His "spiritual actuality," in which he has formed the idea of the beloved, cannot be fitted into the realm of her own existence.

When the girl marries another, the young man is freed from the responsibility of making concrete the idea of love to which he poetically attests, of making it endure the test of time and daily difficulty. He is released, as he puts it, to "belong to the idea" (R, 221). "Hidden" in the "abyss" and flung "above the stars," "in the vortex of the infinite," no one will "call him to dinner" or "expect him for supper." The young poet becomes the elder poet, free to accept the "call of the idea" because he now has "nothing to abandon" (R, 222, 221). The redone repetition in the second half is thus as fruitless as the last, unless the goal is in solitude to love the image of a beloved and an idea of love. Perhaps at least in this case the real other is safe from the false lover's greedy observation and/or his clumsy poetic panic.

In concluding the story, Constantin evaluates the young man's repetition as "the raising of his consciousness to the second power" (R, 229). Is the reader to trust that the young man has indeed gone further? Or is the text, as Kierkegaard originally labeled it, "fruitless"? Much depends on how one evaluates the poet's renewal. The young man remains a poet, but now a poet resolutely separated from actuality altogether. Prior to this point, Constantin explains, the young man has struggled to keep "the whole love affair in its ideality, to which he can give any expression whatsoever" (R, 229). But only after his thunderstorm and her marriage to another can he truly be the unencumbered higher poet. To use again Louis Mackey's lovely wording, the young man is "released not to the sobriety of the actual, but to the inebriation of the ideal."[18]

In *Works of Love*, Kierkegaard calls this the "most dangerous of all escapes," by which one "flies over actuality completely"; such a love "imagines itself to be the highest and most perfect kind of love," unhindered by that which does not easily conform to the poet's spinning (WL, 161). Incapable of reconciling our erotically inebriated vision of another with the basic contingencies of time and mortal frailty, much less the distorted construal our "sagacious" perspective gives to these, we are tempted to "escape" like the young man. As *Repetition* closes, the reader is challenged to imagine alternative possibilities to this conundrum of thievery, poetry, cynicism, and flight. In the last section, Constantin himself merely hints at a "religious" option, wherein, in his estimation, the young man could have gained "iron consistency and imperturbability" (R, 229). While the religious renewal described in *Works of Love* is much more treacherous than Constantin, from outside, can foresee, the entirely different course elicited there offers the only way to proceed.

DIVINE PROTECTION IN *WORKS OF LOVE*

With God's grace, it is not necessary to choose either poetic ignorance or knowledgeable cynicism, because God commands and provides another way of viewing that protects actuality. The adjustment necessary for this vision involves God's role as the true confidant for the relation between self and other. Being the "middle term" that intervenes where self-determined "preference" otherwise stands, God requires of the self a perspective that is the inverse of Constantin's meticulous scrutiny of the other (WL, 58). Whereas Constantin's presence adjusts the young man's idealized, idolized version of his beloved by illumining her mortal fragility and imperfection, God's intervention turns that blinding light of clarity inward on the self, the one to whom the command unequivocally speaks (WL, 90). Just as the poet is anguished by the effect Constantin has on his vision of the girl, so does this "earnest walk" with God cause agony (WL, 77). The command's effect described in *Works of Love* magnifies the shame we experience when we sense that we have indeed invited an invidious third party into the relationship, and it renders that shame intense enough to "reduce [us] to nothing" (WL, 102). The young poet, much in love with his ideal, seeks to assure himself that the love is true and thus consults another. So in *Works of Love* is one continually to request assistance in seeing adequately, but the primary correction involves the lover himself, forcing him out of hiding and into the light of God's "requirement and criterion" (WL, 102). The command is thus like a hall of mirrors wherein one is denied "even the most unnoticed crevice to hide in if you were to be put to shame there" (WL, 248). The testing and doubt of *Repetition* ricochet from the beloved to the inept lover himself.

Constantin and the young man both attempt to hide from the other, Constantin in the shadows and the poet in Stockholm, even while using her as a meal or a muse. Crucial for this turn, whereby the lover is himself implicated (rather than accusatory), is the acknowledgment that one neither consumes another in private nor truly escapes his responsibility to another, for God is always and everywhere present. Taking on God as the third party to one's love places the relationship within an "earnest" context; the lover hears a "task for every moment" rather than "platitudes and fanaticism" (WL, 189). I am consistently to acknowledge God's presence as the one literally between myself and the one whom I love. As the "guardian" for the beloved, God stands between me and the other, commanding that I acknowledge that my beloved is first beloved and protected by God (WL, 189). Here Kierkegaard insists that, although the "object and task" of love involves another person, the "judgment" lies with God (WL, 189). This leaves Constantin and the young man, you and me, without recourse to a place from which we may safely enjoy or contemplate another. Regardless of distance and shadows, the lover is always under God's scrutiny. Even if the other is oblivious to the collusion between ourselves and mistrust (as with the poet), or of our selfish gaze (as with Constantin), God is always cognizant of and judging the manner with which we see another.

By understanding the ones to whom we relate as being first related to God, we come to acknowledge their actual selfhood apart from any image, dream, or plan we have for them. Kierkegaard interprets the command to love one's neighbor as a "redoubling" of the self, forcing one to see that the other is truly other than the self, when what we so often attempt in love is to see the other as an extension of our own wishes and desires (WL, 21). Kierkegaard characterizes properly Christian love as that which "dethrones inclination" with a command to love the other as she is first related to God (WL, 50). Into the consuming selfishness of merely human love, God places this little term "neighbor" whereby we are reminded that the other is God's own, not ours (WL, 53). This is a "test" by which we are to examine our motives toward another whom we profess to love (WL, 54). The individual's desire to subsume the one he loves into his own self, as an "other-I" rather than another self, is thwarted by this reminder-term, "neighbor," whereby each individual is singly related to God (WL, 57). Constantin's and our acquisitive negation of the other, whether from afar or in extreme proximity, is thwarted by this image of the returned and accusatory gaze. The command to love one's neighbor thus transforms even "erotic love" into "matter of conscience" (WL, 139).

God's presence places the command between the individual and the other, requiring self-scrutiny and even fear of impending transgression. Attention to a particular other brings with it an increase in the occasion for sin. Whether due to perfections we may, even inadvertently, purloin, or to perceived imperfections that may tempt us to doubt, the other provides ample opportunity for vice. Given our selfish inclination to distort and steal from the other, it might be understandable for one to wish, like the young man, to be flung far from the task at hand. Yet this "flight that soars above the world" is not the love to which Kierkegaard summons the reader. The "humble and difficult flight along the ground," requires not only fear but also a repentance born of faith (WL, 84). Both Constantin's protective perusal and the young man's disengagement betray a fearful distance from the other who tempts them. Constantin judges himself to be a singular individual, separate from the all-too-easily conforming masses, when in truth he cannot bear the returned, accusatory, gaze of his neighbor. The young man attests to a religious renewal that saves him from the guilt-inducing trauma of his broken engagement. The distance to which one is called in *Works of Love* is distinguishable from either of these escapes, in that a faithful lover remains visible and committed, even with fear and trembling. This sustained engagement requires of the self not only recognition of God's law but a trust in God's grace.

David Cain suggests, in his careful reading of *Repetition*, that, "to have to do earnestly with oneself for very long is to come upon the problem of forgiveness."[19] If guilt before the law were the only aspect of God's guardianship of the beloved, few of us would have the courage to proceed. Because he knows well the abuse Christianity has made of Luther's *sola gratia*, Kierkegaard is wary throughout *Works of Love* to speak of love's task primarily as our reception of grace. But along with an indictment, in *Works of Love*, of *Repetition*'s blundering lovers comes a call for us to face with tenacious hope the realization that the young man evades. There *is* something "darkly hidden in [our] souls" – that is, sin – and we must believe in the possibility of our redemption (R, 201). The infinite debt that we originally and in original ways incur even while "earnestly" trying to love well is "hidden" by Christ, forgiven by God through the work of Christ (WL, 287). As the "fulfilling of the law," Christ enacts the possibility of this other facet of God's presence for the individual: a grateful and persistent trust in God (WL, 102). M. L. Taylor, Gouwens, Caputo, and Crites all aptly propose that the true renewal outside the purview of *Repetition* is repetition through, as Caputo words it, "atonement."[20] Christ's continual work on the repentant and hopeful individual is the persistently necessary key to the true love that eludes the poet, cynic, and thief.

Yet Kierkegaard often moves quickly, in *Works of Love*, through this description of sheer receptivity – that God's grace is the only possible source of hope in our blundering attempts to love.[21] Swiftly, this grace is also again a task, for "we can learn humility from this relation to God," a crushing but not fatal humility before God (WL, 102). While grace enlivens expectancy, the individual's recognition of the infinite debt he has incurred should return him continually to God for forgiveness, limping "as Jacob limped after having struggled with God" (WL, 18). With this humility is to come a commitment again to attempt a truer love for the beloved, to see her as we know we are seen by God through Christ – that is, forgiven. Even grace thus becomes also law for Kierkegaard, pushing the individual invariably to acknowledge how far he falls below the humble gratitude called for in the presence of Christ. We must continually acknowledge our need for forgiveness and seek thereby to forgive the other. When we fail to do so, we are thrown again on the necessity of grace. We are to resist the temptation to be like the young man whose "impatience," in George Pattison's words, "seeks to have done with the whole weight of existence in a flash," and instead resume receiving, trying, failing, and receiving again.[22]

Resilient hope is thus a task as well as a gift. The young man skips over the girl's actuality in part due to his own self-centered need to see her as fitting his ideal, but also in part because he fears the passage of time in which his beloved will necessarily deviate from his present picture of her actuality. Both the cynic and the poet view possibility as an enemy, as that which brings the inevitable devaluation of the other. Thus the young man's love for the girl whips over to despair. The poem he recites repeatedly, as a mantra to sober his giddy desire and solidify his decision to break off the engagement, is of old age. Here, the young man, Constantin, and Kierkegaard's "sage" link hope with youth, reckoning "that everything indeed ends in wretchedness" (WL, 257). The poet decides that the only way out of cynicism is to escape the earth altogether, but Kierkegaard describes a third way in *Works of Love*, whereby one's youthful hopes are transformed, rather than melted down into some "tough slime" (WL, 251). Kierkegaard agrees that hope "has still much more in common with youthfulness than with the moroseness that is frequently honored with the name of seriousness" but insists that the passage of time need not necessarily lead to young love's diminishment and demise (WL, 250). There is a "lightness" about hoping with grace that shifts one's stance toward the future from apprehension to "expectancy" (WL, 249). The lover's "lightness," a "relaxation of the heart" perhaps, involves an irrepressible reliance on God as the third party to secure the future of one's love.[23] The young man seeks out Constantin in order to test and scheme regarding love. Kierkegaard commends instead that one relinquish all machinations and experiments in order to rely on God: "when eternity says, 'You shall love,' it is responsible for making sure that this can be done" (WL, 41). One is called to replace fear of the future with a trust in God's ability to strengthen his resolve to love through time.

The progress we are to make in our effort to trust in God is linked inextricably to our recognition of our own inability to progress. The proper setting for love, Kierkegaard insists, is one's debt before God. Constantin attempts to teach his apprentice his own cynical "alphabet" (R, 145), but the young man is unable fully to master the language. He instead hesitates, "sticking out one foot and then the other," while Constantin acrobatically dives (R, 193). These images are similarly apt for the change to be wrought in the lover when he acknowledges God as his confidant. Kierkegaard admonishes the one who seeks to view the other with a kind of double vision; with one eye the lover tests and "only with the other eye do you see that [the lover] is the beloved" (WL, 165). At issue is not the beauty, truth, or worth of the beloved, Kierkegaard explains, but instead the strength and resilience of the lover's ability to receive and incorporate an alternative language of debt and forgiveness. This "alphabet" entails the opposite of Constantin's miserly vocabulary of examination and doubt. While the "language of sagacity" deems it the "most obtuse and fatuous thing one can do," faithful love is to "believe all things" in favor of the beloved, offering a "mitigating explanation" for what mistrustful experience would deem unlovable (WL, 226, 289). There is an "equilibrium of opposite possibilities," and true love requires that we decide "whether there is mistrust or love in you" (WL, 228). Within this different context, the lover is himself "transformed" to perceive his beloved differently, like an artist who is never unable to "discern a more beautiful side" (WL, 158).

When a mitigating explanation is not possible, the lover is called to "hide" the beloved's sins, as has God for the lover. Constantin's influence on young love exacerbates the young man's wary hesitation regarding his commitment to the girl. If the young man had indeed "murdered" Constantin and silenced the cynic's voice at that critical moment when contemplating his own guilt, he might have received back the real girl (R, 186). If the young poet had chosen God as his confidant, thereby facing his own sin and asking for forgiveness, he might have been able to receive back the girl "despite and with [her] weaknesses and defects and imperfections" (WL, 158). This contrasting perspective of debt and forgiveness enables the lover to pledge his fidelity knowing that, on the occasion when the beloved is truly at fault, the task is still his own. If Christ was able lovingly to "discover nothing" before the Council who condemned him, we are to forgive even the ones to whom we are closest (WL, 288). Given that God sees the log in my own eye (even if I am capable of hiding it from others and myself) and nevertheless forgives me for it, it would be foolishness for me to "discover the splinter" in the eye of the one I behold (WL, 383). Pattison suggests that the "leveling" we experience before God's law and God's forgiveness enables us to love the neighbor with generosity.[24] This "strange way of speaking" whereby I am constantly in "infinite debt" to God requires an adaptation of "attitude and mind" (WL, 178), away from the context of failed repetition, wherein the world is used, tested, weighed, and rejected.

REPETITION, **BUT WITH** *FEAR AND TREMBLING*

From Constantin's perspective, "a deeper religious background" would have allowed the young man to act "with an entirely different iron consistency and imperturbability" regarding the "collision" (R, 229). This is, yet again, a misunderstanding. From the point of view of the elder poet who wrote *Works of Love*, even those who most earnestly seek to receive God's grace merely glimpse true love as it glimmers between the fragmented slivers of our broken attempts. In his chapter on "Recollecting One Who is Dead," Kierkegaard explains that loving the living is perilous because "one cannot see with complete clarity what is love and what is self-love" (WL, 351). Only in loving the dead can one perform this pressing work of self-observation with ease, because the dead can neither tempt nor compel the lover. It is the living, with their beauty and blemish, that render us most incapable of standing resolutely before God with "clean hands" as the young man tries so hard to do. But we are not to find here an excuse to escape, either by sinning boldly or loving above the stars. While one may be best able to step gracefully when dancing alone in a churchyard (WL, 347), the more difficult venture to which we are summoned is to love, carefully and patiently, while crammed inside the rumbling stage coach or, as Kierkegaard puts it, while "in the kettle the coppersmith is hammering on" (WL, 79).[25]

Within the convoluted, confused text of *Repetition*, the reader is given some warning as to the ways that we misstep while dancing with another.[26] The failed repetition there gives only hints as to what might be a more faithful way to proceed. Kierkegaard continues to give us the strands of his own effort to move beyond the pilfering love of the thief and the cowardly suspicion of the cynic, as well as the willed abandon of the poet. Many of the texts in his pseudonymous authorship narrate this tension between our selfish intent and our self-giving involvement, pointing to self-circumspection as a key element of true repetition. Because we are so ready to confuse selfish intent with self-giving involvement (or perhaps increasingly to ignore the difference altogether) every faithful engagement must necessarily involve an element of fear:

Fear and trembling (see Philippians 2:12) is not the *primus motor* in the Christian life, for it is love; but it is what the oscillating *balance wheel* is to the clock – it is the oscillating *balance wheel* of the Christian life. (Supplement to WL, 395; JP III 2383, Pap. II A 370, February 16, 1839)

The love to which Kierkegaard calls us requires us actively to acknowledge that true love itself is necessarily precarious – requiring prayers of confession as well as forgiveness. We are to cherish our loved ones with fear and trembling as the balance wheel for our love, treading warily with the increasing awareness that works we believe to be loving may instead be occasions of our own self-indulgence or preservation. *Works of Love* is a gift precisely because we and Kierkegaard find loving the living to be formidable. Given that even Kierkegaard persevered in his belief that "to love people is the only thing worth living for" (WL, 375), we are to continue our own feebly faithful attempts to heed his exacting call.

Lest we begin to think instead that the solution to the young man's and our own problem is a strong dose of Christian gumption, through which we may gain "consistency and imperturbability" in marriage (R, 229), Kierkegaard gives us, in *Either/Or*, a satirical and cautionary tale. We may be tempted by this point, having read several versions of the same tedious story regarding a young man who fearfully breaks his engagement, to insist that he stiffen his spine, grow up, stop whining, and get married. This is, in part, what Judge William advises in the next two texts. Through *Either/Or* and *Stages*, Kierkegaard prompts us to interrogate not only the cowardly young poet and his voyeuristic mentor, but also the respectable man who, having said "yes" at the altar, lives with his beloved in domestic bliss. Continuing through these texts, we are still to note what Christian love is not, finding the impassable rift between merely human and Christian love evident in the marriage of a Judge as well as in the flagrant transgressions of the Judge's advisee. In what follows, Kierkegaard continues to pester his reader toward confusion, and toward faith.

CHAPTER 4

The married man as master thief
in Either/Or

Believe me, as surely as corruption comes from man, salvation
comes from woman.

(Judge William, EO, II:207)

When B supposes that out of a hundred people who go astray in the
world ninety-nine are saved by women and one by divine grace, it
is easy to see that he is not very good in mathematics, inasmuch as
he gives no place to those who are actually lost.

(Victor Eremita, EO, I:11)

DISENGAGING THE TEXT

We now enter *Either/Or*, that enormous book edited by the pseudonymous Victor Eremita, comprising documents by a dissatisfied sybarite
(known to us as "A"), a complete scoundrel (Johannes the Seducer), a
happily married man (Judge William), and a nameless Jylland pastor.
Kierkegaard published *Either/Or* in two contrasting volumes, or parts,
the first containing essays by A, closing with the exploits of Johannes,
the second "containing the papers of B [Judge William], letters to A"
(EO, II:1). The dichotomous form of the text suggests that the reader's
choice is as stark as the title: choose one volume or the other. It is little
wonder that readers have traditionally understood Kierkegaard to be
prompting a decision between two disparate realms, between the aesthetic and the ethical, between ephemeral pleasure and resolute duty.
Such is the most obvious interpretation of the text.

William's treatises in Part II overtly support this reading. As one whose
"consciousness" is "integrated" (EO, II:177), William differentiates himself from A's diffuse multiplicity and sees himself as wholly extricated
from A's tangle of misunderstanding. His volume is coherent, and apart.
Surmising Judge William's reaction to his publication of Part I, Victor
Eremita says that, given the chance, William "would make me feel that

he had no part in it, that he would wash his hands" (EO, 1:14). But, as Eremita observes with characteristic insight, the reader's "position" becomes "complicate[d]," because, in this book, "one author becomes enclosed within the other like the boxes in a Chinese puzzle" (EO, 1:9). This, Kierkegaard's "old literary device," reveals that William too is trapped within a world of false perceptions. William does indeed have a part in the mess, and, to pile up Kierkegaard's metaphors, he can neither "wash his hands" of it nor efficiently work his own little box free from the puzzle.

The ostensible origin of the book is appropriately odd: the text is a product of Eremita's accidental excavation. One day after purchasing a desk at a secondhand shop, Eremita attempts to open the money drawer, only to find it totally stuck. Finding himself in a "calamitous situation," he takes an ax to the desk, instead discovering a secret drawer that contains the papers "that constitute the contents of the present publication" (EO, 1:6). Although "the result [of his ax-wielding] was not what was intended," Eremita understands the result to "confirm" that "the outer is certainly not the inner" (EO, 1:6). This is a prompt. In Eremita's hatchet job on the desk, Kierkegaard gives the reader a clue to the method necessary for interpreting the text enclosed within. We are, through excavation, to distinguish the interior of *Either/Or*, Part II from its deceptively secure exterior. And if we pry open the book's sealed spaces using *Works of Love* as a tool, we may discover the mistakes within William's supposedly coherent life.

There is a second textual prompt within Eremita's preface. To pry open this text is to pry open one's own life, and the pseudonymous editor's experience should thus warn as well as inform the reader. In preparation for his own "little journey," secure with "everything in order," Eremita goes to fetch what he supposes to be the beneficial contents of the drawer; he attempts to open the desk in order simply to take out money for his holiday (EO, 1:6). To his surprise he discovers instead *Either/Or*. But the trip will not be interrupted; his plan is "unchanged." On the way, he finds a secluded spot, "where I would be as safe as possible from any surprise," and begins to read (EO, 1:6). In spite of his attempt to remain on course for his journey, in spite of his attempt along the way to find seclusion, Eremita's trip and his life are disrupted by the nefarious seducer (EO, 1:9). He finds himself staying up at night, reading the papers, envisioning the seducer himself "pac[ing] the floor like a shadow" (EO, 1:9). Even though we are removed yet again from Eremita – who is, as the mere excavator and editor of the text, "twice removed from the original author" – we who read the book find ourselves enclosed within the confounded puzzle of the text. Those who suppose themselves, like Eremita, to "have nothing at all to do with the narrative," also find their journey haunted (EO, 1:9). The editor and the edited, one author and the next, the reader and the text, one part and another, either and or, all become intertwined and implicated if we read the text as Kierkegaard intends.

After trudging through over four hundred pages of complaints, criticism, and ruthless acts, the religious reader may be tempted to rest, finally, in William's resolute Part II. To "take a hatchet" to William's letters may seem both rudely ungrateful, in that he seemingly refutes A and his dastardly phantom Johannes, and also unduly intrusive, inasmuch as the material for consideration is often his intimate experience with his children and wife. Yet to read Part II of *Either/Or* with *Works of Love* sheds light on the cracks in William's constructed world of moral assurance, and we ignore those fissures at our own religious peril. William's is not the answer to A's queried life, but it is an answer to which Kierkegaard's neighbors, as well as his present readers, too often turn.

Reading the rule of faithful intimacy in *Works of Love*, we discern that William underestimates his own collusion with the aesthete's predatory ways, relies unduly upon the self-giving work of his wife, and overestimates his ability, through duty, to live inculpably. These three mistakes protect William from the requisite crisis of faith. First, by subtly accommodating, rather than overtly refuting, A's aesthetic interest in women, William proceeds along a dubious trajectory. While Kierkegaard "thrust[s] from the throne" erotic love and "preferential love" (WL, 44), William seductively suggests that aesthetics and ethics may share the seat. Second, by positing marriage to a winsome and responsive wife as a resolution to the quandary of ethical existence, William attests to a fraudulent faith. Whereas Kierkegaard reads Christianity as insisting that A stand bare before his maker, William recommends that A procure a female intercessor. Finally, William cultivates the lie that his household sanctuary is the result of his upright adherence to duty.

These false assumptions stem in part from William's optimistic assessment of his present reality. He deems much of what he finds beautiful and soothing to coincide with God's will, in contrast to the warning Kierkegaard gives in *Works of Love* that the world we construct is most often our deceptive attempt to please ourselves. William's version of aesthetic interest is obtusely cheerful, and his domesticated salvation preys upon the solicitous work of his wife. The happily, dutifully married Christian is thus as much a part of the irreligious puzzle as is the seducer.

The extent of William's complicity in the system requires that we read *Either/Or*, Part II as caught – not only sequentially but thematically – between A and the Jylland pastor. William's section is a particularly alluring, and dangerous, dead end. We must move backward to A's musings in Part I on the possibility of tragic guilt – as a blameworthy state out of which one cannot will himself – and forward to the Ultimatum. Both A and the pastor suggest that, in spite of his wife and his stalwart will, William is (as Eremita implies in the quote opening this chapter) *lost*.

A right reading of *Either/Or* requires that we not remain, with William, resolved – that we not stop in the lull of his dutiful world. We must struggle on toward the telos of this pseudonymous text, the Ultimatum, wherein we are told that "in relation to God we are always in the wrong" (EO, II:339). And by interpreting this sermon that closes *Either/Or* as a sign that itself points toward *Works of Love*, we may correct William's claim that duty is the "true temperate climate" for marriage (EO, II:147). If faithful intimacy is possible, Kierkegaard explains in *Works of Love*, it must be based on the alternative reality of an individual's indebted relation to God. While Part II of *Either/Or* does include language about the divine, William's use is deceptive. He writes to A of repentance, guilt, and commitment but misleadingly sees this process as cordial to A's present aesthetic aims and as cohering virtuously in William's own supposedly self-wrought reality. Kierkegaard's description of the effects of God's grace on love in *Works of Love* helps us distinguish faithful engagement from William's alternately muscular and sentimental characterization of domestic order. Rather than having "added a little or subtracted something" from erotic love, God's work in Christ "has changed everything, has changed love as a whole" (WL, 147).

Our faithful humility before God, as described in *Works of Love*, has religious implications as well for women who seek to conform to the merely human realm that men like William create. As Wanda Warren Berry notes, the text shows "Kierkegaard's rare sensitivity to the situation of women within the romanticized patriarchy which the Judge embodies."[1] We should follow Berry's further suggestion that we read the text not only as exposing masculine sin, but also as revealing to women their own predicament within this system.[2] The text is for women a two-fold warning. The female reader of *Either/Or* may, like Eremita, find a murky seducer shadowing her. By finding in William the traces of Johannes's thievery, young fiancées and wives will increasingly detect the shrewd robbery occurring in their own homes. And, through this detection, we may also uncover what Kierkegaard calls our own "abomination," that is, our refusal "to know anything higher" than the esteem of the men we adore (WL, 125). When describing the self-denial of love indentured to God, we thus turn briefly back to the "Silhouettes" of Part 1. In A's ruthless dissection of feminine grief, Kierkegaard attempts to distinguish the generously forgiving vision enabled by faith from women's duped complicity with and active pursuit of men's favor. As William cannot arrive at love unless he first stands, alone, before God, so must his wife refuse any alluring bypass along the way.

WILLIAM'S BAPTIZED THIEVERY

A religiously developed person makes a practice of referring everything to God, of permeating and saturating every finite relation with the thought of God and thereby consecrating and ennobling it. (EO, II:43)

. . . although God, to use a somewhat frivolous expression, is an eyewitness who does not cramp one's style. (EO, II:56)

If we use Kierkegaard's explication of Christian love in *Works of Love* to judge Judge William, we may detect the error in what some deem to be William's advance over A, his more explicitly wayward friend. Though William may, to some extent, grasp that his relationship to his wife is a matter of great ethical import, the love he commends is mired in the false foundation of unchastened preference and is sustained by an asymmetric arrangement between man and wife. Both William's uncritical assessment of first love and his endorsement of marriage's solidity assume an all-too-convenient congruence between the actuality he perceives and God's will. While Céline Léon rightly notes that there are problematic passages in *Works of Love* itself, Kierkegaard can be put to good interpretive use against William's willed ignorance.[3] Kierkegaard himself exposes William as blind to the sinful, selfish, and, in this case, patriarchal, construction of beauty and domesticity.

While, according to William, true intimacy can flourish as "concentric" with "immediate love" (EO, II:30), Kierkegaard forces the lover humbly to acknowledge the continually distorting acquisitiveness of his aesthetic interest in another (WL, 44). In William's apology to A, his wife's beauty is a divine gift for him to appreciate, while Kierkegaard requires the beholder to pluck out the eye with which he assesses another's beauty. And William further fails to note the problematic extent to which his "balance" between beauty and order, aesthetics and ethics, passion and marriage, is poised on the back of his ever-attentive spouse. William claims that the duty and the nature of his wife, a woman "in harmony with time," cultivate a setting in which he can himself achieve harmony (EO, II:308). The pattern of her meticulous solicitude (to which we will turn) contrasts to Kierkegaard's insistence that the individual himself meet "the requirement of self-denial and sacrifice," which is "certainly made infinite" in the "God relationship" that alone "determine[s] what is love between human beings" (WL, 113). Whereas William lauds his wife as his "salvation" – as the means by which he is able to "centralize" and "acquire" himself (EO, II:207, 230) – Kierkegaard prohibits such use of another, demanding that the individual encounter God. We will deal with these errors in turn, beginning with William's insufficiently critical account of aesthetic immediacy, and moving to his account of blessed domesticity.

Whatever Christian marriage should be, it cannot be patterned after Isaac's "humility and trust" in God's superior ability to "choose his wife" (EO, II:44). Or so argues William, who, in order to "do justice to the erotic," amends the biblical story to read Isaac's trust in God as his expectation "that God would surely choose a wife for him who was young and beautiful" (EO, II:44). This assumption that a Christian may properly hope for a young and beautiful lover is a strand linking the seemingly disparate worlds of Parts I and II. There are small but significant clues that William understands the aesthetic as more than merely the "accidental adornment" of the ethical.[4] William's transition into the ethical is not truly an end to the aesthetic stage, as some have read it, but an economical continuation of one's pursuit of pleasure. Céline Léon rightly answers such readings that, "despite his many protestations" to aesthetic indifference, William "is not adverse to subsuming [his wife] under merely aesthetic categories."[5] Throughout the treatise, the reader finds the truth of William's own confession that "the more one is involved with [A], the worse it becomes" (EO, II:6). In *Either/Or*, Part II, Christianity becomes intertwined with the machinations of thievery, albeit a more socially acceptable form of theft than that of Part I.

William assumes the "innocence" of aesthetic assessment and advocates Christianity as the most reliable way for the previously desultory lover to acquire what he seeks (EO, II:49). In his defense of marriage, William argues that faithful matrimony encompasses the "absolute awakening," "the element of the sensuous," the "irresistible force" that the aesthete endeavors to prolong and repeat in his own scattered quest for pleasure (EO, II:42,45). As long as "the beauty implicit in the erotic of paganism" is also "combined with marriage," an aesthete may have his cake and bless it too (EO, II:10). Indeed, William argues, blessed cake is superior. By referring his first love to God in thanksgiving, the lover participates in a "higher concentricity" and, through marriage, heightens his pleasure even in the boudoir: "the higher the heaven is over the marriage bed, the better, the more beautiful, the more esthetic it is" (EO, II:61). This "deeper eroticism" enabled by Christian marriage vindicates Christianity as "the highest development of the human race" (EO, II:30, 31). His advice to A is this: he who is on the market for a lover should turn to God, because God can be trusted to do more than mere justice to the erotic found prior to faith.

Kierkegaard writes in *Works of Love* that a Christian apologetic which "proceeds on the basis that Christianity does indeed teach a higher love but in addition praises erotic love and friendship" is "foolish," "bungling, and confusing" (WL, 45); he might also have added, beguiling. By assuming that a lover's interest in his beautiful beloved is "innocent" and then suggesting that the lover should subsequently saturate that interest with religious gratitude, William presents a conveniently uncritical, baptized aesthetic. William's God does not, as he so revealingly words it, "cramp" a man's style. This version of Christianity confronts neither A's nor his own predilection to see a woman as a source of pleasure, whether shallow and sporadic (as is the case with Johannes) or deep and prolonged (as is the case with William). The sin of acquisition simply does not enter into the discussion, save when William denies its being a matter of concern: A need not fear "the Church's solemn declaration that sin has entered into the world," for "from this it by no means follows that [the eroticism of one's] first love is altered" (EO, II:55). William adds that, if this sort of "earthly love" were to be interpreted as sin, a woman's "whole existence would thereby be annihilated at its deepest root" (EO, II:55). William's view of the erotic and this last comment on woman's existence are linked. If erotic, preferential love is exposed as iniquitous – as most often the result of one's self-centered desire – women's existence, as masculine desire has construed it, is in fact "annihilated at its deepest root."

And it is erotic love's necessary annihilation that Kierkegaard describes in *Works of Love.* Kierkegaard asserts that erotic love blocks the "redoubling" that grants the beheld her own true existence, separate from the desirous fabrications of her beholder (WL, 21). Prior to God's becoming the intervening "guardian" for the loved one, the lover tends to perceive his beloved as an extension of himself; all "earthly love," rather than being a relation, is actually the lover "relating himself to himself" (WL, 189, 55). When faced with God's command that he see his lover as other-than-himself, the lover must become soberly aware of this tendency. His illusion, that the other is a compendium of beautiful particulars for the taking, is fundamentally altered. The tone with which William addresses the matter is thus deceivingly sanguine, and the content of his advice is inappropriately encouraging.[6] Whereas William assures A that "pain" is not "necessary," due to earthly love's concentricity with Christianity, Kierkegaard characterizes love as faithful only to the extent that the lover endures the "self-denial" of God's command to love the other as one's "neighbor" (WL, 53). By denying the necessity of the "separation" inherent in true "confidentiality with God" (WL, 153), William attests to an earthly love. Christianity thereby becomes merely "the highest development of the human race" (EO, II:31).

A more charitable (most often male) reader might counter that William does seem to love his wife for who she is, and that to attribute such selfishness to him is to overstretch the text. However, Kierkegaard does not, in *Works of Love*, describe preferential love as sinful only when evidenced by those who are, like A, clearly misogynist or, like Johannes, brazen seducers. Rather, he warns that each reader who would learn to love well must acknowledge that "purely human love is continually in the process of flying away after, so to speak, or flying away with, the beloved's perfections" (WL, 173).[7] William's obvious failure to acknowledge that spontaneous desire is rarely innocuous and that God must indeed "cool one's passions" (WL, 147, 36) is sufficient to place the religious reader on notice. While it is not inconceivable that William at times does love his wife *as his neighbor* and that he on some level "grants the beloved all [her] imperfections and weaknesses and in all [her] changes remains with [her]," as Kierkegaard commends (WL, 173), Kierkegaard warns us to be more circumspect of self than William at any point suggests. What is more, William is alarmingly obtuse in his failure to note and warn against the clear, indisputable danger A and Johannes pose to their own female "neighbors," suggesting instead that A's faults have "a certain additive of good nature and childishness" (EO, II:8). Finally, as we move on to William's discussion of mature marriage and domesticity, we sense that the aesthetic theft he has failed to note in his discussion of initial desire is not absent in his own life. His piracy has simply become more conventional with time.

William's problematic appraisal of his wife's beautiful particulars may be somewhat indirect, but his parasitic use of her existence as that which sustains his ethical and aesthetic "balance" is flagrant. In his passage on "woman" and her hair, William links his unapologetic approval of "woman's" beauty with the redemptive work for which he admires her: "a woman's luxuriant hair" with its "exuberance of curls" is, in its "beauty," a symbol of her ability securely to connect man to the earthly realm and moor his roving life. As if "flower's tendrils by which she has grown fixed to the earth," a woman's hair is an aesthetic pleasure to behold and a sign of her ability to "present [man] with the finite" (EO, II:313). Much of William's treatise hinges on this grounding work of an attentive woman.

This is a point some readers miss in the text, interpreting God as the stopgap that serves in William's system the Kantian role of ensuring the coincidence of morality and "natural desire."[8] William's advice to A depends on his being able to exist comfortably "at home" on the finite earth. The possibility that "the esthetic, the ethical and the religious [are] three great allies" (EO, II:147) has a prerequisite that beauty, duty, and blessing cohere. And it is primarily William's wife, not God, who enables this coherence. According to William, it is within marriage to a woman that these three "concentric" circles converge; marriage – as "the most beautiful task given to a human being" (EO, II:9) and as part of the very essence of Christianity (EO, II:28) – is a holy, beautiful, dutiful realm for assured human activity. In marriage to a woman, a man is able to experience as "melodic" what would otherwise be discordant in his "eccentric movement" (EO, II:67). He writes that this secure "home-feeling" comes over him as he returns to his abode from a day at the office:

then when I hear the noise and clamor of children inside, and of her as well, for she heads this little flock and is herself so childlike that she seems to compete with the children in shouting with joy – then I feel that I have a home. (EO, II:83)

He continues that his wife knows conversely how to be appropriately "accommodating" when he instead returns "a bit irritable." Apparently, William's wife is so attentive as to perceive in an instant his present mood and to take the shape his disposition dictates, for she is "infinitely flexible" (EO, II:83). These "little matters" of domesticity that consolidate the "meaning," "value," and "beauty" of William's existence are the natural domain of his wife, who has been "created to deal" with such (EO, II:68). Due to his wife's perpetual solicitude and activity ("she always has something to take care of") his home is his "absolute refuge" wherein "time has meaning for [him] again" (EO, II:308).

The "quiet, modest, [and] humming" home to which William returns for sustenance and security is rightly the result of his wife's work, for "she is a woman and in harmony with time" (EO, II:144, 308). As her "luxuriant braids almost touch the earth," she is, by her nature "fixed to the earth," capable of fixing William's own predicament (EO, II:313). And how does this domestic harmony benefit William's wife? According to his assessment, this marital relationship "gives strength and meaning to [her] quiet life," for therein "her weakness is strengthened by her leaning on him" (EO, II:67). She is in marriage to him "enclosed" by a "strong masculine arm" which "firmly and yet tenderly" guides her as they together "dive into the sea of existence" (EO, II:34).

The reader must read between the epistle's lines in order to gain any other impression of his wife's thoughts on the matter. As he so aptly puts it at the letter's close, "her thoughts are hidden in my thoughts" (EO, II:332). The only indication the reader has here of the wife's perspective is filtered through William's occluded vision. He notes in his appraisal of her physical beauty that "she is not as beautiful in the morning as in the evening;" that "a certain touch of sadness, almost of ailment, disappears only later in the day" (EO, II:9). Fortunately for her, by the evening she may again "truly claim to be appealing" (EO, II:9). While William clearly does not do so, the reader may surmise the reason for her waking to each new morning, with its endless list of concerns and attentions, with "a certain touch of sadness." After focusing for much time on William, we will only in closing return to his dutiful wife to consider why Kierkegaard's summons in *Works of Love* may most properly send her running through the streets with shorn hair.

In his defense and to his detriment, William contrasts his favored form of marriage with several he deems to be false. He argues against a marriage of character wherein a wife is as a "guinea pig" selected by the husband in order for him to achieve "a fixed cut-and-dried conception of how he wants to be developed" (EO, II:66), against a marriage of household convenience whereby a man might as well choose "a night nurse" as "a beautiful young girl" (EO, II:77), and against a household wherein the husband secretly creates for his wife a "magic circle" of constructed comfort outside of which she cannot move (EO, II:114). William shows in these passages an inkling of the dangers inherent in domestic life and the potential for use and deception. What he does not grasp is the extent to which his own marriage might be similarly indicted. These passages concern other men, and he uses them to warn A, an individual he supposes to be safely separate from himself. His arguments against these other, erring husbands are to his detriment, however, in that he cannot plead utter ignorance; through these passages he inadvertently adduces his active refusal to inspect his own life critically.

This negligence is perhaps most salient in his discussion of one husband's constructed, "magic circle." In this "silent system" of the husband's making, the wife is the center of a circle that the husband painstakingly and stealthily constructs in order to control her every "perception" and "impression" (EO, II:114–15). What William attributes to this one man's conscious and determined effort could be applied, in a more general way, to the entire milieu within which his own marriage functions – the magic, constructed, sexist circle of bourgeois domesticity. Later, in his notorious tirade against women's emancipation, William testifies against himself regarding the extent to which he is an architect of that erected system:

> . . . if this infection [of women's emancipation] were to spread, if it pushed its way through even to her whom I love, my wife, my joy, my refuge, the root of my life . . . Then I know very well what I would do – I would sit in the market place and weep, weep like that artist whose work had been destroyed . . . (EO, II:312)

If William were a bit more imaginative and considerably more self-aware, he might grasp that the error he attributes to another man might be a fault characteristic of multiple generations. If he were not so imperceptive, Judge William might less readily understand himself and his conventions as squarely matching God's command. He might perceive himself precisely within his own constructed refuge as fundamentally in the wrong before God.

In passing, William likens his marriage to a church wherein he may be "simultaneously priest and congregation" and suggests "that when a person has reached a certain age he ought to be able to be his own pastor" (EO, II:10,70). His unwarranted confidence in his own ability to summon forth and interpret God's presence precludes a truly humbling encounter with his creator. Standing alone before an intrusive God, William might become more aware of his wife's existence as truly other and his own need for extreme assistance. By opening himself up to sincere "confidentiality with God," Kierkegaard explains in *Works of Love*, a husband may hear God's command that his wife is to be loved first as his "neighbor" (WL, 153,141). This "eternal foundation" of God's command is in contrast to the basis William posits in his defense of first love's immediacy and is to sober the lover to distance himself from the beloved sufficiently to take first into account her distinct existence as God's own (WL, 141). William suggests that "the religious is pushed between the true lovers" but denies that "the religious" "separates" the two lovers; rather, "the religious" allows one's wife to "give herself with an exuberance that she had not previously suspected" and allows the husband not only to receive but also to "give himself" (EO, II:61).

What Kierkegaard describes as genuinely faithful marriage goes "beyond" this type of seeming "mutuality" in that there are three in the relationship, with God as the "sole object of love" (WL, 121). This in-trusion of God as a "third party" in between the husband and wife forces each to acknowledge that "it is not the husband who is the wife's beloved, but it is God" (WL, 121). Not only is she a being separate from William's needs and desires, William's wife belongs solely to God. Kierkegaard thus exposes as sacrilegious William's claim to be "everything to [his] wife" (EO, II:81). William's second treatise merely glances the realm of this truth. Although William agrees in a side note that "the meaning of life is to learn to know God and to fall in love with him" (EO, II:249), he overlooks too easily what this might mean for him and for his ever-busy wife. Rather than pausing to consider how the mystic's life of devotion to an exacting God might judge and inform his own, the judge trumps mysticism with what he believes is the necessity of domesticity. William's "animosity toward all mysticism" is a ramification of his insistence that faith and a comfortable marriage coincide (EO, II:245). If it were the case that "there actually were a conflict between love of God and love of human beings," William cannot "imagine anything more horrible" (EO, II:245). Thus swerving mentally to miss the significant hurdles that might reprove and edify his life – that is, God and God's command – William is able to speak with blessed assurance about his own faith and duty. After an illuminating pause with William in church, we will turn to his deceptively robust account of the ethical task.

INTERLUDE: THEFT IN THE SANCTUARY

My practice, namely, has always been imbued with the conviction that woman is essentially being-for-other. (EO, I:432)

. . . for it is a woman's nature to pray for others. (EO, II:314)

William's only report of his worship life is significant. Written as if an aside, his portrayal of his visits to church is crucial for understanding his use of "woman" as a substitute intercessor, for detecting his attempt to place his wife as "naturally" residing between him and God. Similar to Constantin Constantius's visits to the theater in *Repetition*, this vignette reveals much about our narrator's relation to the other.[9] As the cynical Constantin enters the theater hoping to find repetition and then resorts to solitary masturbation using a "young girl's" exposure to inspire his relief, so does the ethical Judge William here reveal his problematic motives and methods for achieving religious inspiration.[10] William confesses that his encounters with what he calls his "devout mother" – the prayerful matron in the parish he frequents – continue to inform his imagination and his marriage (EO, II:316). We may glean from this narrative fragment the trajectory along which he proceeds and also advises A.

The story begins with William's suggestion that, if churches would truly heed the words of scripture that advise a husband to "cling to his wife," they would discover "many prospects for beautifying the church service" (EO, II:313). By replacing the usual parish clerk or sexton with the "beautiful image" of a woman, the church could evoke in men a sense of gratitude for "woman," who is man's link to the finite (EO, II:313). William explains, "it has frequently been my delight to see woman's meaning in this way," and he tells of the "beneficial impression of the congregation" that ensued when he was able to find this meaning exemplified (EO, II:313). During one year of his life he found a church which "appealed to [him] very much," and where he discovered, to his joy, his "idealized conception" both of woman and of the religious embodied in one locale (EO, II:314). While he appreciated the pastor of this parish, who "satisfied the entire ideal demand of his soul," he recounts,

> what contributed to enhancing my joy and made the impression of divine worship in this church complete was another character, an elderly woman who likewise appeared every Sunday. (EO, II:314)

Just as Constantin appreciates the actors in the theater yet requires something more, so William enjoys the pastor's sermons but must find a focal point to immerse himself in the experience. By watching this woman, William "forg[ets] the disturbing image made by the parish clerk at the church door" and is able to focus on "her deep, pure, feminine decency" (EO, II:314).

William uses his matron's presence to participate vicariously in worship, much as Constantin the voyeur participates in the farce by watching a young woman in the audience. Bowing to the matron, William imagines himself and even his counterpart, A, included in her "intercessions"

(EO, II:314). Because "intercessory prayer is so essentially [her] nature," this matron – a "pure" example of femininity – grants by her very presence William's ostensible participation in worship. Coming to the church to worship, William convenes with God only through the woman's intercession for him. Although William's joy is short lived when she is absent from worship (recall that Constantin too cannot enjoy the show once the girl is hidden from view), he often thinks of her, and she continues to "drift into [his] thoughts" (EO, II:316).

When in Part I of *Either/Or*, Johannes writes that "woman is man's dream," that "woman is being-for-other," he has in mind a more immediate use than William's (EO, I:431). As belonging "altogether to the category of nature," woman is "free only esthetically" (EO, I:431). Woman exists to the extent that she is assessed to be sufficiently desirable to warrant man's "proposal." According to Johannes, woman is most clearly woman when a virgin, because a virgin characterizes an open potential for one man's "proposal"; she is not already used by another or currently being used by another, yet she is not, of course, beyond being used (EO, I:430). William's use of his matron and of the one to whom he has himself proposed is more subtle and is a means to a more complex end than Johannes's shallow desire, but it remains parasitic nonetheless. In William's account of himself before God in worship, he reveals the method by which he evades a stark encounter with God's law and with God's only effective intercessor. That William worships God by using a "pure" matron as a focal point is suggestive. If he had instead pondered directly the cross by which we are redeemed, he might not so easily have proceeded with his insubstantial account of sin, repentance, task, and duty. His use of the church matron is a metaphor for his marriage as a whole. By continuing to use "woman" as the intercessor who connects him with the finite, who allows beauty to sit comfortably with task and faith to sit comfortably with confidence, William steals from his wife and forestalls his hearing before God.

AN ULTIMATUM

... the religious is not so alien to human nature that there must first be a break in order to awaken it. (EO, II:89)

There is so much talk about man's being a social animal, but basically he is a beast of prey, something that can be ascertained not only by looking at his teeth. (EO, I:288)

It is in part Judge William's self-comparison with the brazen A and the evil Johannes that allows him such confidence regarding the morality of his marriage. Yet Kierkegaard is unwilling to give his religious readers this satisfaction. In an ironic ethical twist, the sermon closing *Either/Or* hints at A's vindication over the sturdy judge. A, in his conflicted state of laughter and self-pity, may be better prepared to receive Kierkegaard's advice on love than is William. Reading *Works of Love* highlights this twist in *Either/Or*. As Kierkegaard suggests in *Works of Love* using Jesus' parable of the two brothers, the brother who knows himself to be erring is more honest than the one who thinks, falsely, that he has met the father's demand (WL, 92). Although William speaks the language of repentance, confession, and guilt, he considers sin merely residual, and his hope subsequent to that guilt hinges on his own ability to will himself free of blame. He underestimates both his plight and his need for an intercessor.

Here we might consider Eremita's comment on William's false arithmetic regarding who is saved and how one receives salvation. In Eremita's seemingly insignificant editorial note, Kierkegaard links two factors in William's problem: his happy reliance on his wife and his inability accurately to perceive his disorientation. William's soteriological suppositions about his wife's work as a domestic and religious intercessor indicate the extent to which he is actually lost. A, however, does not underestimate his, or our, predicament. What A grants, that the individual may be wandering in a maze out of which he cannot escape, the assured William overlooks. A faces squarely, if sardonically, the possibility that we are all lost. As William himself notes, A does not "step aside for any thought" (EO, II:185) and this unswervingly brutal directness may enable the recipient of the concluding sermon, regarding perpetual guilt, better to grasp its meaning than the sender. William recognizes that A's vision leads him to shout, "vanity of vanities all is vanity, hurrah!" (EO, II:166). In doing so, A proclaims in a different tone what the Jylland pastor insists is the import of Luke 19:41: "And does not this, that it has happened, have the power to make everything else unexplainable, even the explainable?" (EO, II:343). Living in his carefully wrought domicile of assurance, the judge who advises the aesthete misses the treachery of existence.

A aptly likens himself to a pig who can root up truffles but "can do no more with them than throw them back over [his] head" (EO, I:36). Although he may be able to uncover and "take the problems on [his] nose," A is then capable only of flinging them about. A's disconnected notes on reality cannot point a way out of this Chinese puzzle. But it is in part his ability irreverently to uncover problems beneath the surface of perceived actuality that allows A a more apt vantage point than the positive William. In wondering, "what if everything in the world were a misunderstanding," and confessing, "God knows what our Lord actually intended with me or what he wants to make of me" (EO, I:21, 26), A does indeed, as William notes, "revel in shaking all the foundations" (EO, II:121). And from amidst the rubble of his self and the world around him, A harbors no illusions regarding who he and we are. One of Kierkegaard's obscure clues, hidden in Part I, is within A's treatise on the tragic. When speaking to his brethren of death, A produces a provokingly eccentric (and incoherent) paragraph pointing the reader back to the sentence preceding, regarding the ineluctably tragic element of human guilt (EO, I:151). He explains, if there is such a thing as "hereditary guilt" then purely subjective categories will not suffice; the individual is mired in muck deeper than that of his own making. Or, to use the previous example, if all that we think that we know is a misunderstanding, there are no reliable foundations (EO, I:150). The tragic, A explains, thus precludes a simply Pelagian solution (EO, I:144).

A suggests that, when someone within this conjectured, tragic, reality instead attempts "to gain himself in the superhuman way our age tries to do it, he loses himself and becomes comic" (EO, I:145). Although A cannot solve the conundrums of the text and of our lives, he does, in contrast to William, grasp that the reality we most immediately perceive is not easily understood, willed, or blessed. And here one may reasonably guess that A's reaction to William's arduous Part II is yet more laughter, for William becomes by A's definition a comic figure. According to William, hereditary sin leaves but "a little depression," a remnant trace that need not unduly become the focus of one's concern (EO, II:190). While William concedes that this residual depression does indicate that "no human being can become transparent to himself," he has hale advice about resolving even this problem (EO, II:190). He explains that "in the intention" sin can be "perceived as surmounted" (EO, II:97); and thus one's willed self-judgment may be a guide even in the more ambiguous of situations. On the occasion of near ethical confusion, William writes down "briefly and clearly what it was that I wanted or what it was that I had done and why," and then is able later, if "my action was not as vivid to me," to "take out my charter and judge myself" (EO, II:197). Even one's atavistic tendency to "deceive oneself" is therefore manageable with some effort (EO, II:197). A writes of his utter lack of clarity regarding God's intention for him, while William is resolutely self-assured.

Intertwined with William's optimism is his evaluation of dutiful relations. By understanding duty as "precisely the divine nourishment love
needs" and as "an old intimate," a "friend" and "confidant" to one's
love, Judge William suppresses a love commandment that would otherwise judge both him and us (EO, II:146, 147). On his account, the lover
who is in the throes of intimate love hears the command "not as something new" but as "something familiar" and in fact as that which assists
in love's climax (EO, II:146). In the midst of this encouraging dialogue
A's voice intrudes critically to inquire,

But what does it mean to commit oneself to love? Where is the boundary? When
have I fulfilled my duty? . . . In case of doubt, to what council can I apply? And if
I cannot fulfill my duty, where is the authority to compel me? State and Church
have indeed set a certain limit, but even though I do not go to the extreme, can
I not therefore be a bad husband? Who will punish me? Who will stand up for
her who is the victim?. (EO, II:151)

After asserting that A himself is the one who will know, punish and
vindicate, William stifles A's voice, saying "enough of that." Plowing
ahead, William insists that with the "treasure" stored in one's "own
inner being," the self may "choose itself" and, William insists, is able to
choose itself well (EO, II:177).

Yet William, being also interested in the religious, supplements his
discussion of duty with his own rendering of guilt, repentance, and reception. One technically "receives" oneself through repentance
(EO, II:217). In order to choose "the absolute," one chooses himself in
his own "eternal validity," which means, one "repents himself back into
himself" and back into history "until he finds himself in God" (EO, II:216).
Through this acquisition which is reception, the individual centers himself ethically, and becomes "in the most absolute continuity" with both
the infinite and finite (EO, II:249). Along this way, one does indeed at
times "feel one's own guilt," and one should, with "magnanimity" and
"courage," also "repent of the guilt of the forefathers" (EO, II:239, 218),
but we must not go overboard here. Sin may at times be limiting, but
it is also limited; and one should not become overly concerned with
transgression.

In his discussion of the mystics' error, William answers A's treatise on
the tragic possibility of insurmountable guilt. To follow the mystics and
"repent metaphysically is an unseasonable superfluity," for, as William
explains, "the individual certainly did not create the world and does not
need to become so upset if the world should actually prove to be vanity."

Such "metaphysical judgments" do not "ethically determine" the self's relation to the finite (EO, II:248). Even if all we think we know turns out to be a whirl of chaotic confusion, the self is neither indicted nor fundamentally hindered. The person "always" has "a point to which he holds fast, and that point is – himself" (EO, II:253). Duty thus comes from within, and allows for both "inner serenity" and a "sense of security" regardless (EO, II:254). How are we to do our duty if in fact we perceive with A that "all is vanity"? We simply will, providing we each hold fast to our self. And what of the victimizing to which A refers in his previous, intrusive inquiry? William's language of "magnanimity," "courage," and "high-minded[ness]" indicates that the choosing self is figuratively above sin as a permanently problematic state. As Louis Mackey so well puts it, William "thinks that a man can get behind his whole history and push."[11] What if an individual is in fact, in spite of all his suppositions, a bad husband? He may repent through will and become inculpably dutiful by choice.

Given that William himself understands his wife as the anchor who holds him fast, his words on self-sufficiency ring hollow. Moreover, as is the case with his felicitous coincidence of beauty, comfort, and blessing, William's intertwining of duty, repentance, and confidence is dangerous. Through his realignment of repentance with self-assertion William interprets gumption as righteousness, and makes of God a mere accessory to self-birth. As he so heretically phrases it:

Through the individual's intercourse with himself the individual is made pregnant by himself and gives birth to himself. (EO, II:259)

By offering a version of guilt and repentance whereby an individual can gain himself and go forth with confidence – by making faithful existence seem a matter of sheer will – William ignores both the extent to which he depends upon the labor of his wife and, more importantly, the extent to which his easy use of her is a symptom of an all-enveloping quandary.

Perhaps here we may fear for William himself inasmuch as he will eventually perceive the cracks in his domestic bliss. Currently, he may "thank God that [his] life has been so uneventful" that he has "only a faint intimation of [Nero's] horror." But eventually this "happily married man" may more intimately know the truth of his statement that Nero is "still flesh of our flesh and bone of our bone (EO, II:188). While today William may effectively both will himself ignorant of the exploitation within his own marriage and consider himself capable of activating his own rebirth, the illusion requires an effort difficult to sustain.

The "Ultimatum" closing the text suggests that his herculean attempt at self-justification may be weakening. If he does, as he reports, read the "Ultimatum" while thinking of himself and of A, William may discover that the one circumstance under which he concedes that a man should not marry – "that is, when the individual life is so entangled that it cannot disclose itself" – precludes his own marriage and rebuts his own treatis (EO, II: 117).

It is unclear whether William believes there to be congruence between his own words on humility and repentance and the Jylland pastor's sermon on perpetual guilt. William does warn against the "certain secretiveness" by which one attempts to avoid "humiliation," and he insists that when one instead is able "to will to be sound, honestly and sincerely to will the true," true love flourishes (EO, II:105). But again the way for one to accomplish this humility is through self-wrought courage. While "humility" is a "helpful and constant disciplinarian" for one's love, one can rest in the "true assurance" that the movement toward humility is his own (EO, II:111). And the version of security William proclaims to be the result of humility works against humility itself. In contrast to the preacher's insistence that one sit and stay with the thought that one is never "in the right relation to God," William suggests that humility can readily lead one to "have the cheerful boldness to believe in his own love" (EO, II:344). This is consistent with William's confession early on that, in his relation to others, he "persist[s] in the conviction" that he is a "humble instrument" of "divine providence" and is thus able to understand God as "guid[ing] everything for the best" (EO, II:13). With William's form of humility before God, then, he is able to say assuredly that he has "nothing for which to reproach [himself]" (EO, II:13). Missing is William's sense that the "certain secretiveness" he warns against may infect his life. Whether trusting in God's providence or in his own ability to judge the decisions he meticulously reports in his ledger, William believes that there is a way for him confidently, as Eremita suggests, to "wash his hands" of the situation.

Particularly given the fact that William is blind to the sins of his own self-centered circle of domestic comfort, this confidence is comical. If William does begin to submit himself to that "probing consciousness that [truly] scrutinizes itself," as his enclosure of the "Ultimatum" suggests, his prior confidence may become less comic than tragic. Before God, the preacher argues, "every uplifting thought that once made you so rich in courage and confidence" is rendered as a mere "jugglery that a child believes in" (EO, II:344). Unable to "penetrate [the] consciousness" and caught in a downward spiral of "duplexity," the previously confident man tries to scramble back up the ladder of his providential and dutiful acts, only to find there is no reliable foothold. The choice then is either agreeing to be "nothing in relation to God" or "having to begin all over again every moment in eternal torment, yet without being able to begin" (EO, II:346). Our culpability, the preacher explains, is qualitatively deeper than our ability to hoist ourselves out of the predicament.

To quote Louis Mackey again, William "takes his guilt as a moral challenge, when in fact he would be better advised to see it as a moral defeat."[12] Because William's version of faithful love requires that one be able to take a truthful accounting of himself and then repent accordingly, he encourages one to fashion a false and precarious foothold, a location from which he can safely "judge his act" as "right in the present moment" (EO, II:346). Given that his morally secure locale is none other than his home, in which his wife is ever busy and attentive, his hope appears more parasitic than self-reliant. Contrary to the seeming continuity between William's letters and the preacher's sermon, William's account of his "balanced" life can be read as his sustained avoidance of true religious humiliation and as his willed unfamiliarity with the damning secrets of his own domestic life.

THE "TEMPERATE CLIMATE" FOR LOVE

When, however, the God relationship determines what is love between human beings, the love is prevented from stopping in any self-deception or illusion, while in turn the requirement of self-denial and sacrifice is certainly made infinite. (WL, 113)

Reading *Works of Love* with *Either/Or* not only exposes William's certitude as hubris but also allows us to differentiate more clearly his aesthetic and moral appreciation of others from love enabled and chastened by faith. With his desultory truffle tossing, A is not a reliable guide for the lover seeking faithful intimacy. But at least A's confusion and thievery are readily evident; he does not mistake himself for a righteous man or even for an expert lover. It is in part William's use of religious language that makes his treatise more threatening. One could not mistake A for one who takes Christ seriously, but distinguishing Christ-centered love from William's version requires more effort and even "a hypochondriacal inquisitiveness," as William terms A's form of inquiry (EO, II:8).

In A's close dissection of sorrow, he suggests that "only the experienced observer suspects that in this particular house things are quite otherwise at the midnight hour" (EO, 1:173). In order to determine where William diverges from Kierkegaard on love, the reader is required also to suspect and observe, but not with the detachment A evinces. In this inquisitive section, we must return purposely to that which is also our own illness. By moving more explicitly to Kierkegaard's summons in *Works of Love* as it relates to our comic/tragic hero, we are well reminded that, unlike A, we are not "catching a fly" and watching dispassionately its imprisonment (EO, II:289). Kierkegaard makes painfully clear in *Works of Love* that the sins to which William seems insensitive infect each reader as well as the epistle's author. The system that entraps William imprisons us all. While debunking the illusion of baptized aesthetics and the moral law as a "temperate climate" for anything, much less love, we must also submit our own lives and loves to scrutiny. We need be reminded that an acute detection of William's faults may, without adequate self-inspection, also lead the reader astray. Criticism that merely tears down another but does not also criticize the critic cannot rightly be the "truth that builds up" (EO, II:354). This *nota bene* is not only for the male reader. While within a patriarchy women are more often vulnerable to the symptoms we discuss in the "final word" below, at least this female reader is susceptible as well to William's maladies of predation and false-confidence.

Linked to William's dismissal of Isaac's story is his notion that "true marriage" begins with the "freedom and necessity" of erotic interest in another (EO, II:43–45). Although the lovers subsequently thank God for the other as a gift, the "surprise" of erotic first love is, William asserts, "involuntary" and thus not the apt point for "taking counsel with God" (EO, II:43). By reading this moment of desire as a bare fact, as "innocent" and "free" (EO, II:45, 49), William misses the lover's self-serving construction of beauty. Kierkegaard warns that the moment before erotic interest is neither unwilling nor benign and insists that the lover consult with God prior to desire. The command that we love each person we see as first (not subsequently) our neighbor is in effect to "blind" us – to expose our predatory interest in another's beauty as an aberrant form of love. As the lover is watching, surveying, and appraising, the command rudely intrudes, forcing the perusing one first to be "all ears to the commandment" (WL, 68).

The commandment's intervention is to force the lover to acknowledge and if not to check then significantly to mitigate the self-interest and other-negation inherent in erotic love. While Kierkegaard's warning is applicable for all of us who wish to love rightly, the villainy of erotic interest is particularly obvious in the patriarchal world of *Either/Or*. Within a culture that determines some to be rightly the beholders and others inherently the beheld, the male lover may disregard entirely this facet of God's command. In the very act of looking upon another in order to decide whether or not to love, the lover is, in this patriarchal system of selfishness-writ-large, able to ignore that "the defect could be in him or in the wrong conception" of love (WL, 162). When faced with God's command that the beheld is separate and distinct from any evaluation of worth, beauty and attraction, the lover is instead to become "rigorous" toward himself; he is to turn that appraising eye inward and detect the treachery of his own love (WL, 157).

A is thus to some extent accurate when, in the middle of William's ode to erotic Christianity, he interjects that "in Christianity the beautiful and sensuous are negated" and that it is "a matter of indifference to the Christians whether Christ had been ugly or handsome" (EO, II:47). William's attempt to wed aesthetics and faith ignores the extent to which Christianity does indeed require that the individual suspect and interrogate his aesthetic evaluations of the other. William's "esthetic that returns in its relativity" after the individual chooses duty (EO, II:177) is insufficiently transformed. Christ's command that we love each person first as our neighbor is radically to deconstruct our self-serving patterns of supposedly harmless evaluation and interest.

Yet in *Works of Love* our moral assessment of others fares no better than does our erotic appreciation of them. When William is not extolling the salvific powers of "woman," he understands himself to be saved through courageous self-exertion, and his esteem for others is built on this foundation. Relating his introduction to religion, William explains that he discovered "the immortality of [his] soul" while staying resolutely with his task of memorizing a catechism (EO, II:270). This well characterizes his approach to the eternal significance of others; one's worth is exemplified by one's "work." Through effort, one is able to "carry out one's task," and this proves one "higher than nature" (EO, II:282, 296). Thus, as he looks out his window, the judge appreciates each according to his potential to accomplish an assigned duty. Each individual has a "concrete task for life," thus inspiring Judge William's approval (EO, II:275). Whereas accomplishment is in large part the basis of William's ethical regard for others (EO, II:296), his imagined interlocutor is in an odd way closer to the truth when he supposes that "whether [one] accomplishes something or does not accomplish something is entirely beside the point" (EO, II:294).

In *Works of Love*, Kierkegaard explains that because God is "an eternity ahead" of any relatively minute act of love we can muster, our sense of self-congratulatory worth or success is a chimera (WL, 102). The one who loves truly, in contrast to William's window musings, does not with self-confidence esteem the other as similarly efficacious, but instead, finds himself greatly indebted before God and loves each and every neighbor out of gratitude (WL, 51). Although William's regard for his neighbors is potentially "universal," it is based on worth or capacity-in-common rather than humble gratitude (EO, II:257). William encourages A to "give birth to himself" and to esteem others as those who are similarly capacitated (EO, II:259, 282). The faithful lover, according to Kierkegaard, is through God's law and grace to know himself instead as infinitely indebted and to know each other as also fallen and blessed.

Kierkegaard speaks of this in explicitly Christological terms when describing Jesus' work as the "perfection" of love's law. With God's work in Christ comes an "everlasting chasmic abyss between the God-man and every other person" (WL, 99, 100). In the face of this chasm to continue speaking unabashedly about one's own or humanity's innate capacity to be "victorious" or to "conquer" (EO, II:275) is to endorse an illusory path to righteousness. Being "reduced to nothing" by God's "criterion" in Christ, the lover must acknowledge the infinitude of our universal, original debt to God and his own accruing debt before Christ's perfection (WL, 102). Universal regard for ourselves or our neighbor is to have at its source a notion of this utter dependence on grace.

While William's world of moral regard for self and other may for some time remain intact, a significant glitch in his "struggle with the cares and necessities of life" could send the whole system spinning (EO, II:286). Currently he may know that he is "everything to his wife" and may think his "consciousness" resolutely "integrated" (EO, II:81, 177), but William's treatise assumes that this will continue to be the case. If William encounters a catechism he cannot effectively memorize – if he encounters a chink in his self-wrought moral reality that he cannot fill in with more courage or determination – the life to which he attests may crumble. Or, to mention what is perhaps a more likely scenario, if his wife eventually refuses carefully to contort her form to fit his mood, William's esteem for her and his hope of "salvation" through her may collapse. As Louis Mackey suggests, "when [marital] conflicts occur, they cannot be resolved by moral computation in a way that meets the Judge's ethical demand," for "immediacy conspires to righteousness as little as it does to beauty."[13] William admits that, as he grows older and is faced with how to "extricate" himself from "spiritual trials," he increasingly seeks a more reliable "judge" or "expert" to assess his progress; what is more, he looks "up to this umpire" and continues to "covet his approval" (EO, ɪɪ:287).

Such self-judgment and coveting, combined with William's strange hybrid of self-confidence and spousal reliance, make his marriage rife with the possibility for the "loathsome rash" of "comparison" (WL, 186).[14] In what is perhaps the most apologetic and poignant section in *Works of Love*, Kierkegaard diagnoses the internal instability of a marriage such as William's. Kierkegaard explains that when we attempt ethically to bypass our infinite debt to God's grace, we are tempted to "look around" – to "compare [our] lot" either to our previous lot, to the lot of the person closest to us, or to our neighbor's lot (WL, 185, 184). As he suggests, "comparison's sidelong glance all too easily discovers a whole world of relationships and calculations" with which we assess and shore up our sense of ethical achievement (WL, 183). If the self-reliant individual seeks to assess his own progress in this way, he may turn on himself with no solace. If the seemingly self-reliant individual who in truth depends upon his spouse seeks to assess his own progress through comparison, he may turn on her for inadequately shoring him up. Seeking approval, wishing for signs of advance and determinations of providential blessing, the erstwhile lover finds in his relationship or in his partner the deficiency he fears (WL, 35, 36). Once love is infected with this scourge, comparison "turns inward" and destroys the very "marrow" of love (WL, 186).

There is hope for William, and for us, but only inasmuch as the Judge and we heed the closing sermon. Rather than attempting at each moment to determine our progressive distance from each prior moment, seeking our own or an "expert" judge's approval (EO, ɪɪ:286, 346), we are to enter into an "infinitely free relationship with God" by "acknowledg[ing] that we are always in the wrong" (EO, ɪɪ:352). Refusing to "gauge his relationship with God by a more or a less, or by a specification of approximation" allows the lover to cease the vicious cycle of comparison against which Kierkegaard warns us (EO, 2:352). As David Gouwens notes of William, he misses the real implication of the sermon he encloses, which is "if one is always in the wrong before God then one cannot fulfill the ethical law."[15] The Jylland pastor's sermon thus hints a way out of the Chinese puzzle: the individual stands alone before God and knows himself to be in the wrong. This is a very Lutheran notion of virtue, wherein the first and continual question is "how is one to stand before God?" again to quote David Gouwens.[16] Rather than ignoring his predicament, depending on "woman" to save him from it, or ethically willing himself free, the lover must find himself indicted, infinitely, before God.

What the sermon does not make explicit, however, is that the individual is not only incriminated but ransomed. Kierkegaard avoids bringing Christ's justificatory work clearly out into the open in his discussion of this freedom that comes with absolute culpability (perhaps lest the reader skim eagerly to find the escape clause), but Christ's work is the presupposition underlying our indebtedness. Faced with the condemning and yet also salvific work of Christ, the lover is to know himself incalculably beholden to God (WL, 179). This "strange way of speaking" requires an entirely new "attitude and mind" (WL, 178). True love requires one to live in an alternative "element," a habitat quite unlike William's "temperate climate" of duty, whereby one stays soaked with a sense of "infinitude, inexhaustibility, [and] immeasurability" (WL, 180). This is a crucial facet for Kierkegaard's entire explication of love: one must live in debt in order to love well. Our "duty" is precisely to know ourselves as extravagantly ransomed transgressors of duty (WL, 187).

This is to put an end not only to our eager self-justificatory computations but also to our ludicrous attempts to interpret our lover as indebted to us (WL, 189). (Recall that William alternatively perceives his wife as his refuge and his ward.) In our universal debt, we are all only indebted to God, "who, so to speak, lovingly assumes love's requirement" (WL, 189). Given that "comparison is the most disastrous association that love can enter into," the faithful lover must keep an "eternal vigilance, early and late," to stay in this context of debt rather than of calculated estimation (WL, 186, 179). The truest progress a husband can make is in confessing himself lost and found – redeemed not by "woman" or through ethical parthenogenesis but by the amazing grace of God.

This alternative climate of indentured love is not nearly so temperate as William's own, apparently serene, marriage. Christ's work of heightening and fulfilling the law gives testimony to the fragility of truly faithful intimacy and deepens the lover's sense of indebtedness before God. By exposing each individual in the marriage to "God's requirement" that we love the other first as our neighbor and thus as separate from our own needs and desires, Christ's command is to sober us to the often ill effects of our affection (WL, 112). The knowledge that God is the "guardian" of each beloved exposes as iniquitous all systems, writ large or small, wherein a beloved is subtly deemed the servant of or intercessor for her lover. By making intimacy itself a "matter of conscience," Christ's presence in the bedroom exposes each marriage as encompassing a myriad of occasions for sin (WL, 137, 142). Rather than being a secure realm of undaunted, blessed activity – a locale of "home-feeling" wherein one may be assured that all seemingly disparate facets of life are "melodic" (EO, II:67, 83) – one's abode is exposed as a potential den of self-delusion.

God's presence in Christ is precisely to cramp one's style, in various ways. One's proclivity to assess, evaluate, use, and (when she is unappealing) ignore one's lover comes into sharp relief with Christ's love (WL, 168). The lover's tendency, "just as pernicious as an ingrown toenail," to encourage his lover to turn only toward himself, fostering a "small-mindedness" that "holds together with small-mindedness" (WL, 272), is clearly in breach of God's law that true faithful intimacy is to prompt each individual upward to God and outward to each neighbor (WL, 61). The temptation, in intimacy, to love one's beloved only as her becoming presence at the dinner table makes life more commodious clashes starkly with Christ's banquet summons to the limping, bleeding, and sputtering outcasts on the outskirts (WL, 81). A lover's habitual familiarity with a wife "whose thoughts are hidden" in his own (EO, II:332) is suspect, given that God commands of each individual a new, potentially discordant, task for every moment (WL, 189). Even a couple's reminding one another in faith that they are to love one another first as each is related to God can become, without caution, a routine evasion of God's command (WL, 37).

And this is only randomly to mention a few of the obvious pitfalls facing one who would be both married and faithful, according to Kierkegaard. Confronted with these and many other harrowing prospects for original and inventive transgression, the lover is to experience himself as chastened and lost . . . yet also redeemed. The cycle of infinite debt is to continue as both lovers know themselves accruing and depending on grace as their source of strength and hope, lest either begin relying instead on self or other. This very knowledge of perpetual debt is to contribute to both lovers' ability better to love, ensuing in a faithful narrative that is, in David Gouwens's words, "joyful but also fearful" as we precariously "stand before the living God."[17] Because I am myself transgressor and victim, predator and prey, user and used, and am redeemed only through God's justificatory grace, so am I to see with new sympathy and forgiveness the obviously sinful neighbor with whom I awaken each morning (WL, 295). The truly apt climate for love is thus neither beauty nor duty, but real repentance and grace.

A BRIEF WORD IN CLOSING TO THOSE OF THE FAIR SEX

Look! There she stands in all her imperfection, a more inferior creature than man; if you have courage, snip off those abundant curls, cut those heavy chains – and let her run like a crazy person, a criminal, to the terror of people. (EO, II:313)

Having noted several facets of faithful marriage in *Works of Love*, we must turn back to A's "Silhouettes," because reading *Works of Love* with *Either/Or* should enjoin William's wife. With Kierkegaard's summons to indebted, forgiving love in *Works of Love* comes a warning for all Cordelias, wives, and novices to refuse the pernicious circle of evaluative observation and asymmetrical servitude their men have created. To employ William's words in a way directly contrary to his purpose, we are to cut both our beautiful curls and our domestic chains. This summons is to the young, foolish girl and the older, resigned wife. Both Johannes (overtly) and William (covertly) assume that women and their beautiful locks are to be observed and appreciated aesthetically. Even though William's evaluation of his wife's comeliness is within the context of committed fidelity, his continued aesthetic interest in her as the beheld is a key point in his defense of the institution itself (EO, II:9). In William's world, even as a man declares "for better or worse," he need not worry that indeed there will be much worse; the marriage vow only makes a woman all the more pleasant to behold (EO, II:34).

And, in William's estimation, a woman's rightful work is to make her husband's life beautifully harmonious. Her dutiful work is effective to the extent that she serves to ground her husband's often-disconnected life (EO, II:298). It is difficult to know who is a more exacting judge, God or man, but in a society ruled not by God, but by man, approval and appreciation is more immediately advantageous. In a world constructed to please men, women are rewarded to the extent that we make our lovers' interest and then our husbands' comfort the measure of our existence. As A's descriptions of forlorn women relates, the temptation is great within this constructed reality for women to perceive themselves as viewed and to consider masculine interest, gratitude, and approval as the primary measures of existence. The love to which Kierkegaard calls the individual in *Works of Love* is based on the individual's relationship to God in Christ, and it judges all our attempts at gaining masculine approval to be idolatry (WL, 125). We briefly close by interpreting A's ruthless dissection of feminine grief as Kierkegaard's attempt to distinguish the tenacious love enabled and strengthened by faith from women's duped complicity with and destructive pursuance of men's favor. As William cannot come through faith to true love but by standing bare before his maker, so is his wife to refuse a patriarchal detour.

In A's preface to his "Silhouettes," he offers a warning to all who enter that there will indeed be dragons past this point:

> Foresworn may love at all times be;
> Love-magic lulls down in this cave
> The soul surprised, intoxicated,
> In forgetfulness of any oath.
>
> (EO, 1:166)

The female reader may read this as a notice on the entry-way to a world of masculine power, betrayal, abandonment, and feminine despair. Drunken with their adoration for their lovers, each woman in this chapter forgets the oath between herself and God, and each then has no recourse for solace save her own cultivated illusions of her deceitful lover. This motif of God's being thrown over for a man is explicitly the case with Donna Elvira, who leaves a convent for Don Giovanni, but it is implicit as well for Marie and Margarete, whose language for their villainous lovers is the language of idolatry. The severity of their heretical reverence builds with each vignette, from Marie, who hears Clavigo as accusing her with the phrase "O you of little faith," to Donna Elvira, who, loving Don Giovanni "more than her soul's salvation," "casts away everything for him," to Margarete, whose love for Faust is, to her own mind, "worship" (EO, 1:185, 196, 213).

Particularly in this section Kierkegaard grants A a notably biblical imagination, emphasizing the religious implications of the sketches. Each woman's description of her love is phrased in scriptural terms, culminating with Margarete's petitions to Faust. She pleads with Faust, "satisfy the hungry, clothe the naked, revive the languishing"; begs God to "incline [Faust's] heart" toward her; and calls herself both "clay in [Faust's hands]" and "a rib from which he formed me" (EO, 1:213). Finally, she concludes, "he was my all, my god, the origin of my thoughts, the food of my soul" (EO, 1:213). In Margarete's litany of petitions, A strings together verses from Matthew, Psalms, Romans, Genesis, Jonah, and Hosea to form a chain of blasphemous love. These passages, originally on God's creative and redemptive grace, change in this context to become clear manifestations of Margarete's total dependence instead on her lover. We miss Kierkegaard's point if we note only that each woman has, like Margarete, "completely disappear[ed]" behind her betrayer (EO, 1:210). "Silhouettes" is not only about loss of self but also about loss of one's soul. The oath forgotten, supplanted and distorted in this venue of perverted love is each woman's covenant with God.

The context for these women's tortured attempts to forgive and offer "mitigating explanations for" their lovers is significantly different from the forgiveness Kierkegaard describes as the result of living within one's debt to God's grace (WL, 281). In their self-interrogations, A's shadowy women attempt to find some self-indicting explanation for their abandonment lest they be forced jarringly to rethink the patriarchal context of their existence. The sexist way to salvation posited by their world and to which they each creatively wed themselves leads them elastically to reconfigure their idols as still worthy of their devotion (EO, 1:180). Unable to imagine her life committed to another source of self-justification, each woman seeks to exonerate her man as the proper grounding for her existence.

The elasticity and resilience of their love might seem initially similar to Kierkegaard's description of the love which, indebted to God, "hides a multitude of sins" and abides in spite of the faults of one's lover (WL, 289). Such true love realizes that we are "called neither to be judges nor servants of justice" (WL, 293) and these women do indeed have "an interest in the accused that is incompatible with strict justice" (EO, 1:185). But the veneration of A's profiles is a grotesque distortion of God's command for love to "abide" as Kierkegaard describes it in *Works of Love*. Love truly abides only in the context of one's absolute focus on God as one's judge and redeemer. *Works of Love* may be read as offering a more somber summons than Wanda Warren Berry's humanist/existentialist antidote to the "sadomasochism" of "Silhouettes."[18] The ethical self-birth of William is no more possible or faithful for women than men. Rather, before God we too are lost and found. In this context, we are, each of us, first God's own; each heart is "without limit bound to God" (WL, 148). True, I am, in this God-relationship, judged iniquitous. But I am also exonerated only through God's grace, not because I dutifully stand by my man. Further, the forgiving and mitigating love I give another is given to him as he is also profoundly sinful and saved, not to him as if he is in any way my superior.

This requires that one throw over male evaluation as a system of judgment and redemption. A well notes that these women's vicious attempts to acquit their men of wrongdoing can "only by a break" be "brought to a halt"; each woman must "cut short this whole movement of thought"

(EO, 1:188). The setting of the silhouettes – a cave of intoxicated and idolatrous love – exposes merely secular forgiveness as a cyclical perpetuation both of men's role as the evaluators of women and of male affection as the true telos of women's lives. Abiding, forgiving, indebted and true love originates from the alternative trajectory of faith in God. Each woman must refuse to worship Priapus and know that she is appraised, accountable, judged, and extravagantly saved by God alone. Only within this setting of God's direct lordship over each individual, with no intercessory gauge other than Christ, can a woman rightly love and faithfully forgive.

In *Either/Or*, Kierkegaard depicts the devious connections between William's "humming" domesticity and the world of Don Giovanni, Faust, Clavigo, and Johannes. The former is in fact more dangerous, in some ways, because William is almost able to pass himself off as a Christian, thereby dulling the wedge that must come between woman and the system. But by using *Works of Love* to detect William's home life, we perceive how his wife is in as grave a danger as Donna Elvira, Margarete, or Cordelia. Kierkegaard warns, in *Works of Love*, that one's relationship to God must always be at the forefront of one's mind, must always be the grounding for one's love, and must be the focus of one's existence (WL, 129–30). If, as William admits, his wife "always has something to take care of" (EO, II:308) and stays ever busy in her attempt to create a "melodic" life for him (EO, II:83), how may she find the time or energy to love God? Rewriting William's story of the absent-minded professor is apt here. He comically relates how a husband is saved from his misguided obsession with an infinitesimal vowel mark by his persistently solicitous wife. While beckoning him to lunch, she reveals that the mark is instead merely a tiny grain of snuff. What Kierkegaard reminds us, and what William conveniently misses, is that a wife, by perpetually preparing her husband's salubrious meal, may lose sight of the otherwise infinitesimal moment in time when she is called to sit at the feet of her redeemer.

The most insidious facet of this system is that William's wife may not, while buzzing around within this magic circle, even perceive that her creator is summoning her. Believing in her role as the anchor that keeps him tethered to the finite, William's wife may, in a way more quiet and modest than Margarete, lose her soul. By carefully conforming herself to William's expectation that she be his "absolute refuge" and a "natural virtuoso" of the mundane, his wife may "dance" and "sing" with "an indescribable lightness" but be slowly, almost imperceptibly, descending into hell (EO, II:308). Knowing no other measure for her existence than her husband's equanimity, she believes herself to be living a justified life. And the vicious, magic circle continues . . . If you instead have the courage, snip off those curls and cut your chains, perhaps to the terror of your husband; you have nothing to gain but your faith.

CHAPTER 5

Seclusion and disclosure in Stages on Life's Way

... the lover has with his beloved the most priceless amusement and the most interesting subject of study in his life.

(Constantin Constantius, SLW, 55)

As far as I am concerned, the emphasis must be placed elsewhere – whether I was actually capable of giving my life the kind of expression that a marriage requires.

(Diarist, SLW, 195)

This mode of answering, to swing away from the direction of the question . . . in order instantaneously to press the task as close as possible to the questioner, what he has to do – this is characteristic of the essentially Christian.

(WL, 96)

INTRODUCTION

Stages on Life's Way, which Kierkegaard subtitled "Studies by Various Persons," is a set of texts "compiled," "stitched together," "forwarded to the press, and published by Hilarius Bookbinder" (SLW, 1, 4). This book is an interlocked, "stitched together" world of various characters, many of whom we have already met in earlier chapters. And each previously noted occasion for confusion and error becomes extreme here. William Afham (a new character) narrates the first section, entitled "*In Vino Veritas*," wherein the Young Man and Constantin Constantius (from *Repetition*) gather for a private banquet with Victor Eremita and Johannes the Seducer (from *Either/Or*), along with the (new) Fashion Designer, to consider, over wine, the truth of "woman." Upon leaving their clandestine party of libations and monologues, the men sneak up on Judge William (of *Either/Or*), whose "Reflections on Marriage" comprise the second part of the text. Finally, by way of a diary entitled "Guilty/Not Guilty?" we enter the tortured world of another young man (whom we will call the Diarist), who attempts, but then fails, to be engaged. The text concludes with interpretive remarks by the Diarist's self-proclaimed puppeteer, Frater Taciturnus. The relation of each character and each section to the others is obscure, but, if Hilarius Bookbinder's "learned friend" is to be trusted, there is a relation. He suggests that "there must have been a fraternity, a society, or an association" of which our various characters were members (SLW, 6). The tie that binds this book is not blessed. These men are associated by way of their various attempts to avoid the other, by perpetuating seclusion and precluding disclosure.

William Afham prefaces his own tale of wine and truth with an enigmatic discussion of reflection and seclusion, wondering, "how can the beaten and frequented be reconciled with the out-of-the-way and the hidden?" (SLW, 16). Existence, "the essential," "the idea," all require that the self be adept at the "art" of critically reflected memory, an ability to "conjure away the present" and be "absent" even while in the presence of another (SLW, 13). How can life's demand for reflective solitude cohere with the ineluctably relational facets of existence? How can the frequented be reconciled with the hidden? William Afham, whose surname means "by himself," gives thanks to a "friendly spirit" who has "protect[ed his] stillness" and granted him "a hiding place" all his own (SLW, 17). But, as he suggests, "recollection's bookkeeping is a curious thing" (SLW, 11), and the protective spirit who grants secrecy may not necessarily be on the side of truth; it may, rather, be a means for duplicity. An individual's motive for seeking a solitary place in which to reflect and write does matter. One may eschew the influence of others on one's own "reflective bookkeeping" in order to attend carefully to the truth, in order to perpetuate self-delusion, or for even more sinister purposes. William Afham, who is alone, thanks his friendly spirit for preventing the "interruption" of another into his own silent retreat, noting, "only someone who sought solitude unworthily can benefit" from such a disturbance (SLW, 18). Our narrator thus mentions fleetingly that the "surprise" of another's voice, intruding on one's self-enclosed reflection, may correctively "disturb" the invidious "secret" bookkeeping with which an individual becomes preoccupied. Reading *Stages on Life's Way* with *Works of Love* in view, we provide such an interruption.

In this collection of papers, a "fraternity" of men considers the "beaten and frequented" institution of marriage and whether life may accommodate contact with that other who truly interrupts a man's reclusive bookkeeping – woman (SLW, 6). The texts within well depict various means by which a man may avoid a true encounter with the other.[1]

The banquet revelers explicitly exclude anyone lacking the requisite tool (whether "cigar," "pipe," or "divining rod"), thus ensuring that no one "impertinently insists on being an actuality" over and against their manhood (SLW, 23). William the Married, unlike William Alone, believes himself joined to an other but in the course of his treatise reveals his dependence on a feminine fabrication of his own spinning. The Diarist, in his earnest reflection upon life, acknowledges the genuine otherness of the beloved but, in mistrust of himself and her, chooses to seek solitude through an elaborate deception of self and other. Although the way of each man is mistaken, their missteps are instructive. Especially in the Diary, we have occasion to note the close resemblance between one man's apprehensive retreat from reality and the sober self-examination Christianity requires. By interrupting each man's thoughts on marriage with the command to love, we may insert the other back into the text and spoil the inappropriately inclosed reserve of each. When the actual (female) neighbor thus enters this fraternal discourse, we may perceive the truth of Kierkegaard's epigraph: "Such works are like mirrors: when an ape looks in, no apostle can look out" (SLW, 8). Each reflection reveals each man to be more nearly simian than saintly (SLW, 8).[2]

Every mistaken stage in this book of wrong ways begs for Christian correction. By reading *Stages* with *Works of Love* we may hear God interrupt Constantin's carefully orchestrated feast, insist that William the Married has more to worry about than he has even begun to imagine, and call the dear Diarist out of his idea and into an authentic encounter through self-disclosure. In *Works of Love*, Kierkegaard seeks to bring God's command so close to the reader as to avoid any possible diversion or excuse for not loving the other. While bona fide engagement is a fragile possibility for many reasons, objective and subjective, the one task on which the individual must focus is "to acquire the true conception of love" (WL, 236). Constantin and his guests speak of the misrelation between men and "woman" that precludes involvement, and the Diarist tortures himself over the inherent, intractable misunderstanding between himself and the one to whom he must commit. But in *Works of Love*, Kierkegaard urgently reminds us that the only impediment to our engagements with which we should be concerned is the "misrelation" or "inversion" in our own understanding of love (WL, 31, 40, 162).

Because their inquiry is more blatantly vicious than that of the Diarist, the celebratory misogynists of "*In Vino Veritas*" may be exposed with less effort than William or the Diarist. The Diarist's missteps are most difficult to dismiss; his self-scrutinizing reflection is askew, but almost imperceptibly so. The contrast between the Diarist's recurring apprehension and William the Married's unshakable confidence may instruct us as we attempt to meet Kierkegaard's call in *Works of Love* for a genuine, honest construal of love. The Diarist seeks seclusion in part because he, in his own disoriented manner, rightly recognizes that true love with another requires both self-examination and a sober acknowledgment that the beloved is a stranger. Although William the Married bypasses the Diarist's temptation to flee, he does so largely by virtue of amorous luck, idealizing the other and underestimating the treachery of love.[3] After interrupting each man's evasive treatise with God's command, we will consider how God's presence as a confidant (rather than as the Diarist's idea) might facilitate an (albeit arduous) marriage for the Diarist, and for those of us who similarly struggle.

DIVINING RODS AND UNMENTIONABLE CRAVINGS

It is a sad but altogether too common inversion to go on talking continually about how the object of love must be so it can be loveworthy . . . (WL, 159)

. . . the idea of woman is only a workshop of possibilities. (SLW, 76)

To spend any amount of time distinguishing a true construal of love from the words of Constantin and his cronies may seem like overkill.[4] But, as the narrator explains, these "nocturnal revelers seen in the morning light" may have "an almost *unheimlich* [disquieting] effect," and Kierkegaard intends the reader to be alarmed by this first set of stages (SLW, 81). It is not incidental to Kierkegaard's purposes that we enter the book through the stark depiction of vice at the banquet. These men's words are "stitched together" with the treatise on marriage and the Diary because "*In Vino Veritas*" is associated, in some way, with what follows (SLW, 6). The celebrants' explicit attempts to shield themselves from the reality of the other, avoiding the "frequented" while musing on intimacy, introduces blatantly the fear and avoidance of otherness more implicit in William's marriage and the Diary. In this way, Kierkegaard introduces an issue that is central to the text: the avoidance of actual interaction.

As Johannes asserts, there is "nothing more nauseating" than to have one's fantasies broken by "immediate" and "impertinent" actuality (SLW, 23), and the whole banquet is set up to allow each man to reach climax without interaction. Every "worthy member brings with him" an "unmentionable craving," and Constantin's intent is to "awaken and incite" that craving with no threat of surprise (SLW, 25). Smoking his own cigar, Victor notes that "there should never be any women at a banquet," and William Afham (our resolutely solitary narrator) cheers (SLW, 24). The absence of contingency is crucial, for who "has not sensed the anxiety that something might suddenly happen, the most trifling thing" that would "upset everything" (SLW, 27). Keeping their "wrist[s] flexible" so as best each to serve "the lamp in his hand," they begin their masturbatory musings on "the relation between man and woman" (SLW, 27, 31). Each with his "divining rod" may enjoy the evening, for "all one needs to do is wish" (SLW, 27, 28). The entire setting is constructed to provide for male pleasure by ruling out interaction, interruption, and consequence. The content of each man's speech follows according to this form, precluding a time "when men and women banqueted together" and portraying with extremity the evasion of genuine intimacy (SLW, 30).

There is one among them who fails to enjoy himself, at least in the way intended. Our narrator recalls that the first speaker in this lineup, the Young Man, had a "loving sympathetic demeanor" that "involved no one" (SLW, 21). This description points to a problem in the Young Man's way: his manner of loving the other, while seemingly innocuous, involves no one. There is no other to whom he gives his love. Unlike those who follow him, the Young Man does not seek to construe "woman" in order to deny her reality. Rather, the love to which he attests is "pure," self-enclosed in his "thought," and independent of actuality (SLW, 46). His reasons for remaining alone reflect his refusal to infer the other as merely of interest for his fulfillment. The other with whom an individual interacts is, as a human being, "a complete entity" herself, and thus intimate interaction cannot be merely a game of finding a complementary piece (SLW, 43). The Young Man explains that actively to take note of such an other involves risk; apprehending "the impression" of an other requires a "surrender" of "control" (SLW, 32). Before such a venture, he explains, one should be aware of the multiple "fox traps" of erotic love (SLW, 38).

Through the Young Man's voice, Kierkegaard introduces an important facet of the Diarist's apt apprehension regarding his engagement with another. The stakes facing the lover and the beloved are perilously high. While others may bumble through this very "narrow path" as if it were instead a "broad way," the Young Man refuses to ignore the "spiritual trials" inherent to the endeavor (SLW, 46). He thus "does not dare to walk, to put his foot on the ground" or, as he also suggestively puts it, to smoke his pipe (SLW, 38, 33). Rather than walk confidently, wielding his "divining rod" or smoking his pipe, the Young Man resolves to remain above the route altogether. This, our first speaker of wine and truth commends a stance subtly off from Kierkegaard's requirement that the individual take serious note of love's danger. If he is to love, the Young Man explains, he must know the task well (SLW, 35). By acknowledging the traps and trials involved, the Young Man reveals his acuity, but his solitary resolution in *Stages* is no more loving than it is at the close of *Repetition*.[5] While Kierkegaard also seeks earnestly, throughout *Works of Love*, to point out the dangers inherent to engagement, he insists that one must put his foot to the ground and commence walking the per-ilously narrow way of loving well on earth. We will return later to this precarious, pedestrian love.

While the Young Man keeps himself afloat in the clouds rather than harm himself or others, the speakers who follow him assert that reality, in the form of "woman," may be tricked, consumed, subsumed, and negated. The Young Man flees the consequence of love by remaining alone. His fellow banqueters deny the other's consequence by sys-tematically excluding her. Insisting again that "between two such different entities no real interaction can take place," Constantin steers the men back to the trajectory set when he excluded women from the occasion (SLW, 48). Constantin proclaims that women exist to the extent that men perceive them, and the speakers proceed to work off this assumption (SLW, 48). He construes "woman" as a man's "most priceless amusement" – an opportunity for men's "jest" – because she is in her youth "a demure miss . . . constructed in one's imagination" and, later, a "broken-in horse" who still may be "teased" (SLW, 52, 53). Joking to his "fellow conspirators," the Fashion Designer scathingly suggests that "woman does have spirit" and is quite "reflective," for, he continues, is she not able infinitely to transform all that is sacred into that which is "suitable for adornment" (SLW, 67)? As the "high priest" of this sustained joke at women's expense, the Fashion Designer vows that, eventually, "she is going to wear a ring in her nose" (SLW, 71). The Designer's task in life is to materialize Constantin's and Johannes's imaginary construct: woman exists for men to view, enjoy, and "prostitute" (SLW, 71).

For his part, Johannes the Seducer commends another use of "woman," who is "a whim from a man's brain, a daydream" to be enjoyed craftily in order to avoid repercussions (SLW, 73, 75). It is im-perative, he explains, that a man not become entangled with an actual woman; she must be handled carefully so as to "evaporate and dissolve into that indefinable something" that is her essential form, "like a tem-porary character whose time is up" (SLW, 80). Ultimately, both he and

Johannes sum up the discussion by noting that, really, in order to be of any use to her lover, a woman must, in effect, be dead (SLW, 61, 80). She must be construed in such a way that she does not, actually, exist. The other must be perceived only as an extension of the perceiver.

Thus, over their wine and mutton, these men reveal the many means by which we may avoid and even slay the reality that is the other. By envisioning the other in this manner, as nothing of real ethical conse-quence, and by reconstructing meticulously every potential interaction as "only forgery," an individual may be, as Victor puts it, "better safe-guarded than if he entered the monastery" (SLW, 65). The monastery is, therefore, not necessary. In their construction of intimacy, there is no need for the Young Man's abstinence; we may imagine ourselves alone even during an embrace. By willing the theoretical exclusion of the other from reality, the banqueters may take with them, as a memento of the occasion, their host's carefully constructed gift of isolation. Each one is enabled to continue imagining himself alone, holding his "lamp," able to grant himself every possible "wish" *sans* interruption. Each man may remain effectively secluded and undisclosed, even while entering another.

Once construed as a cipher, the other is open to infinite interpretation; she is the explicit topic of conversation and celebration, but for a partic-ular purpose. In "*In Vino Veritas*," woman is the focus, but only in order that she might be rendered completely available. As Victor Eremita ex-plains, by becoming "an undefinable quantity" made "blissful in fantasy," woman is simultaneously a "'hurrah' and nothing." This, he determines, is a fate worse than being a slave and therefore something (SLW, 59, 56). We may elude the returned gaze of a real other either by denigration or by elevation; either way, we resist real intimacy. Keeping Eremita's interpretation in mind, we now turn to William's prolonged "hurrah."

OBJECTIONS TO THE MARRIED MAN'S ANSWER

Thus woman has a possibility that no man has, an enormous possibility . . . and the most terrible of all is the witchcraft of the illusion in which she feels so happy. (Victor Eremita, SLW, 62)

. . . jesting aside, marriage in many ways really is a venture in natural magic. (The Married Man, SLW, 90)

Stitched alongside "*In Vino Veritas*" is "Some Reflections on Marriage in Answer to Objections." William Afham, our narrator, relates that these "nocturnal revelers" come upon William the Married and his wife while the two are hidden away in an enclosed arbor, "much too secure to think of themselves as objects of observation by anyone but the morning sun" (SLW, 82). This, Kierkegaard's narrative segue between the two sections, provides an interpretive link from "*In Vino Veritas*" to William's "Reflections." Although the banqueters, in word and deed, exclude the other from the table while William shares tea with his wife, William's treatise also betrays an attempt to exclude the other's real, disturbing, presence.[6] As Kierkegaard has us revisit this couple, he intensifies themes from *Either/Or*, Part II. Not taking sufficient account of God's command, and of the self-critical humility that is to result from an encounter with God, William's defense of intimacy is, again, built on overly buoyant suppositions. His "venture in natural magic" at times touches tangentially the love Kierkegaard describes in *Works of Love*, but it is William's wizardry, not his acknowledgment of God's presence, that keeps his domestic situation happily "humming" (SLW, 159). Inappropriate solitude remains at issue, as we move from the banquet to the marriage arbor. As William explains, "a married man who writes about marriage writes least of all to be criticized," and the trees which shelter his marriage from observation metaphorically imply precisely that problem (SLW, 94).

Kierkegaard indicates again, through this essay as through William's contribution to *Either/Or*, the small but significant missteps that occur, to the detriment of self and other, when one loves without God as the intrusive third party to one's marriage. Only when God enters that sheltered *tête à tête* with the command that William acknowledge his wife first and continually as an other may William perceive the extent to which he himself is fallen and unable to get up, even strengthened on the milk of her kindness. William's parasitic understanding of "womanhood" denies his wife's existence as distinguishable from her role as his nurse. And his subsequent advice to "Cheer up," be "courageous" and accept the "assured blessedness" of marriage is reckless, considering the gravity of his and our condition (SLW, 111, 112, 161). Given that we who come to the arbor are stumbling because we have inherited original sin, the true "sickness unto death," rather than a tendency toward foot callouses, we need divine help, not natural magic (SLW, 129–30).[7] We will return to the religious import of this (obscure) reference below.

But before finding fault with Judge William, we should note the extent to which his problematic call to love resembles Kierkegaard's own in *Works of Love*. William speaks almost with Kierkegaard's own voice when he insists that, in true love, "resolution is present from the beginning"

(SLW, 103). If the lover instead allows his resolve to "tag along behind" while he tests out "probability" and seeks to determine "outcome," the lover is "lost" (SLW, 103, 105, 110). This "mirage of perdition" that "frequently prowls around when the making of a resolution is at stake" leads a person to chase after chance rather than love (SLW, 110). As God "always does business *en gros*," love is insecure unless sealed from the onset against change (SLW, 110). A lover must thus avoid assiduously the tendency to "inspect whether the beloved meets the abstract conception of an ideal" (SLW, 158). Any "reflection of this sort" is "an offense" to the resolution that secures one's love (SLW, 158). William thus concludes that a lover must "always [be] in love," or else he will never at any point truly love; love must be "a given," must be "assumed" in order to be lived (SLW, 122–23). Even a husband's periodic, "adoring admiration" of his beloved betrays a kind of inappropriate "separation" from his love whereby he stands back and appraises (SLW, 158). There is "a criticism dormant in this admiration," and it is thus "an affront," a "kind of unfaithfulness to the beloved" (SLW, 158). Much here could be transposed onto Kierkegaard's own insistence in *Works of Love* that we must "abide in love," "avoid comparison," and refuse to appraise the other.[8]

Even though William here addresses the problems of mistrustful appraisal and comparison, the love William defends is significantly off-kilter from Kierkegaard's. There are traces in the treatise of the resolute, non-comparative love to which Kierkegaard calls us in *Works of Love*, but undergirding William's system is a self-serving ideal of womanhood. This ideal, to which he holds his wife, collapses the distance between his needs and her existence (SLW, 91, 133–34). William immediately, unfortunately, amends his prohibition on a husband's appraisal of his beloved: "*on the other hand* there is a feminine lovableness" – "essentially that of the wife and mother" – which "dares to be admired," for it is "the lovable substance of her nature" (SLW, 158–59, emphasis mine). Through the "incorruptible humming of quiet joy" that is marriage, a woman is "transfigured" to reflect the true "beauty of [her] soul," and a man may rightly appreciate her for this maternal, solicitous beauty (SLW, 159, 160). With it, woman "has the joy of continually equipping" and "strengthening" her husband (SLW, 144). Although a husband is not otherwise to stand back and evaluate the extent to which his wife meets the ideal that best fits his own desires and needs, he is allowed this particular type of appraisal. The problem of the beloved's otherness is bypassed because a wife becomes, in marriage, *essentially* and continually that which conforms to her husband's "abstract conception of an ideal" (SLW, 158). This is not appraisal, William implies; this is merely a husband's recognition of a married woman's natural aptitude.

William has advanced little beyond his advice in *Either/Or*, with his continued refusal to worry over the possibility that his trajectory of faith, marriage, maternal solicitude, and spousal joy will reach a significant hurdle. As he has construed the situation, a husband is to have resilient faith in the state of marriage (not, we note, faith in God). While the composition that is marriage may "contain a very difficult passage," William himself has only a "presentiment of the terror" that might prompt him to flee (SLW, 111, 92). This married man's explicit advice to the lover is to be of good "cheer" and to keep plowing ahead with his faith in domestic harmony (SLW, 111, 161, 163). There is no need for ponderous worry about this or that transgression. A man's earnest conviction is his justification, and thus at the altar, "the church will proclaim him to be a lawful husband" (SLW, 91). That we might find ourselves in, or will ourselves into, a situation that is unjustifiable, and out of which we cannot resolve ourselves, is a possibility beyond the scope of William's immediate concern.

An instructive refrain through the last pages of his treatise runs "that a young man in love is happy goes without saying" (SLW, 161, 164). If one is uncertain about his love, his justification, or his resolve, he should take "comfort" in knowing that "he is just like other human beings" (SLW, 164). And here William ever so briefly considers that a person might be "singular" in a way that does not "promptly come off in the washing of resolution." It might possibly be the case that someone is soiled beyond the scope of such laundering. This exception should not be his, or our, concern, however. William states "I shall not pursue this here." For, as he explains, "difficulties of that sort have no place in a general consideration" (SLW, 164). We who resemble other human beings need not worry. "Hip, hip hurrah!" – the "exception" to his rule of happy marriage "vanishes" (SLW, 164, 165). While there may in fact be the genuinely exceptional one, who "has attired himself in misunderstanding" and is thus in "a void from which mankind shrinks," William declares that "the terror is now far removed." He then departs to "have lawfully as [his] own" she whom he has been "authorized" to take (SLW, 183). For, as he suggestively explains, what a husband enjoys with his wife is "infinitely more precious" than anything he might enjoy alone with his "pen" (SLW, 184).

Explicitly, William advises a prospective husband first to take "resolution's bath of purification" and marry (SLW, 164). The subsequent step, he implies, is to bathe oneself in the "mother love" of one's wife (SLW, 134). In this implicit advice, William both underestimates the depth of our estrangement, which prevents our use of another as a salve, and ignores the import of God's command, which precludes such use. In order to note this significant fissure in his text, we must trace one obscure passage regarding foot callouses. By noting a posted advertisement hawking a cure for this condition, William indirectly reveals his ignorance regarding our fallen predicament. With humor he notes that, on the poster, the grateful father of a family cured by the treatment inadvertently exposes his daughter to ridicule:

[t]he members of the family [cured] were specified, and among them there was a daughter, who, since like an Antigone she belonged to this unfortunate family, was not exempted from this family evil either. (SLW, 128)

Thinking (still "humorously") on her plight, William considers the situation more generally: What if the lover or his betrothed suffers an intractable condition that is not obviously apparent and thus not immediately disclosed? For example, what if one has inherited foot corns? "Yes, it is difficult, it is difficult . . . no one can know for sure about them, whether someone has them or has had them or is going to have them" (SLW, 129). He continues wondering what this might mean for an afflicted woman and her blissfully unsuspecting lover, for a flawed husband and his unwitting wife.

Although he sees this poster three times, William barely glances past the meaning therein. After briefly thinking on the potential for one's inheriting a condition that would afflict a marriage, he quickly shakes off this way of thinking and gathers his confident wits about him. Similarly to the manner with which he ends his section on the "singular exception," William here insists to himself, "But enough of this" (SLW, 129). William transforms the serious into the trifling by musing comically on the advertisement, rendering our hidden inheritance of error virtually inconsequential. He then stops himself before detecting a crack in his system. William brushes quickly past a question that, for Kierkegaard, requires our full stop. This textual prompt is subtle, but crucial.

In part due to his trivialization of that which is hidden, William is able to cling securely to the immediate, human comfort he has in his wife. Connecting William's light-hearted treatment of the advertisement with his subsequent discussion of his wife's work on him, the reader may note the interlocking errors in William's advice. With his sanguine estimation of his own plight and her goodness, he shifts quickly to her redemptive work on him. Because he deems that neither he nor she may have an undetectable and significant fault, he is able to keep their magical domesticity operative. Evidence, whether of his wife's inherent goodness or of his own confident resolve, is unnecessary: "For I know what I knew and what I am repeatedly convinced of – that there within my wife's breast beats a heart, quietly and humbly, but steadily and smoothly, I know that it beats for me and for my welfare" (SLW, 130). Yet she not only breathes for him, she also transmits vitality. He attests,

And I am a believer: just as the lover believes that the beloved is his life, so I spiritually believe that this tenderness – like mother's milk, which, as also stated in that little book, natural scientists maintain is lifesaving for someone who is sick unto death – I believe that this tenderness that unfailingly struggles for an ever more intimate expression . . . I believe that if I were ill, sick unto death . . . that it would summon me back to life . . . (SLW, 130)

That same feminine breast in which her heart beats dispenses a balm. Through her, he "absorbs peace and contentment" (SLW, 130). Indeed, her "tenderness" has "many times" saved him "from the death of despondency and evil torment of vexation of spirit." The "sickness unto death" to which William refers twice in this section can be cured through the rejuvenating powers of "woman" (SLW, 131). She is the one who "provides the solution for the worried person" and is "the best eulogy on existence by being *life's beautiful solution*" (SLW, 134, my emphasis). This, Kierkegaard's second textual prompt, is blunt.

It is this "mother's milk" of life, solicitude and security that distinguishes the young flirtatious girl from a woman like William's own wife, and that allows his domestic life to cohere (SLW, 134). Through marriage, a woman is able to become "life's beautiful solution," a lover from whose breast flows life-giving sustenance, not only for her children but also, importantly, for her husband. William's implicit advice on marriage here joins his explicit call for each potential husband to remain resolute. In order for the "natural magic" of marriage to work, a man must believe securely that marriage can "transform" his wife into one who can cure him of his "sickness unto death" (SLW, 134). By first dismissing as an "exception" a serious impediment to matrimonial harmony and then treating with levity the potential for undisclosed barriers to domestic bliss, William is finally able to posit "woman" as the tie binding together a man's resolution and his happiness.

STAGES ON LOVE'S WAY?

When compared to the slimy Seducer, the flamboyant Designer, or caustic Constantin, William seems to approximate Kierkegaard's description, in *Works of Love*, of the faithful lover. Does not Kierkegaard commend there a love that "believes all things," that resolutely hopes in the goodness of the other, that "presupposes" that love is continually present in the other? There are two crucial distinctions between Kierkegaard's and William's conceptions of love. First, Kierkegaard warns from the onset and throughout *Works of Love* that the faithful lover must assiduously avoid the temptation to see the other as an extension of himself, as an appendage created to serve his needs. The term "neighbor" is to act as a conceptual wedge between the lover and the beloved, reminding him that she is an indeed an other self, unto God (WL, 21). William's estimation of "woman" is not carnal (as is Johannes's) or sardonically comic (as is Constantin's or the Designer's) but it is based nonetheless on an understanding of his wife as "essentially" for another, namely him. He presupposes, believes, and hopes that her heart beats for his sake. "Woman" is still, in William's treatise, a "hurrah and nothing," to use Victor's perceptive phrase.[9] His treatise effectively eclipses her existence as an entity apart from their domestic life together, as fallen and redeemed before Another to whom she is ultimately accountable.

The second distinction between William's and Kierkegaard's advice on love involves the basis of William's ability to abide in his love for his wife. Through a happy coincidence of his own resolve and his wife's conformity, William is able to continue believing that she is "life's beautiful solution" (SLW, 134). But in *Works of Love*, Kierkegaard explains that one is only able to abide in love if one remains fixedly in a relation of debt before God (WL, 180). To put a critically Christian twist on William's assertion: we are to disturb, rather than reassure, ourselves with the fact that we are "just like other human beings"; i.e., we are irresolute sinners before a forgiving God (SLW, 164). This "certain transformation of attitude and mind" that Kierkegaard describes involves our recognition of the debt we each owe, infinitely, to God (WL, 177). We who are fallen and indebted are consequently forbidden to evaluate the other's worth, whether that evaluation leads us to dismiss her (as do the banqueters) or to idolize her (as does William). Love is no more in its element in William's defense of marriage than it is at the banquet. William's underestimation of his own predicament and his overestimation of his wife's purity provide a brittle foundation for marriage. According to *Works of Love*, his inability to understand his wife as a separate person (herself fallen and redeemed before God alone) and to acknowledge forthrightly his debt to God indicates the false assumptions undergirding his present affection. On the other side of the Diarist's pertinent fear of self and other we will return to a more sober, Christian, conception of a love that can endure full disclosure and our realization of grave error.

INTERLUDE

Each reflection up to this point in *Stages* differs from Kierkegaard's; the ways in which they differ reveal the hazards of thinking alone. While the crowds are maddening, solitude may also warp. As William Afham observes, "recollection's bookkeeping is a curious thing" (SLW, 11), and although authentic understanding requires that we each ponder in stillness, for each and every moment of reflection there is an occasion for self-delusion. This is why, for Kierkegaard, a treatise on love must continually ricochet the question of the other back to the potentially deluded questioner himself (WL, 14, 90, 96). The reflective reckoning of engagement must take place with the love command in view, lest we become preoccupied with our own hunger and transform love into a matter of the coherence between our taste and the object's fare. Each of our previous speakers (excepting the Young Man) makes use of the "stillness," "secrecy," and "hiddenness" of recollection to his own advantage. During their clandestine caucus on erotic love, Constantin and his guests swerve away from love itself to reflect on the factor preventing "real interaction," that is, "woman" (SLW, 48). By excluding the other from the conversation and focusing on the extent to which she satisfies each man's craving, these men construct a hermetically sealed space for their iniquitous deliberation; the other may not enter. For his own part, William the Married is wed but not truly engaged. The "life immersion" that is his domestic existence (SLW, 89) negates his wife as an other who exists apart from him, leaving him safely alone with his thoughts, needs, and wishes.[10] Up to this point, it is only the Young Man who seems to have sat earnestly with the disturbing thought that an individual is not alone when he is with an other. His apt fear compels him to be truly, unthreateningly alone. As we move to the reflections of the Young Man's close cousin, the Diarist, we consider whether an individual's solitary self-disclosure before God may transform reflection itself.[11]

THE DIARIST'S RETREAT

Might it be possible, might my whole attitude to life be askew, might I have run into something here in which secretiveness is forbidden . . . (SLW, 223)

After prying open the Diarist's buried box and finding the key inside, the narrator comments that "inclosing reserve is always turned inward in that way" (SLW, 189). The Diarist entrusts his tormented reflections on his engagement to paper alone; his reflections on himself, love, and his beloved remain locked inside his head and within this sunken container. Of all those who hide in this stitched-together collection of papers, the Diarist is the most adept. Yet it is also the case that his secretive avoidance of frank discourse reflects more his apt appraisal of his predicament than his desire to enjoy (Johannes), mock (Constantin), or use (William) his beloved without fear of reproach. The Diarist's self-enclosure and broken vow are the results of his terror before the great responsibility that is engagement. From the beginning, he understands himself to be "the one acting"; the success or failure of his engagement is a question posed to him alone. But unlike William (who deems himself an actor but also justified), the Diarist deeply suspects himself as "the guilty one" (SLW, 198).[12] The others avoid their accountability and thus this apprehension from the onset, by construing the other either as an infinitely malleable trifle (the banqueters) or as gloriously, "essentially," *for* the one to whom she is "lawfully" wedded (William).

The Diarist refuses both the seducer's and the husband's options, but neither will he disclose himself to this other who binds him and before whom he is responsible. Recognizing the numerous dangers both to her and to himself, the Diarist vows to "flee back into my interior being and leave nothing, not a trace, in the outer world" (SLW, 201). The Diarist's stages are along yet another wrong way, subtly distinguishable from the way of honest and fragile intimacy in *Works of Love*. The Diarist explains that he wishes to retreat to the "monastery" in order to "find peace" (SLW, 198). Kierkegaard will not let him escape God's vexatious call to love the other so easily. By shedding light on the Diarist's self-reflection, using God's command for disclosure, we may illumine the sliver of space between fear and faith. We may note the difference between the walk of an individual who, due to fear, is alone with his idea, and an individual who is alone, in faith, before God.

Within the first few entries of his long, painful account, the Diarist manifests several clues to his secretive existence. Even before he begins to flee, the Diarist is already quite gifted at deception (SLW, 195–96). He explains that he is able convincingly to present "a candid face and an openhearted nature," even while involved in an elaborate "sleepless and thousand-tongued reflection" (SLW, 196). We should note here that he names the generic one with whom he converses on such deceptive occasions "the opponent," who must be kept uncertain as to whether she "is coming or going" (SLW, 196). In this way, the Diarist explains, "one attains one's security" (SLW, 196). This apprehension and this pretense are at the heart of his initial feelings for her ("I have secretly and clandestinely been absorbed in this love"; SLW, 202) and continue throughout the affair. Dodging the other's potentially keen gaze, the Diarist flips through multiple possibilities while leaving the beloved ignorant of the turmoil within him. She must not be allowed to know his "suffering," his "suspicion," or the "craftiness of [his] understanding," and, to this end, the Diarist is able to mimic both reassuring confidence and disarming confusion (SLW, 196, 198, 199). Although he is, halfway through, unmasked in a fencing game, the young man is incapable, from the onset, of bare and vulnerable engagement (SLW, 300). By considering the multiple reasons for and ramifications of his frightened maneuvers, we may better perceive the fault line between love's apt caution and doubt's undue timidity.[13]

The Diarist explains from the beginning that "the reason [he is] so cautious, cautious to the very last moment" is the manifold possibility for error in his engagement (SLW, 202). Purposefully imagining "many a terror," he determines "not to do the slightest thing without calculation," lest he underestimate "the storms" ahead for him and his beloved (SLW, 202, 203). Along the way, his realization that he is "almost happier in [his] hiding place" seeps into the crevices of his presentiments and, ultimately, wins out (SLW, 206). In his engagement, the Diarist has "come so close to actuality," but he accurately perceives that – due to the work of time, her error, and his frailty – there is also an insurmountable "distance" intrinsic to such involvement (SLW, 205). He finds himself therefore "happier in the distance of possibility"; and, in the end, this is where he resides (SLW, 206).

It is important that we parse his calculations. For while his apprehensions overlap, we may differentiate and evaluate several of his central concerns. First, although he claims that his "soul is resolved" to "imagine everything lovable about her," one cause of the Diarist's caution is his sneaking suspicion that his beloved is less than he had first hoped (SLW, 206). Second, the Diarist suspects that he himself is damaged beyond marriageability. His own sternly willed resolve to "earn a liveli-hood of joy for her" may not, he speculates, be sufficient to sustain them both (SLW, 197). Finally, and related to the first two, he surmises a fun-damental "misrelation" between his and her conceptions of existence and, subsequently, of love itself (SLW, 244). Each of his misgivings is, to some extent, apt, but the resolution he chooses is wrought from the stuff of further calculation, deception, and fear. We will first read through his fears, then examine his elaborate plan to deceive his betrothed, and then consider a "third position" whereby he and she both may be "remade" as each alone before God (SLW, 220, 320).

In order to get an inkling as to why the Diarist begins to look askance at himself and his beloved we should note the absurd ideal to which he, at least initially, holds their love:

> when I belong to her, I shall be able to concentrate my whole soul on making her as happy as it is possible for me. I ask no more in the world than that my soul might still have one abode where joy is at home, one object upon which I can concentrate in order to make happy and to be made happy. (SLW, 206)

In order for his hope and joy to be realized, the Diarist must be single-minded and she must be perfectly receptive. He must "concentrate" his "whole soul," and she must be capable of returning his concentration with perceptible levels of euphoria. The Diarist's quite perceptive con-cern that each of them may not be up to this colossal task comes to bear on his vision of his betrothed. Seen through the extreme funnel created by the Diarist's ideal, the girl seems small indeed. The "demon of laughter" and the "craftiness of the understanding" increasingly com-bine in his scrutiny of her as an individual who cannot secure his hope for a safe and jubilant abode (SLW, 198, 199). This appraisal of her behavior and her motives is interspersed throughout the entries. She must indeed not be loving, given her behavior; she seems to wish "to wound some-one who is tortured to death" (SLW, 212). He allows himself to consider that "she fancies herself to have become commonsensical," that she may be "thinking" and herself "reflecting" on their relationship, that she may in fact be "proud," and then orders himself to "Stop!" for he has "no factual information that justifies" his suspicions (SLW, 214, 216, 235).

But the suspicions take hold. As he explains, what he most wants is for her to "express herself a little more so that [he] can see what is taking place within her" (SLW, 235). (We will return to the hypocrisy of this wish.) Even though he has worked arduously to conceal his tendency to judge, he guesses that she (trenchantly) "regards [him] as a very sharp critic" and that she in turn "stifles" her thoughts (SLW, 235). Regardless of what she does or does not reveal, mid-way through the engagement he concludes his "report": the one to whom he is engaged is "only an ordinary dollar," "a little miss," who "lacks the integration that beautifies," who has "a secret pride" and whose "fidelity is of a dubious kind" (SLW, 237, 268, 308, 356). He progressively determines that "externally she cannot now be [his]" and, finally, that, by "playing false in the religious," *she* is to "blame" for the whole mess (SLW, 239, 393). In view of this "actuality" he has himself created, he resolves instead to create again the ideal that first drew him to her. Trying on a guise of indifference, he vows to "steal her [untainted] image" as he is free to "see it in [his] imagination," gazing at his hope of her rather than what he has discovered (SLW, 334).

But we must note that the Diarist also places himself under the microscope. Whereas the Young Man argues vehemently (here and in *Repetition*) for his purity, and the banqueters and William the Married deflect self-criticism by speaking (in various ways) of "woman," the Diarist faces head-on the task of self-examination. He retreats with his pen and his paper but does not thereby avoid self-inspection. The early passage wherein he confesses, "I fear no one as I fear myself," sets the tone for much of what follows (SLW, 207). He continues, "Oh, that I do not make a false step," and pledges to detect in himself any sign of "deceit" (SLW, 207, 208). His tangle of apprehensions includes three fears: that she will be "far happier without [him]," that he will in particular use his art of deception "to prevail upon her," and that his tendency toward "calculation" will spoil the whole affair (SLW, 206, 207, 208). Throughout, he is anxious not to "make a false step!" and thereby injure her and indict himself (SLW, 208).

The Diarist's assessment of the many potentially false steps leads him to walk in a strange way indeed, as he attempts simultaneously to avoid fraudulent deception *and* reckless candor, cruel detection *and* irresponsible ignorance, undue distance *and* inappropriate familiarity. That, in spite of all his efforts, the engagement spins recklessly out of his control propels him repeatedly to his room where he may reflect on the affair in the form of the diary itself. He finds himself "sleepless" in the maddening confusion of his motives, "because I cannot know for sure whether I love or do not love" (SLW, 232). "Perhaps," he thinks, "I have not loved her at all; perhaps on the whole I am too reflective to be able to love?" (SLW, 231). He attempts to deliberate back upon himself to distinguish "corruption" and "hypocrisy" from "chivalry," wondering whether he may be "even to the point of nausea ensnared in self-deception" (SLW, 317). When his beloved perceives his impending retreat and more passionately "surrenders" herself to him, the matter becomes ever more perilous. The "narrow pass" of "responsibility" becomes more than he can bear, and he determines over time that he must use his wits and his powers of subterfuge to set her free and, not incidentally, free himself of her (SLW, 316). It is in the midst of this engagement that the Diarist finds himself most vulnerable to his own scrutiny, and he vows, with increasing resolve, to get himself back to the monastery.

OF SECRETS AND SALVES

In his section "A Leper's Self-Contemplation," the Diarist reveals two significant clues for understanding the despair ensuing from his estimation of himself and of her (SLW, 233). First, whereas William the Married flippantly jests about an undetectable proclivity for foot sores, the Diarist imagines himself as Simon the leper, who is literally covered with infectious sores and therefore should rightly "fill the desert with [his] shrieking and keep company [only] with wild animals" (SLW, 233). In this section of the text, we note that the Diarist accurately perceives the depth of his disorder and quickly recognizes that he is beyond his beloved's curative powers. The entry following their first kiss finds the Diarist initially seeking in her a salve for what plagues him:

A girl with a joyful temperament, happy in her youth! And she is mine. What are all dark thoughts and fancies but a cobweb, and what is depression but a fog that flies before this actuality, a sickness that is healed and is being healed by the sight of this health that is mine since it is hers . . . she can say, as an apostle said to the paralytic, "Silver and gold I do not have, but what I have I give you; stand up and be well!" (SLW, 211)

His beloved must be pure joy, happiness, and well-being in order through the union to impart health to this leper. The Diarist's hope in this frail, human other is taut to the point of breaking precisely because he is so acutely aware of his predicament. Unlike William's faith in "natural" marital "magic," the Diarist's anticipation of conferred health is ephemeral. He finds that his "dark thoughts" return with a vengeance and that she is not, in fact, an apostolic redemptress. She cannot enact the proclamation "Stand up and be well!" Even in love, the Diarist remains paralyzed. Even in love, he remains a leper.

But, unlike Simon the leper, the Diarist is not yet alone in the desert; his beloved is still with him. This story of infectious disease is also about the individual's courageous disclosure, before an other, of that communicable disease. The Diarist, taking on Simon's voice, condemns Manasse, another leper who uses a salve to render his infection invisible, running then to the city and secretly endangering everyone with whom he interacts. Simon instead remains in the desert, holding fast to his hope eventually to sup with someone who knows his disease and yet does not fear him (SLW, 233). Simon's resolve in this story not only stands in contrast to William's willed ignorance of his plight but also implicitly indicts the Diarist's own behavior. In the story, Simon the leper refuses to deceive. The Diarist, unlike Simon, opts for deception. He cannot believe her capable of supping with one who is unclean. Appropriately recognizing that she cannot heal him, the Diarist continues to hide from her the gravity of his affliction. Not finding in her a salve that would cure him and currently unable to live alone, the Diarist does in fact accept a path similar to Manasse's, putting on his mask to hide his affliction from a beloved he cannot trust. Only when we return below to *Works of Love* may we find the other who can enable the sinfully paralyzed to walk. And we find warrant for Simon's hope that a leper may uncover his face before his friends.

The tangled, deceptive web the Diarist instead weaves around himself and his beloved ensnares them both. The entire relationship becomes ever more snarled in a mess, as the Diarist attempts to construct a way to work her free from him. In his entries, the Diarist conveys his growing resolve to preclude her receiving a "reliable conception of [him] and of [their] relationship." She is under no circumstance to receive an "authentic interpretation" of his hopes, plans or fears (SLW, 246). Indeed, those very plans and fears become of a piece with his deception. Although he complains that it is a "torment to have to observe a phenomenon when the phenomenon itself changes in relation to the observer," the Diarist overlooks this pivotal moment for reflecting on the effect of his dishonesty on his engagement (SLW, 234). His machinations infect his observation and their interaction. He wonders at her "circumspect reticence" and wishes that he might know "what her state is in a deeper sense," but his otherwise discerning mind is unable to make the important connection between his own deceit and her determined impenetrability (SLW, 250). As quoted before, the Diarist's most fervent wish is that she would "express herself a little more so that [he] can see what is taking place within her," that she would "sit still" while he examines her relation to him, but he himself sets up the affair to be an elaborate artifice, precluding the revelation of truth (SLW, 235). Her "stifle[d] freedom of expression," as he words it, is hardly accidental (SLW, 335).

Whether the beloved also actively chooses the pretense fundamental to their interaction the reader cannot know, but the Diarist takes up that question as an undercover detective accepts a perplexing case. Claiming that he is using "ingenuity in the service of righteousness" rather than "in the service of deceit," the Diarist carefully orders his feet not to "leave a betraying clue" and his hand not to betray what is "hidden" in his "heart" (SLW, 267, 265). She must not know that he is monitoring her, nor is she to know the "sympathy," "fear," and "suspicion" that motivate his surveillance (SLW, 273, 372, 198). There is, in all this, scarcely any chance for real intimacy. We barely catch sight of a missed opportunity in the story when the Diarist is literally "unmasked" and wounded while fencing (SLW, 300). Although he dismisses his beloved's poignant response as sheer sentimentality, the reader may guess that the irony of the moment is not lost on her. Seeing some recognition in her face, he concludes, "the whole thing does not count if the mask falls off" and quickly returns to the game. He cloaks himself "at [her] entryway" in order to "renounce every expression," daring not to "alter [his] features" and offering instead "a cold and callous front" (SLW, 300, 336, 349, 350). He regulates every minute facet of his behavior to ensure that "no truth glimmers through the deception" (SLW, 332).

This young lover, in a myriad of ways and for various apt reasons, does not trust himself, his beloved, or their love. Before proceeding, however, we should note that the Diarist has refused at least three other wrong paths on the way. First, while he wistfully glances momentarily at a marital ideal (similar to William's) which neither of them can approximate, he refuses to remain poetically, romantically duped. His scrutiny of himself and of her, although alternatively masochistic and cruel, is preferable to a flimsy overestimation of their ability to love one another. A second path that the Diarist refuses is that of the seducer or spoiled husband. Though the Diarist cannot trust his beloved, she is for him a separate entity to whom he is responsible. He explicitly refuses, from the onset, to "whirl her off like an abracadabra" or use his deception in order to create "a magic word" or "a rune" that would transform her into an extension of himself (SLW, 198, 202). Neither will he allow her to fashion herself into a devoted, submissive wife. The type of marriage wherein she thinks herself "indebted" to him – where she is "devoted" to the point of prostrating herself (figuratively and literally) before him – is not an option (SLW, 226, 312). He would rather cause her suicide by breaking their engagement than allow her to think him her benefactor (SLW, 370). The only one under whom a person should surrender herself is, he insists, God (SLW, 235). Like the Young Man at the banquet, the Diarist holds as a prior assumption the fact that in the calculation of responsible intimacy, she counts in and of herself; interaction is not the meeting of one and a half (SLW, 43).[14] Finally, the third, erroneous, option that the Diarist will not choose is a marriage built on deceit. He refuses to pretend that she is not a stranger to him or that there is not a deep "misunderstanding" between them. And he will not countenance a marriage plagued by her confusion and his mistrust (SLW, 351, 355). It would be a "profanation" of marriage for him to "vow" to love her while not simultaneously bringing her into his confidence, "for it is a deception that marriage does not tolerate" (SLW, 355, 375). It is here that he finds himself: unwilling to dismiss her, loath to dominate her, unable to understand her, incapable of making himself comprehensible, and, quite sadly, "stranded" (SLW, 375).

THE PRAYER OF A DIARIST

In other words, the Pharisee thinks he is speaking with God, whereas from what he says it is clear and distinct enough that he is speaking with himself or with another Pharisee. (SLW, 238)

At one point the Diarist wishes but that his "pen were a living thing" (SLW, 307). The form of his (lack of) communication, between himself and his inanimate paper and pen, fits the content of his account. His text is not a discourse, his engagement is not, ultimately an interaction, and his prayer is not, finally, a prayer. It is only through accident, and against his fervent wish, that the Diarist reveals his thoughts to the reader at all. The Diarist escapes from revealing himself to his beloved, and his concluding resolution with his "idea" of God is not a revelatory encounter, either. Although the Diarist thinks he is speaking with God, it is clear enough that his "religious" resolution is consistent with what has come before. Standing alone in the midst of the whirl of guilt and suspicion, he seeks alternative ways to answer his fundamental question, guilty or not, and finds in the "idea" an apt escape clause.

But along his mistaken route, the Diarist catches sight of an alternative manner of being whereby he may, with courage, reveal his reflections, speak honestly to his beloved, and receive and accept forgiveness. He at one point surmises that he has indeed "run into something" in which "secretiveness is forbidden." And he momentarily realizes that he must "break [himself] of the habit of walking in this way" if his "journey" is to be "pleasing to heaven" (SLW, 223). He who has "with most extreme effort" become "a master in [the] art" of deception must take to heart that his "method is completely wrong" (SLW, 223). While true prayer and self-revelation do not, by any estimation, make one a "yodeling saint" who proclaims that life is "wonderful," they thwart the solitary bookkeeping that precludes engagement (SLW, 259).

From early on in his engagement, the Diarist surmises that there are "religious crises" at stake (SLW, 216). As his relationship to his beloved renders his "life-view ambiguous," he casts about for some reliable mooring, and his search does indeed hold implications for the state of his soul (SLW, 216). Unable to "advance," not knowing with certainty of what he should repent and how best he may "recant," the Diarist finds himself "*in suspenso*" (SLW, 261). He hopes that the matter will soon be "resolved," and he will thus be "free again" (SLW, 261). He tries to secure himself through a careful assessment and arrangement of his intentions toward her. The fact that he gives her only snippets of the truth and reveals nothing of himself is justifiable, he determines, *only* if his fabrications are for her own good. "Inclosing reserve, silence," is a legitimate "teleological suspension of the duty to speak the truth" *if* the liar has the hearer's care in view (SLW, 230). Because the Diarist believes that his deception is only licit if he does indeed practice it out of love for her (SLW, 230), he sets the details of his life in order logistically to make room for her: "Everything I buy, I buy double. My table is set for two; coffee is served for two . . . for me it is a matter of integrity, which I take with the greatest earnestness" (SLW, 295). By taking note of her existence and his responsibility toward her, he hopes to make his "balance sheet balance down to the last penny" (SLW, 295). Through this careful accounting, he seeks to reassure himself that, in his clandestine scheming, he has "not [his own] welfare in mind but hers," as his Lutheran rule book requires (SLW, 230).

The narrative interlude about a tortured man from Christianhavn, who may have sired children but cannot know for sure, sets the tone for the Diarist's struggle to rectify his own yearly ledger with his beloved (SLW, 276). Even while giving vast amounts to the children of Christianhavn, the potential father finds his efforts tragically comical, given "his own enormous account" (SLW, 284). Just so, the Diarist discovers the "solidarity between guilt and innocence" in his own life and cannot make his column of figures tally up to an indisputable sum of integrity or culpability (SLW, 301). When an individual goes about detecting "life's pathological elements absolutely, clearly, legibly," he begins to perceive the distorting prevalence of "sin" rather than disjunctive "bungles," and it is difficult for him continually to maintain that existence is a clear, decipherable "system" (SLW, 291, 292). The Diarist discovers over time that, if he is going to find shelter from the whirl of confusion around him, he cannot do so by counting, cutting, computing, and pasting his (or her) portion of virtue or vice. While he continues intermittently to "demand" that life will "make clear whether [he] was trapped in self-delusion or [he] loved faithfully," he ultimately chooses a route apart (SLW, 384).

Several months into the engagement, the Diarist confesses: "What I have shaped myself to be with all my passion appears to me to be an error," and then continues, "I cannot be remade now" (SLW, 320). If his intentions toward her are not pure sufficiently to warrant indisputably his passionately deceptive shape, he must find another route out of the mess. If there is hope for him, by his estimation, there must be a defensible "third position" in the "theological proceeding" against him (SLW, 220). The Diarist relies increasingly on his detective "report" of his beloved: "with regard to the religious, " she is "only an ordinary dollar" (SLW, 237). Returning again and again to the difference between her "buoyancy," and "childlike happiness," and his own depth, the Diarist determines that he must "choose the religious" (SLW, 222). Judging her own reflection to be "only single," whereas he adequately grasps their situation, he is able to justify his working out matters above her, so to speak, hidden behind "the category" or "idea" to which she cannot aspire (SLW, 303, 304). Because he "has the category and the idea" on his side," he must make himself impervious to her pleading (SLW, 356). The third position he fashions for himself is that of the justified religious martyr, forced to deceive and desert his beloved for the sake of his own religious conscience. With this solution, what is good or ill for her does not, ultimately, matter. Carrying with him a "divine counterorder," the Diarist must "retreat," regardless of the cost to him or to her, and take upon himself the task of going "through repentance" toward "freedom" (SLW, 261). As he eventually concludes, he may not justify his broken "ethical commitment" to her by means of "any calculation of probability." Rather, he must assume "the ultimate possibility of responsibility" (SLW, 394).

In repentance, the Diarist hopes to make his "way back over the chiasmic abyss that separates good and evil in time," to transform himself into "nothing, nothing at all" (SLW, 353). Whereas the Young Man at the banquet (and in *Repetition*) makes his escape from actuality to eternity through innocence, the Diarist finds freedom through a hybrid of resolute repentance and religious self-justification. He is justified in leaving her; after all, "she does not have infinite passion but only to a certain degree" (SLW, 349). His deception is warranted, given that "there is a language difference between" (SLW, 312). But, nevertheless, he finds himself whirled backward into a pit of "misunderstanding," and the only way out is repentance (SLW, 351). This movement is the final stage in the Diarist's irreligious way, and it bears the marks of his previous pattern of evasion. He confesses, immediately prior to the "religious structur[ing]" of his existence: "When the right thing becomes doubtful to me, I have usually said my name aloud to myself, with the addition: One may die, one may become unhappy, but one can still preserve meaning in one's life and faithfulness to the idea" (SLW, 346). The Diarist explains that he has "lost the very substance of [his] existence," the "secure place of resort behind [his] deceptive appearance," and the "religious" method he employs is akin to his repeating his name "aloud" to himself, with the addition of an "understanding" that vindicates his "honor" (SLW, 351, 353). "Only religiously" is he able to "become intelligible to [himself] before God," he surmises, but the religious communication he finds is akin to an inverse Tower of Babel (SLW, 351).

He burrows deeper and deeper into himself in order to find that which is not "acquired" from another but rather his own. Unable "to structure [his] life ethically in [his] innermost being," the Diarist is "forced back further into" himself and there, utterly apart from actuality, he finds "religious" truth (SLW, 351). He may rest here assured that his new self-understanding is not "chattering blabbing," for, he asks, "to whom should I speak?" (SLW, 351). Following the lead of his own, hidden, untranslatable "reminders," he is able to reach an "eternal certitude of the infinite" (SLW, 378). While it is true that burrowed deep into himself and his Diary he is no longer able to deceive another or to be deceived by another, the Diarist is still capable of self-deception. In his attempt to become "nothing at all," turned inward to such a degree that his existence leaves no footprints, he is safe but deluded.

FROM DIARY TO DISPATCH

When does eternity begin? What language is spoken there? Or is there perhaps no speaking at all? Could there not be a little intervening time? Is it always high noon in eternity? *Could there not be a dawn in which we found understanding in intimacy?* (SLW, 390, my emphasis)

Given that the Diarist has not found God's confidentiality to be the determining encounter for all subsequent encounters, the Diarist continues to judge his beloved, deceive the world, and proceed with his withdrawal. We may surmise that the Diarist's conversion is amiss from what follows it. The "understanding" he has with God is but his deeper entrenchment into a self-enclosed monologue, and it thus issues forth in yet more secrecy with his beloved (SLW, 351). At this crucial juncture wherein he is forced to cease his efforts at ethical calculation, the Diarist comes ever so close to the possibility of an "understanding in intimacy." Moving from the "starting point of knowledge" that is "wonder," he tangentially brushes the prospect of real prayer (SLW, 348). Where "wonder shipwrecks one's understanding," he explains, one may begin to speak to God as "the only one who does not become weary of listening to a human being" (SLW, 348). It is this shift that the Diarist cannot make. He cannot take even God into his confidence. His "method" for reaching the "holy city" is still "completely wrong" even though he is still walking "with most extreme effort" (SLW, 23). Although he deems his life to be "religiously structured," he does not encounter God as an other to whom he must reveal himself, as he is, in "actuality" (SLW, 351).

Having not truly found God in his inward turn, having not risked the truth before God as his confidant, the Diarist cannot risk the truth before his beloved, either. This follows the trajectory of his enclosing apprehensions. In entries scattered throughout the Diary, the Diarist considers then despairs of real disclosure to another. Not able to trust even the one he supposedly loves, he despairs of finding any other in whom truly to "confide" (SLW, 219). Given that every possible "third party" with whom he could consult regarding his predicament would judge his acts as "villainy," the Diarist cannot possibly speak (SLW, 224). He later "assure[s]" himself "how absurd it would be if [he] sought out any confidant" (SLW, 347). Finally, "realiz[ing] clearly that [his] depression makes it impossible for [him] to have a confidant," he determines that he cannot possibly marry his beloved, for marriage requires the truth (SLW, 374). In the midst of this last resignation, the Diarist envisages that, if he "did have a confidant," that intimate would advise him to "constrain himself and thereby show that he is a man" (SLW, 375). It is imperative, he imagines the third party insisting, that he conceal his "depressing idea" before his beloved (SLW, 375). His imagined confidant requires secrecy, not disclosure.

There is an alternative way not chosen but woven delicately through the Diarist's text. Soon after reflecting on the occasion when his fencing mask fell off, the Diarist comes face to face with his betrothed at church. There, surrounded by reminders of God's presence, he is "so easily tempted to regard the matter eternally" and almost finds himself therefore capable of "speak[ing] the truth." But he wishes anxiously, "not in time . . . not yet" (SLW, 301). In worship, having recently recalled the experience of being laid bare in a fencing match, he glimpses an alternative implication of "the eternal" whereby one is able vulnerably to unveil oneself. But he continues rather to say to himself, "the truth . . . [but] not yet" (SLW, 301). Whether "arrang[ing] occasion[s] and pos[ing] situational question[s]," "dropp[ing] a few hints in a joking or chatty tone," or sending a missive indirectly through mutual friends, the Diarist continues guardedly to evade the possibility of truth, giving her instead "little dose[s] of untruth" (SLW, 267, 272, 338). Not trusting her ability to comprehend and progressively determining that "her fidelity is of a dubious kind," he disguises himself and precludes honesty (SLW, 356).

If the Diarist had connected the moment of being unmasked and the moment of insight at the church with a previous moment, wherein he contemplates forgiveness, he might have started on the (narrow and precipitous) path toward intimacy: "what if the word 'forgiveness' between us were to be earnest, the earnestness of judgement, and not a ball we both hit in the game of erotic love while fidelity jubilated over its victory" (SLW, 228). Deeming his beloved to be "out of step" and thus incapable of grasping "that it is being faithful to reject illusory relief," the Diarist does not himself embark on the hard work of self-revelation, confession, and forgiveness (SLW, 228). Fearing that she will not understand him in his "entire makeup," he decides that forgiveness between them would be hollow, "dubious," and merely "illusory relief" (SLW, 383, 228).

If the Diarist's repentance before God had been a dispatch rather than a journal entry, he might have caught sight of that "little intervening time" in eternity that makes a narrow path for intimacy: God's forgiveness (SLW, 390). Turning inward to the point of oblivion, the Diarist does not repent before an other; he does not repent before one who may offer remission. Within both "Solomon's Dream" and the "Leper's Self-Contemplation" are crucial clues to the Diarist's inability to accept this route of forgiveness. In the former section, Solomon, who "was able to separate truth from deception," finds himself struck dumb by the possibility that "to be singled out by God one has to be an ungodly person" (SLW, 251). But Solomon's dream stops with the image of his father, David, crying out in "despair from the penitent's soul" (SLW, 251). For Solomon, and for the Diarist, there is neither debt paid nor sinner redeemed. Rather, there is one "rejected by God" (SLW, 251). Or, as is more the case for the Diarist, there is one who preemptively avoids coming before God in fear of the encounter and its consequence. As we have above noted regarding the Diarist's dialogue as a leper, he himself is unable to trust his beloved to sit and sup with him regardless of his dangerous, infectious malady. Here, as in Solomon's dream, the Diarist's vision of the soul before God is aslant. Praying that God would "hear him if his heart is still not infected," the Diarist/Leper imagines himself as "blessed" precisely in his willingness to suffer his disease righteously, with an uninfected heart (SLW, 234, 233). In both stories and in the Diarist's eventual "religious" repentance, there is not the possibility of one's beseeching God *while* infected, duplicitous, and malformed. There is no hope for the sinner. It is not surprising that the Diarist, in turn, cannot free himself to speak the truth of his culpable affliction before his own fallen beloved. Incapable of full disclosure before a God who redeems, the Diarist continues to flee from the one who, as he rightly notes, cannot effect his redemption.

LOVING THE LEPER WITHIN

When, however, the God-relationship determines what is love between human beings, the love is prevented from stopping in any self-deception or illusion, while in turn the requirement of self-denial and sacrifice is certainly made infinite. (WL 113)

Ah, it is enough to make one lose one's mind. (SLW, 312)

As is implied by the quotes which open this chapter, the Diarist's self-critical turn resembles much more closely the "essentially Christian" than either the revelers' self-serving, other-negating speeches or Judge William's confident, cheerful charge forward. Given that "the God-requirement" is "infinite," the way of faithful intimacy requires of us our sober, somber estimation of our own incapacity to love. Before correcting the Diarist's way, first we must note that the Christian stages on life's way are excruciatingly difficult – a point William blithely misses and we may be tempted to overlook. The Diarist insightfully likens our relation to God to a Syrian hermit's effort to stand on a small platform upon a tall pillar. The hermit's life consists of "bending himself into the most difficult positions and frightening away sleep and searching for terror in the crises of balance" (SLW, 253). Whether the best metaphor is the Young Man's "fox traps" or the hermit's wavering platform, our attempt to exist honestly before God requires not mere stamina but an ability to reflect earnestly on our own resilient tendency toward sin (WL, 18). As Kierkegaard depicts in *Works of Love* with meticulous detail, "divine authority . . . fastens its piercing look" upon each one of us and is "as if all eyes," finding within us every small and great evasion of God's command that we acknowledge and love the other (WL, 97).

We are "in fear and trembling before God" to fear ourselves, detect our own "crises of balance," and, with effort and grace, attempt to adjust accordingly (WL, 15). In *Stages*, Kierkegaard narratively depicts a myriad of ways that love can go awry when the lover evades the command to acknowledge, see, and forgive the other. With the interruption of God's command, we are able to detect the self-deception and danger in the text, but we are moreover to note the ways that we too swerve off balance or step flat into a snare. We are, like the banqueters, often tempted to consume the other in a secluded, solitary lair. We are, like the Happily Married Man, tempted both to underestimate our sin and to use the beloved as the felicitous resolution of our own crises. And therefore, with the Diarist, we are called to reflect piercingly on our own incapacity even to approximate the infinitude of God's command. This is, by Kierkegaard's estimation, a requisite and continuing task for the Christian. Is it, indeed, enough to make one lose one's mind.

But, as the Diarist inadvertently reveals, such reflective self-inspection, when divorced from an encounter with the God who, through Christ, shoulders our debt, may dangerously lead us either to seek self-justification through a careful calculation of the beloved's own faults or to escape God's call altogether in a frantic burrowing inward, away from actuality. As Kierkegaard characterizes a true encounter with God, one perceives together the overpowering magnitude of love's task *and* the well from which all love must draw strength (WL, 9). Yet again, we enter the language of "infinite debt" (WL, 102). If we attempt to remain engaged without our immeasurable debt before God constantly in view, love "wastes away and dies" (WL, 180). Incapable of the hope that enables courage that enables disclosure, we who inadvertently or willfully remain on the other side of redemption watch our love trickle out or become murky with distortion.

Love's demise may take many forms, but the Diarist manifests two obvious symptoms which Kierkegaard links to our lacking a sense of indebtedness. First, the Diarist "commits treachery," as Kierkegaard puts it, by bringing a criterion to bear on his beloved:

Life certainly has tests enough, and these tests should find the lovers, find friend and friend, united in order to pass the test. But if the test is dragged into the relationship, treachery has been committed. Indeed, this secretive inclosing reserve is the most dangerous kind of faithlessness. (WL, 166)

Kierkegaard describes this "secretive inclosing reserve," whereby one examines the other, as a sometimes subtle but destructive "lack of honesty" and as a definitive sign that love has gone awry (WL, 151). As if speaking specifically about the Diary, Kierkegaard notes "how mistrustingly one must conduct oneself in order to make the discoveries" about one's beloved (WL, 283). Hoping to save ourselves from the fox traps or secure our footing on the pedestal, we go about calculating the probability of the lover's fidelity, worth, or beauty (WL, 254). Second, the Diarist, and we, are tempted, if we perceive accurately the treachery of intimacy, to escape. Not knowing the one to whom we can turn for sustenance, not perceiving grace simultaneous with the command, he and we may burrow deep or, as Kierkegaard puts it, attempt to fly "above the world" (WL, 84). Noting that the beloved is ineluctably untrustworthy (after all, she too is fallen), recognizing that we are not up to the task of love, we may, like the Diarist, decide that "none of us is worth loving" and flee (WL, 158).

It is clear that the Diarist is not adept at the "strange way of speaking" and has not experienced the "transformation of attitude and mind" that accompanies the realization of God's infinitely excessive forgiveness (WL, 178). Perhaps fearing that his fate would be that of David in Solomon's dream, he does not truly reveal himself before God or unmask himself before his beloved. His self-inspection leads him instead to ever more elaborate scheming to detect her faults, clear himself, and find a "religious" way out. For Kierkegaard, Christian self-reflection is inextricably linked to our faithful self-disclosure in prayer, and it is to enable our taking the risk of vulnerability before another. The only way that we can begin to disclose and to engage is through a very specific relation to God. Kierkegaard depicts by way of the Diarist what plagues many of us who, finding ourselves unforgiven, suspect others and hide from God. In a strange way, the Diarist's determination that "like loves only like" – and that thus he should find a lover whom he can "understand" and whose way in the world is one with which he may "deeply and essentially sympathize" – is a warped inversion of Kierkegaard's insistence that we forgive the sinner before us because we know well our iniquity (SLW, 222; WL, 386). But rather than find himself a sinner in the hands of a forgiving God, the Diarist persuades himself that he is a religious martyr temporarily engaged to a shallow girl. His "religious" method of escape is especially pernicious at the point where he justifies his deception of her by determining that he has "the category and the idea on [his] side" (SLW, 356). Finding no way out of the whirling confusion around him, finding that these two who are to wed are instead strangers, he falsely pulls rank on her. Unable to know God as the confidant to whom he may disclose all, he continues to dwell on her misunderstanding and to remain silent.

In the context of our infinite debt before God, the beloved is allowed to be merely the human beloved. She need not be expected to act as that confidant who understands one fully and whose forgiveness has eternal significance, because there is another to whom we are instead accountable and on whom we are to rely. Kierkegaard explains that, when the lover recognizes his debt to God, God himself "lovingly assumes love's requirement," as a "guardian for the beloved" (WL, 189). This facet of Kierkegaard's description has many implications, one of which is that the heat is turned down on our relationship with this fallen stranger to whom we are ourselves engaged. Our debt assumed by God in Christ, we are enabled to venture self-disclosure even while simultaneously praying that the beloved will treat our honesty with care. Living in the midst of God's grand, eternal abundance, and our infinite gratitude, the love that we show another is not contingent upon the minute or large particulars of the beloved herself (WL, 157). Kierkegaard speaks of this similarly when discussing the "belief" in love consequent to our recognition of debt. If we know ourselves as existing in the midst of a radical gift, we may perceive the love we show another as also within this context of free, gracious bestowal (WL, 242). This is to free the lover to love regardless of the potential outcome of his gift. If reciprocity is required, the love bestowed is not a true bestowal, and we betray ourselves as outside the proper framework for love. The Diarist's arduous attempt to "imagine many a terror" and to gain an exhaustive list of the "storms in which" his love will be tested all prior even to his risking a meeting with her is here exposed as a significant misunderstanding of love's task (SLW, 202). His meticulous efforts to gauge her reliability and religious depth before committing to her, wanting a "defect removed" or a "perfection added . . . as if the bargain were not yet concluded," are exposed by Kierkegaard as symptoms of a mistaken way (WL, 165).

What rightly troubles the Diarist is that he *is* truthfully alienated from his beloved and that she *is*, as a person, to be held to the same requirement of faith. Although the Diarist is culpable for bringing mistrust into the re-lationship from the beginning, he is likely correct that his beloved would not fully understand him even if he did truly unmask himself. But when the Diarist asserts that he has the religious on his side against her, fig-uring himself as one and a half to her individuality, he betrays dubious confusion. Although he correctly perceives, unlike the misogynist ban-queters or William the Married, that his beloved is truly a stranger to whom he is nevertheless responsible, he exacerbates their alienation by considering his religious reflection superior to her own. Her "reflection is only single," he reports, and he wonders at the difference between woman and man, toying with the idea that perhaps "infinite reflection is not essential for a woman" (SLW, 302, 303, 306). To his credit, he is not long willing to be "consoled" by this option whereby she would remain "beautiful" even though inferior (SLW, 306, 307). He rejects the "illusory relief" that would ensue were she not also expected to meet the requirement of faith (SLW, 228).

The Diarist is right not to excuse his beloved metaphysically from "the requirement," but he betrays his religious error when he decides that he himself cannot "exist intellectually" in his "category," unless she "is able to exist in the same thing" (SLW, 305). Believing that his existence itself is an "indirect judgement" on her, he finds marriage to his beloved impossible (SLW, 305). For him, "like loves only like," and marriage requires intrinsic compatibility (SLW, 222). He missteps here in the text (and we misstep here in this life) in at least two related ways: according to Kierkegaard's words in *Works of Love*, the fitting consideration is not the other's faith but our own, and we are always wrong to think that faith tips the balance in anyone's favor. Regarding true love's refusal to compare, genuine faith is to turn the lover inward again to inspect himself, not outward to discern his beloved's depth or lack thereof. The assumption about the other properly coincident with faith is that the other is "equal" to oneself "before God" (WL, 60). She is not worthy to the extent that she has similarly probed the depths that brought him to the (so-called) religious. Rather, she is worthy in her own right, before God: "unconditionally every person [even his buoyant beloved] has this equality and has it unconditionally" (WL, 60).

It is for a reason that Kierkegaard forces us past William the Married's insistence that love is "happy" and through the Diarist's anguish. It would be to invite yet another form of self-delusion were we to think that inter-rupting the Diarist's treatise with God's command loops him and us back to William's beautiful, enclosed garden. Self-disclosing, self-reflective prayer before God may enable us to know ourselves as indebted and to risk the dangers of intimacy, but our beloved remains, to some extent, a stranger. And our love for the one to whom we are engaged remains, to every extent, dependent on grace. Only the uniquely blessed (or, what is more likely, the happily oblivious) find themselves intertwined in marriage with another whose understanding is daily and ultimately compatible with their own. As herself fallen and also called by God in a way undetectable to others, the other continues, even in faithful intimacy, to prevent, by means of her very existence, a "union."[15]

Living simultaneously with an other and with God is, by Kierkegaard's very apt estimation, less like the Judge's "solution to the worried person" and more akin to Frater Taciturnus's image of "lying out on 70,000 fathoms of water" (SLW, 134, 445). By noting what Taciturnus calls the Diarist's "dialectical treading water," we are to resist any notion that faithful love "goes so smoothly" that "Point eighteen follows upon or after Point seventeen" (SLW, 452). When faced with the prospect of supping regularly and "having daily arguing from" the other, we may note, with the Diarist, "how dangerous it is for a thinker to be in love" (SLW, 305). The occasions for error within marriage are inexhaustible, from evading self-disclosure to judging the other, from believing ourselves despicable to thinking the divine balance tipped in our favor. It is here that Taciturnus states, "From the religious point of view, the greatest danger is that one does not discover, that one is not always discovering, that one is in danger" (SLW, 469). But, Kierkegaard adds, just as there are 70,000 fathoms of water, or 70,000 fox traps, or only seven square inches on the Syrian hermit's high pedestal, God's love is infinite. Only as we self-reflect before this God are we enabled to approximate the vexatious balance that is loving the other.

CHAPTER 6

On the way

Even if there were nothing else to prevent the poet from singing about love for the neighbor, it is already enough that beside every word in Holy Scripture a disturbing notice in invisible writing confronts him that says: Go and do likewise. Does this sound like a poet-summons that calls upon him to sing?

(WL, 46)

So also with the road sign "Christendom." It designates the direction, but has one therefore arrived at the goal, or is one always only – on the way?

(WL 48)

INTRODUCTION

Each time we have, in the previous five chapters, distinguished faithful from fallen love we have had to do so with a disclaimer. If we think at any point that we have actually "gone and done likewise" – if we find "rest" and "comfort" in the thought that by "doing what we can" we have met God's command to love the neighbor – we are almost certainly wrong.[1] The "Go and do likewise" we hear "beside every word in Holy Scripture" is, in a significant sense, to render us speechless. Droning on resonantly about the true life of a loving Christian is, as Kierkegaard insists, to confuse the matter. So although in this concluding chapter we sum up and clarify the matters covered previously, we must not deceive ourselves. Faithful love does not go so "smoothly" that "Point eighteen" follows immediately upon "Point seventeen," as Frater Taciturnus warns, and we must be careful lest we mistakenly conclude that any point in the Christian life ineluctably precedes or follows any other (SLW, 452). We are continually to cultivate what the Frater calls a "Socratic horror of being in error," and assiduously avoid the "modern foolhardiness" whereby we think that, if we describe the movements toward and aspects of faithful love with sufficient clarity, we have thereby become what we have described (SLW, 484). Even the most perspicacious description of love cannot serve as an incantation. The transformation evoked by these texts is decidedly not like the change "in the fairy tale [when] one becomes a bird by saying certain words" (SLW, 484). Again to layer Kierkegaard's metaphors, the way of veritable love is sufficiently precipitous to preclude encouraging melodies about our love, our trans-formation, or the road to faithful intimacy. Most of the time, we who call ourselves Christian are wandering aimlessly or reveling shamelessly along another route altogether; on our best days, when we are in fact facing the goal, we are "only – on the way."

With this caution implicit on every page, we must still "designate the direction" toward which Christianity points, employing as our guides the characters Kierkegaard has wrought in his pseudonymous works and in *Works of Love*. The men and women of the texts we have covered, through their cruelty, blustering, idolatry, and anguish, give us clues about where we too go wrong in our love. And, by revealing the many ways that merely human love may go awry, they give force to Kierkegaard's call in *Works of Love* for us repeatedly to turn toward God. Having taken note of the various pathways attempted and proven "fruitless" (as Kierkegaard wrote of *Repetition*) we may better navigate toward the One in whose presence we are both humbled and indebted.[2] Exposed by God's law as the idolatrous, cynical, selfish, perverted, and perplexed creatures that we are, we often try to clamber out of our predicament through the other, misguided routes Kierkegaard describes. Rather than turn-ing vulnerably toward God in repentance, we may, like Constantin's young man or de Silentio's knight of resignation, seek to elevate our-selves above existence and grasp the infinite. Instead of confessing our sin before God, we may like William elevate our beloved in order to find in her our "joy," our "refuge," and the "root of [our] life" (EO, II:312). Or, many of us try, as the Diarist does briefly, to heed William's advice and take the "washing of resolution," wherein our iniquity is, by dint of our dutiful will, "promptly" removed (SLW, 163). Finally, we may decide, as do Margarete and her sisters, to attach ourselves to our lovers and evade the question of innocence and guilt. The road they all miss and that we seldom attempt is an "earnest walk" alone before God (WL, 77).[3]

The import of these texts is not only theological, but also specifically so-teriological. By tracing these paths together, we are able to discern more clearly and fully Kierkegaard's attempt to bring the reader to Christ.

Kierkegaard's description of a life in debt and in profound dependence on God reveals that, if we hope to love, we must fall to our knees before the One who intercedes on our behalf. Each one of the characters whose story we have heard misses or avoids this encounter. The Diarist notes that his "whole attitude to life" is fatally "askew"; to paraphrase Constantin, "underneath" each of these texts is a grave "misunderstanding" that reveals much about our own skewed suppositions (SLW, 223; R, 136). Whether wrangling with guilt and innocence like the young man and the Diarist or reckoning ourselves washed through resolution like the Judge, we avoid the somber proclamation of the Jylland pastor: "you may argue with God only in such a way that you learn that you are in the wrong" (EO, II: 344). The way of love, glimpsed in these texts only insofar as the principal characters avoid it, requires that we first know ourselves, like Tobit's Sarah, fundamentally and irreparably "botched" (FT, 104).[4] And given the reality of our infinite guilt, we require divine deliverance. The alternative context described in *Works of Love* necessitates that we turn toward the one whose redemptive work reveals each guilty individual to be "under divine confiscation" (FT, 77). By Kierkegaard's account, in order for us to approximate the law of love, we must both resign ourselves to Christ – whose life proves us incalculably "in the wrong" – and know ourselves, through Christ's death, as indentured to God.

In this chapter we return, for a final time, to the characters whose misbegotten love exposes our need for grace. Some of these pseudonymous personae are able to discern the depth of their confusion and guilt, however falteringly, and we will track the mistakes that ensue as they attempt to find a route out. Retracing their efforts, we find that a full repetition, once more from the beginning, is in fact necessary. None of the routes described in these pseudonymous texts allows access into the precarious realm of faithful love. We will therefore reconfigure the Christian route described in *Works of Love* and parse the effects such a turn is to have on our love. Reading *Works of Love* with all four of the pseudonymous texts behind us, we are able more fully to discern the manifestations of our alternative encounter with Christ as our judge and as our redeemer. Perceiving the impassable gap between that which is true and that which we currently try to pass off as love, we must resign ourselves before Christ as our judge. With Christ's command to love the neighbor as an "other," we are made aware of the sins we commit daily when we, like so many of Kierekegaard's characters, ignore the distinction between self and other. We are thus to be self-circumspect and penitent in love, cautious of the many ways we steal from or fuse ourselves to the others closest to us. My repentance is further to humble me and prevent my selfish evaluations of my beloved, whose character I have most opportunity to inspect. Recognizing that we have no recourse but to hope in God's forgiveness offered through Christ, we are, like Tobit's Sarah, to accept the radical gift of salvation. This redemption determines that my beloved and I are each, through Christ, bound first and fundamentally to God alone. We are thus denied our attempts to fuse what God has definitively rent asunder. Given that our salvation in Christ reveals each of us to be no more and no less than justified sinners before God, faith further precludes comparison and inequality, and is to enable our free disclosure to and forgiveness of one another. But, finally, because it is not as if "Point eighteen" neatly follows "Point seventeen," we continually find ourselves convicted by Christ's law, confessing anew.

WHAT LOVE IS NOT

It is what the age wants, to become dizzy over the abominable and then fancy itself to be superior. They will not get that from me. (JP IV 5705 [Pap. IVA 181 n.d., 1844]).[5]

A strand that runs throughout the authorship and that Kierkegaard weaves directly into *Works of Love* is the tenacity of our self-delusion and error. At the most basic level, there are two manifestations of fallen love, consumption and self-abasement, whereby we ignore the distinction between self and other. The main means by which Christianity reveals this tendency to us is Christ's command that we love the other "as yourself" (WL, 17). Kierkegaard describes the import of Christ's law by reckoning the term "neighbor" as a factor that "redoubles" the self in an interaction, thereby demarcating the individual we otherwise attempt to acquire for ourselves or to whom we attempt to fuse ourselves (WL, 21). As he explains, "this 'as yourself' expressly contains a requirement" for the lover, that is, that I know the other as separate from myself (WL, 21). In so describing the effect of the command on our love, Kierkegaard exposes our default mode of "relating" as rather a negation of relationality. We love as if there were only one self involved in the loving, either by pulling the other into ourselves or by blending our own self into the aims and wishes of the other.

First, with our voraciously subjective perception, we draw the other into a world wherein we are the center. What I suppose to be love through this form of self-delusion is, most often, merely a case of my loving myself

(WL, 52). Whether clumsily (like *Repetition*'s young man) or with crafted intention (like the men of "*In Vino Veritas*") we mentally subsume the other into the realm of our own aims, desires and wishes, denying her existence as "the other" (WL, 21). The term "neighbor" in Christ's command is to interrupt our selfish assumptions and force us to acknowledge the other, distinct entity before us. Second, like the women of A's "Silhouettes," we allow ourselves to be drawn into a world of another's making, giving an individual the power only God should have over our lives (WL, 125). Christ's command that the other remain truly other-than-me also exposes my subsuming as transgression. By dwelling with these errors in turn, we may for a final time note what love is not, as well as the way Kierkegaard rhetorically implicates all forms of merely human love.

Most of the men in these stories, by focusing on another individual with intent to encroach and consume, enact the first of the errors described above. In the case of the merman and Johannes, the danger is physical and thus clear. Each man not only construes the beloved as an extension of his desires but also seeks to draw her into his domain in order to possess her (FT, 97; EO, 1:314). By way of the "Seducer's Diary," Kierkegaard stretches the space of time that is momentary for the merman, relating the process by which Johannes "pull[s] the bow of love tighter in order to wound all the deeper" (EO, 1: 349). Through this unapologetic seducer, Kierkegaard explores the process by which the other becomes encompassed by the acquisitive lover. As Johannes, with characteristic candor, words it, the girl whom the lover chooses is "chosen" precisely in order that she may be literally "overtaken," (EO, 1:317), and with both the merman and Johannes the danger to the one "chosen" is not figurative but actual. Agnes will be dragged back to the sea and Cordelia will be "attacked" (EO, 1:360). The "neighbor" in these instances is not only subsumed through vicious perception but also violated physically.

We are not to stop here in righteous horror. Through the eyes of Constantin and of the other men at the banquet, Kierkegaard compels the reader to uncover the theoretical subtext common to all forms of selfish perception. Crucial for Constantin's quest in Berlin is his systematic construal of the other as that which exists for his enjoyment or scorn. Unlike Johannes, Constantin does not desire explicit seduction, but his interest is relatedly iniquitous. Albeit from a distance, Constantin uncurls his tentacles to draw others figuratively into the range of his appetite. While Constantin's victims suspect nothing (indeed, their credulity is necessary for his enjoyment), Kierkegaard suggests that by mentally transforming the other into a thing to be devoured, Constantin, like a "beast of prey," extracts something from the other (R, 153). Johannes and Constantin join forces in "*In Vino Veritas*" to commend that mental process which secures the perceiving individual at the axis of his own subjective universe. Philosophically reconstructing the other into a conglomeration of interesting or laughable particulars, the lover is able mentally to create an impermeable, self-centered system. In Johannes's seduction of Cordelia, Constantin's removed voyeurism, and the banqueters' theoretical exclusion of the other, Kierkegaard relates the connections between physical and mental violation. He attempts rhetorically to close the gap between the actual rapist and us who perceive rapaciously.

It is not a tremendous leap from these obvious transgressions of Christ's law to the less overtly startling errors of *Repetition*'s young poet and Judge William. For the young poet and for Judge William, the female other is (to use Victor Eremita's words) "an undefinable quantity," in effect a "nothing" that can be made "blissful in fantasy" (SLW, 59, 56). The young poet and William, although their paths later diverge, both reveal their iniquitous kinship with the other men in their respective texts, each by using his beloved as if she were a "rung" on a "ladder" (R, 138). William and the young man each imagine their beloved as a "goddess" or a "savior" in order to use this constructed and thus malleable entity to become a happy husband or a beautifully melancholy poet (R, 139, EO, 11:207). For the young man, the concrete girl is "merely the visible form" for what he seeks, and William's love has as a presupposition his wife's attentive adherence to his wishes (R, 141, EO, 11:83). In William's blessed life with his chosen one, there are links to the poet's desire to love a girl whose existence provides harmony for his own dreams and expectations. Indeed, William calls his wife's ability "tenderly" to meet his needs her "rich bridal dowry" (SLW, 131). As we have noted, the use of the other in William's case is subtler than in that of the Seducer, and William, unlike *Repetition*'s poet, stays below the stars in order to marry the girl. We have reason to suspect that William does not love his beloved as his "neighbor" but rather inasmuch as she is willing and able to provide him with a reassuring "feeling" of "home" (EO, 11:83). But it is hard to say which route – an escape from the beloved through poetry or a marriage to the beloved through self-deception – Kierkegaard finds morally preferable; both are equidistant from the truth. While *Repetition*'s young poet attempts to "clip" himself in order to become "commensurable," it is William's wife whose existence is clipped in order that his life might cohere (R, 214).

Kierkegaard's subtle but significant connections between those who prey voraciously and those who use discretely lead us each to question the assumptions undergirding our own love. Reading downward on the obvious continuum of vice, from Johannes the seducer to Constantin the voyeur to the poet to the happily married man, it is a small subsequent step to question the worth of our own love. Each person must "first learn from [Christ] what love is, in the divine sense," and this lesson proves us to be "not merely all Jutlanders" but "all robbers," as Kierkegaard considered phrasing it.[6] This predatory form of "self-love" is to be thoroughly thwarted by a true encounter with the commandment that the beloved be the "neighbor":

This as yourself does not vacillate in its aim, and therefore, judging with the unshakableness of eternity, it penetrates into the innermost hiding place where a person loves himself; it does not leave self-love even the slightest little excuse, the least little way of escape. (WL, 18)

Using the same metaphor of criminal acquisition, Kierkegaard explains that "purely human love," even when seemingly innocent, "has something thievish about it," and it is the work of the term "neighbor" to reveal to us even the small ways we subsume the other into our own world of desire and purpose (WL, 173). We are, by way of Christ's commandment, denied all other ways of "escape," and forced to face the error of our ways.

This warped idea of the other as one who exists primarily (or only) to the extent that she resolves the lover's quandaries, furthers the lover's aims, or quenches the lover's desire corresponds inversely to the perversion plaguing A's women. The flip-side to their lover's transgressions, each woman accepts her role as a "rejuvenating potion" for her lover, diluting her identity as an individual in order to be of use to the man she adores (EO, 1:206). Margarete is the nadir of A's series in *Either/Or*. She "completely disappears in Faust," no longer a self distinguishable from the lover to whom she clings (EO, 1:210). But as is the case with Johannes, we are not to stop, gaping in horror at A's fallen women. Again linking the stark with the subtle, Kierkegaard hints that William's "modest, humming" wife is similarly endangered; inasmuch as she also intentionally conforms her existence to a man's needs, she is Margarete's sister (EO, II:144, 83). While we are only able to read through the occlusion of William's own writing, we may surmise that his wife has some inkling of her plight. (For example, she exhibits a "a certain touch of sadness, almost of ailment," when she wakes to each new day of work;

EO, II:6.) The reader may hope that William's wife finds clever ways to wring herself free, but if not, she faces the same danger as the shadowy women of A's stories. As William's wife seeks solicitously to meet the demands of the system in which she is entrenched, her violation is less disreputable than Margarete's or Cordelia's, but she is still in danger of losing her soul. The command that she refuse her beloved's efforts to fuse her self into his falls as heavily on her as on the women seduced. For Agnes and the other seduced women, the command comes as a call physically to refuse their lover's advances. For William's wife, the command requires that she disavow the moral system that permeates their marriage. We will return below to her only hope for doing so – and ours.

Whether actively concocting a system whereby the beloved is an appendage, more innocuously assuming it, or passively accepting it, all of these characters exhibit, in ways more and less flagrant, the transgression exposed by the term "neighbor." In the pseudonymous texts Kierkegaard connects the large and the less conspicuous ways our own "ungodliness" "collide[s]" with Christ's command (WL, 110). The narratives challenge the common "misunderstanding" that an encounter with Christ's law only corrects the glaring errors of a social deviant like Johannes and a branded woman like Margarete. The links Kierkegaard fashions between lurid and mediocre forms of sin expose our moral preoccupation with the "abominable" as an evasive maneuver.[7] We who wish to love well must surrender ourselves to the command and all its implications, allowing Christ's words thoroughly to test our motives. While we might wish rather to become better lovers by distinguishing ourselves from the disgraceful, we will not get that from Kierkegaard. His texts interrupt our meditation on the outer boundaries of deviance in order to reveal to us our own sin. The command is a "clue" that forces us to "make discoveries" about our own predicament, discoveries that are "alarming to others and humiliating to oneself" (WL, 53). Under the law's rule, we may no longer regard ourselves as "superior" to the seducer but instead are called to detect the tendency within ourselves that proves him our kin. Under Christ's command, we are no longer to wag our heads in judgment at Margarete or any other duped, abandoned mother but rather discover that we are, ourselves, similarly deceived.

MORAL VERTIGO

But what does it mean to commit oneself to love? Where is the boundary? When have I fulfilled my duty? ... In case of doubt, to what council can I apply? . . . State and Church have indeed set a certain limit, but even though I do not go to the extreme, can I not therefore be a bad husband? (EO, II:151)[8]

Even though we do not go to the extreme, we are indeed bad husbands and wives. To what council can we apply? As Kierkegaard swirls the possibilities around the reader, we are to be confused. A's disconcerting response to Judge William's irrepressible confidence is characteristic of a strain in the pseudonymous texts and in *Works of Love*. With the "dialectic of truth," Kierkegaard seeks to "turn [our] comfortable way of thinking topsy-turvy," a requisite move given that we are often in "the cellar," oblivious to our disorientation.[9] Precisely because Christians too often suppose ourselves to have a "Du relationship" with reason, Kierkegaard throws up various "obstacles" to understanding in his texts and, with re-gard to love, repeatedly confounds our quest for reliable, human council (WL, 199). Indirectly in the pseudonymous texts and directly in *Works of Love*, Kierkegaard challenges our reliance on the "certain limits" set by "State and Church." We are to suspect that the behavior deemed proper by the magistrate and the pastor may be a world apart from what is truly required of us. The crises of proper human performance and right knowledge twist together particularly in the pseudonymous texts, as we become uncertain about our ability to perform the good we know, while simultaneously doubting that we actually perceive correctly the good we are to do. The treatment for our condition must therefore be of a dif-ferent order than Judge William's healthy dose of will-strengthener, and the moral alteration we require lies on the other side of our realization of ignorance and ineptitude. Indirectly implied in the pseudonymous texts is the possibility that "every uplifting thought that once made you so rich in courage and confidence [is] only a fancy, a jugglery that a child believes in" (EO, II:344). If we, like A, reflect on this possibility, we experience something akin to moral vertigo.

A and de Silentio both require the reader to interrogate comforting appearances, and we may read their iconoclasm as instructively irksome. These two characters are irreverent cousins to the brother Kierkegaard borrows from Matthew 21:28, who says "no" to God's command out of "a concerned distrust of himself" (WL, 92). Unlike the brother who replies with a "sleep-inducing" yes, both A and de Silentio are "almost afraid of [themselves]." Through their insomnia Kierkegaard intends in us a type of disturbing, moral "awakening" (WL, 93). Evoking the "anxiety and trembling that disciplined the youth," de Silentio seeks to provoke his otherwise staid readers toward a "proficiency in doubting" using the example of Abraham (FT, 7,6). If what appears to be murder may in fact be love, then might it not also be the case that what appears to be love is quite the contrary? Kierkegaard's rhetorical use of Abraham in *Fear and Trembling* is similar to the use he makes (through the sermon by the Jylland pastor) of Christ's condemnation of Jerusalem. Our "courage and confidence" in what appears to be true is in both cases splintered (EO, II:344). Listening to de Silentio's contrast of Abraham and the merman, we are prompted to "scrutinize in sleepless vigilance every single secret thought," and "in anxiety and horror" detect "the dark emotions hiding in every human life" (FT, 100).

Through A, Kierkegaard mimics a cynical voice on the same theme. Having in youth noted that "wisdom was whatever the majority assumed it to be," A, in various ways, incites the reader to ask, "What if everything in the world were a misunderstanding?" (EO, I:21, 34). If so, my life may be "like the word Schnur in the dictionary," nonsensical in its range of possible meanings, leading me ultimately to shrug wondering "God knows what our Lord actually intended with me or what he wants to make of me" (EO, I:36, 26). Because de Silentio's text merely touches on the topic of sin, and A eschews sin as "not an esthetic element," neither pseudonym can do more with their observations than "throw them back over their heads" like a pig tossing truffles (EO, I: 36). But, as Judge William notes of A's skepticism, it can be characteristic of "the most light-minded" or the most "heavy-hearted of men"(EO, II:151). Taken in a different tone, de Silentio's and A's words can be read as Kierkegaard's effort to burden a man's heart.

Several of Kierkegaard's characters lead the reader to the precipice where A laughs and de Silentio shudders. The young poet's bafflement over his own guilt or innocence in *Repetition*, the women's shattered expectations in "Silhouettes," and the Diarist's tortured attempt to reassemble his splintered love in *Stages* all serve rhetorically to underscore the crisis we face when thinking earnestly about love.[10] In *Repetition*, the young man finds himself in Berlin, with neither the girl nor his love, and demands, "Who tricked me into this whole thing and leaves me standing here?" (R, 200). He finds that there is no explanation for the mess and wishes that someone would "invent a new word" to clarify his guilt, innocence, or madness (R, 202). He vows to remain absolutely still, not daring to "stir from the spot" lest he make his life even more "ludicrous" (R, 202, 214). Each of A's abandoned women finds herself also alone, and they too "deliberate," "interrogate," and "examine" in order to forge some "meaning" out of their incomprehensible predicaments (EO, I:170, 191).

Having molded her life according to her beloved's wishes, each woman cannot fix blame on her lover even for her abandonment and instead spirals through the irreconcilable facts regarding their love, his treachery, and her guilt (EO, 1:188). Finally, in the Diarist, Kierkegaard creates a character who must struggle close-at-hand with the possibility de Silentio considers from a distance: might one delusively think himself loving when he is instead a murderer? His "demand to life" is that "it would make it clear" whether he is "trapped in self-delusion," "even to the point of nausea ensnared in self-deception," or that he is in fact loving (SLW, 384, 317). His plight is our own as he remains "sleepless," unable to distinguish "chivalry" from "hypocrisy," love from its opposite (SLW, 232, 317). Incapable of making himself "comprehensible to any human being," he attempts to find God, and fails (SLW, 350). Each of these characters seeks in vain to find sure footing in the whirl of moral inquiry. In their crises we are also to be thrown off kilter, and, in their mistaken attempts to achieve balance we are to recognize our own futile efforts.

CRAWLING IN VAIN

The infinite, the eternal, hence the true, is so alien to the natural man that with him it is as with the dog, which can indeed learn to walk upright for a moment but yet continually wants to walk on all fours. (WL, 245)

Kierkegaard's various characters endeavor by different means to find their way out of a moral morass of inconclusive guilt and innocence. Patterns emerge as we consider their methods, similarities that in effect carve out ruts in the terrain of their and our behavior. Whether trying to propel themselves over their moral confusion, using the innocence of another to still the chaos, plowing resolutely forward through the (underestimated) quagmire, or, through self-effacement, hiding underneath another, Kierkegaard's characters miss the only relation within which love exists.[11]

First, there is the method of self-elevation. Turning a critical eye toward the beloved and maintaining a high estimation of themselves, several of Kierkegaard's characters seek to "grasp" a religious route out of their impasse (FT, 40). De Silentio's knight of resignation, the young poet, and the Diarist all try to hoist themselves above the fray. Second, Kierkegaard narrates a way in which we deem the beloved "utterly, utterly, utterly innocent" and thus rely on her to solve the previously insoluble (FT, 95).

The Diarist and the merman each consider and then forgo this option, whereas William heartily combines it with the third method: dutiful resolve. According to William's treatise, we are, in the face of apparent moral incongruity, to march forward. In his related attempt, the Diarist tries diligently, for a time, to conform his intentions and even arrange his cutlery so as to ensure his legitimacy. Finally, A's women employ a fourth method, whereby one subsumes herself underneath the aims and wishes of the other, and in effect crawls beneath the question of culpability. After rehearsing each of these tactics, we are better able to hear that the only way toward love runs right through the center of impending moral bedlam. To rephrase the children's song, the truth is too high, too low, and too wide for us to get over, crawl under, or go around. It is only through our profoundly disorienting encounter with Christ that we may begin, haltingly, to love.

There are significant similarities between the irreligious progression of de Silentio's knight, the earnest work of the deluded young poet, and the Diarist's false resolution. Each one aspires to legitimacy by association with the eternal, but all three do so through presumptive ascent, rather than humble descent. In de Silentio's description of the knight's "movement" is the paradigm for both the young poet's and the Diarist's failure to progress. Shortly after falling in love with a princess, de Silentio's knight quickly becomes "totally absorbed" instead in his own experience and believes that he must "transfigure" his love for the girl into "a love of the eternal being" (FT, 44). In this way, the knight hopes to propel himself above the "lower natures," of which the actual girl is a part (FT, 43, 44).[12] Thinking himself thereby rightly to have moved beyond the "particular something" (namely, the girl) who initially prompted his "passion," the knight determines that "all by [him]self" he has "renounce[d] everything" and has achieved "blessed harmony" and "love for the eternal being" (FT, 49). It is by way of a related renunciation of the other and elevation of the self that both the young poet and the Diarist seek to find their own moorings. *Repetition*'s poet determines that his love "cannot find expression in [mere] marriage," and, by way of Job, declares himself, in spite of his broken commitment, "in the right" with "clean hands" (R, 207, 214). This dubious self-declaration is beyond debate, given that it is a matter of his "personal relationship" with God, a qualification which disallows "any explanation at second-hand" (R, 210). While the poet moves slightly beyond de Silentio's knight in that he considers briefly the possibility of his own guilt, his work is again an upward struggle toward the "absolutely transcendent" and that illusive "spot" of inculpability (R, 214). Rather than standing condemned before God, the poet wishes to approach God in order to avoid condemnation.

The Diarist dwells, almost interminably, with the reality of his own possible condemnation, but his movement still bears a resemblance to that of his distant cousin, the knight of other-resignation. Also seeking a "new word" whereby he will not be "blameworthy," the Diarist pulls rank on his beloved, whom he deems to be, "with regard to the religious ... *valore intrinseco* [according to intrinsic value] only an ordinary dollar" (R, 202; SLW, 257). With "the category and the idea on [his] side," the Diarist weighs her paltry sum against the "idea," appraising her "voice in order positively to assure [himself] that [he has] done the right thing in keeping [himself] from hearing it" (SLW, 356, 377). His effort at self-justification contributes the material for his "religious structur[ing]" (SLW, 351). He moves inward to seek a truth that "cannot be an illusion" because it is indisputably distinct from the shallow girl to whom he has compared himself. The "moment of understanding" comes, for the Diarist, at the point when he is able clearly to distinguish his "innermost" conversant (himself) from the voice of the "ordinary" girl (SLW, 351, 257). Climbing upward toward truth in God, the Diarist seeks a counterfeit standard of faith. All three of these characters resign the beloved in their misguided attempts to elevate themselves above the moral turmoil that they each rightly perceive.

The other side of this coin, whereby the individual secures his own status through a self-elevating comparison with the beloved, is the effort to secure an "utterly innocent" beloved to be one's intercessor (FT, 95). Although neither one ultimately uses the beloved in this way, the merman's and the Diarist's retreats from the girl bear the mark of this idea. According to de Silentio, either Agnes is "utterly, utterly, utterly innocent," and therefore stands in crushing contrast to the fallen merman, or else she is not, and is therefore incapable of intercession. Incapable of self-disclosure before an innocent Agnes, the merman returns to the sea. And the Diarist, determining that the beloved is insufficiently innocent to cure him, returns to himself. For both of these characters, the hope for using their beloved in this way is short-lived. After the first kiss, the Diarist briefly imagines the "bliss" to which he could, through the girl, be initiated. By the "sight of her health," he initially hopes that he will be "healed," and that she will be "as an apostle" to "the paralytic," through her work allowing him to "be well" (SLW, 211). In this wish, he asks "no more" (and no less) than that she might provide for him a link to that "one abode where joy is at home" (SLW, 206). On determining that she is not faultless but instead harbors a "secret pride" and exhibits "a dubious" form of "fidelity," the Diarist decides that the girl he has chosen "lacks the integration that beautifies" (SLW, 268, 308, 356). It is then that he moves on to the method described above, that of hoisting himself over her, and all of actuality, in order to find an autonomous position before God. Both the merman and the Diarist come upon the chance and then the impossibility of using a merely human other to tether themselves to coherence.

William does not grasp the impossibility of merely human intercession. Between his stories about attending church and his description of his wife's work on his behalf, William implicitly and explicitly advocates a method of parasitical salvation. In both *Either/Or* and *Stages* William tells stories of his contemplation (while in church) of maternal purity, and of the renewed confidence he experiences on such occasions. Watching a young mother in church tend to her little boy, he determines her to be "like a flower" that "under microscopic scrutiny" becomes "lovelier and lovelier" (SLW, 137).[13] He explains that, through this observation, his faith in maternal solicitude is strengthened; such "motherly solicitude" allows one to "forget the dissonances of life" and is, therefore, "life's beautiful solution" (SLW, 133, 134). For William, it is maternal love that bridges the rift between what should be and what is, providing the individual with the "solution" to life's "dissonances." With its ability to harmonize the discord, this love is the key to William's earlier renewal as a young unmarried man visiting a church (recounted in *Either/Or*). His experience of the "venerable matron" not only "drift[s] into [his] thoughts" on marriage but continues to infect his perspective on the resolution of his and our condition (EO, II:316; SLW, 133). William is able to "go on" precisely because he "spiritually believes" that he may find that which is "lifesaving for someone who is sick unto death" in his wife's "rich bridal dowry" of "tenderness" (SLW, 130).[14] If his wife continues to hold up under William's "microscopic scrutiny," we are to wonder whether, in William's resolved life, there is even any "gap" for God to fill.[15] This false method is, for Kierkegaard, the most insidious in that an individual may hum along securely with little premonition of his soul's impending peril.

William's supplemental method of dutiful resolve suggests that the "magic" that holds his domestic "circle" together requires either that we minimize the rifts in the moral life or that we acquire more willpower than any mere human can muster (EO, II:114; SLW, 90). Even leaving aside the incriminating fact that, as it stands, William's form of resolution is more reliant on "mother's milk" than on his own strength, his account is problematic. The "religious view of life constructed upon ethical presuppositions" apparent in William's treatises presupposes that the "ethical presuppositions" cohere harmoniously in our minds and in our wills (EO, ii:162). The "internal and external dangers" to love, about which Kierkegaard warns, become, in William's account, akin to minor foot problems (SLW, 162, 129). To put the same point differently, William is able to "resolve" the "paradoxes" of ethical existence by dint of his own "courage" only because he weakens the strands that are paradoxically knotted (EO, ii:111). Whereas Kierkegaard posits an unyielding tension between preferential and Christian love, William attenuates both, rendering duty "not something new" but "something familiar"; marriage is a "happy" "synthesis of falling in love and resolution" (EO, ii:146; SLW, 109). Duty may "give the assurance that in all eternity no obstacle will be able to disturb love" (EO, ii:59). While for Kierkegaard any assurance lies only in the midst of great obstacles, utter confusion, profound repentance, and radical grace, for William our fears are quelled by way of the "divine nourishment" of "duty," love's "true temperate climate" (EO, ii:147, 146).

Although William seems currently capable of taking "resolution's bath of purification," many of Kierkegaard's other characters continually (and perceptively) discern that William's bath is insufficient (SLW, 164). Their forays into the world of his treatise are instructive. The method of dutiful resolution he espouses runs up against the other characters' sneaking (and often howling) suspicions that duty, earnestly considered, is not so clearly discerned or neatly met.[16] A's queries to William – "when have I fulfilled my duty?" and, even if I meet what I think God demands, "can I not therefore be a bad husband?" – haunt the other characters as they attempt in various ways to know and to will William's method (EO, ii:151). De Silentio conscientiously turns Abraham's story around, peering intently at every facet in his effort to learn studiously and follow resolutely Abraham's example of radical obedience, only later to conclude "Abraham I cannot understand" and "in a certain sense I can learn nothing from him except be amazed" (FT, 9–14, 37). The young engaged poet sits, "clipping" himself in an effort to "take away everything that is incommensurable" and thereby "become commensurable," only to find that "the next morning [his] beard is just as long again" (R, 214). The Diarist's work, following immediately as it does on William's treatise, is the most rhetorically clear in its refutation of William's confidence. The Diarist seeks with "integrity" to configure his life so that his "balance sheet" may "balance down to the last penny" only to find that his "enormous account" outweighs his exertion (SLW, 295, 284). Like the benefactor from Christianhavn who thinks himself responsible for children he cannot find, the Diarist discovers that his "earnest" "accounting for [each] year" is but a "joke" when compared with what he owes (SLW, 284).[17] Realizing that "the person who sins in one thing sins in all," the Diarist concludes that he (and the reader) must refuse William's "lie" and instead remain "ashamed" (SLW, 292, 291).

The fourth route toward illegitimate certainty is, in most of Kierkegaard's texts, more implied than narrated. We know very little about Agnes, except that she trusted the merman. We know nothing about the young poet's fiancée, except that she was prudent enough to marry someone else. The Diarist's sweetheart apparently recognizes the poignancy (and irony) of the occasion when her metaphorically cloaked beloved is unmasked and wounded while fencing, but she too remains for the reader a mystery. But through A, Kierkegaard pointedly turns the focus on a form of other-preoccupation that plagues "the girl" rather than the muse, knight, recluse, or seducer.[18] Each woman in "Silhouettes" seeks a way to resolve the dissonance resulting from her lover's treachery, and the mercy they lavish on these men is both an evasion of their predicament and a secular distortion of Christian forgiveness. The trajectory of their love is, from the beginning, idolatrous, but their choice of mooring subsequent to their abandonment is damning. The solution to their version of moral vertigo is to dispense with "strict justice" in favor of "an intense interest in the accused" that "cannot stand up against a single objection" (EO, 1:185). Each woman, by submitting herself and all her moral claims beneath her interest in her lover, seeks to negate the standard for "objection" whereby her lover might be indicted. By making her lover "the whole world, more than her soul's salvation" Donna Elvira "cast[s] away everything" for her beloved, including the rule of justice that would brand him a thief, and she vows to remain in that realm (EO, 1:196). Because "nothing has meaning for her . . . except Don Giovanni," she and the others love within an impermeable but amoral universe. With resolute determination, each woman refuses the explanation that her lover is "to blame," crawling below justice in order repeatedly to "acquit" him and patch together the idolatrous system fractured by her idol's behavior (EO, 1:185).

Either/Or's A surmises that "only by a break can it be brought to a halt" (EO, 1:188). Only "by her cutting short this whole movement of thought" may she make another "beginning" (EO, 1:188). She may escape, but only by refusing the system forged through a man's desire and treachery and perpetuated by her determination to avoid his indictment. A suggests further that the break must occur "in the power of [her] own willing" (EO, 1:188). Each woman must, through some miracle, discover that she does in fact have a will external to her lover's – that she is not "an insignificant little plant" at the disposal of a man, that she is not "clay in his hands," and that her stifled protest is not mere "presump[tion] toward the potter" (EO, 1:213). But the source for such power lies outside A's and the women's purview. Because Margarete has allowed Faust to become "the origin of [her] thoughts" and the "food of [her] soul," and Donna Elvira has loved Don Giovanni "more than her soul's salvation," both are incapable of making another beginning (EO, 1:213, 196). Neither are able to hear that every man is a mere "human being" and that no man is rightly an "object of faith" (EO, 1:209).

Margarete despairs of her ability to will on her own: "What am I that I dare to be so bold" (EO, 1:213). There is one solution to her quagmire that Kierkegaard refuses her, and us. Margarete may not stand up coura- geously with Judge William and march boldly out of her predicament. Not only would this be useless advice, given that she is almost certainly incapable of such a feat, but she would then only be trading one false method for another, deeming her life to be clay in her *own* hands. While William might (if he were not patently sexist) recommend that Margarete "give birth to herself" and thus emerge victorious, Kierkegaard offers a radically different answer.[19] And here we must leave Kierkegaard's char- acters behind. *Either/Or*'s A slyly hints that the answer to the problem of "Silhouettes" "falls outside of [his] concern entirely" (EO, 1:188). The only hope for Margarete, as well as for Kierkegaard's many iniquitous men, falls outside of the world of his pseudonymous texts.

INDENTURED TO GOD

From this foundation [Christ's command], Christianity now takes possession of every expression of love and is jealous for itself. (WL, 140)

While in various ways they attempt to "grasp" upward, find consolation, justify by calculation, and hide from the chaos, not one of these characters is able to see that the only true way runs right into the middle of the storm. Although Kierkegaard's characters, in the midst of moral maels- trom, make periodic reference to the "God-relationship," none is able to surmise the religious solution that is a "heart bound to God" (WL, 149).

The one through whom they become infinitely indebted and eternally indentured to God is beyond the scope of Kierkegaard's religiously inept characters. In their disorientation, several characters falter toward and trip over this rupture in the foundation of human understanding and, subsequently, fall into the realization of our grave propensity toward error. The Diarist for example, in his story of Solomon, is able to conjure up the image of a man totally bewildered and guilty before God. But redemption eludes each one of them. There is one clearly discernible reason behind the futility of their efforts. Every text we have read is forged in the vacuum of Christ's absence. Unable even to guess that there is a Christian interpretation of their crises of guilt and innocence, error and truth, most of Kierkegaard's characters flounder. By denying the crises, William believes himself justified, but the fissures in his own system imply that it may be merely a matter of time before his home itself cracks.[20] All of the characters miss that there is One – a simultaneously terrifying and redeeming One – to whom they must disclose themselves. This is the only One who can bring about their absurd justification. The secular and religious confusion layered through the pseudonymous texts provokes the reader into making the choice that continually eludes the Diarist and the poet, the solicitous woman and the consoled husband: to exist as beholden to God through Christ. Each must disclose fully his or her sin before God and accept redemption in Christ. This relation, only glimpsed between the fissures of their fractured lives and loves, has multiple implications for our own love.

In a passage within the longest chapter of *Works of Love*, Kierkegaard links Christ, the abyss of human sin, our infinite debt, and the Christian transformation of intimacy. This dense section repays our close attention. As the only one for whom "love was totally present," Christ is both the "explanation" and the "transfiguration" of the command to love (WL, 101, 102). Christ's command (his "explaining") and his existence (his "being") perfectly correspond, and thus in him the law finds completion (WL, 102). There are two subjective effects of this completion on the individual: astonishment leading to repentance, and faith. Through the revelation of scripture, we discover that "there was no moment" when Christ's obedience to his own command faltered; he perpetually acted out of love for the neighbor and never stood addled or idle while "time slip[ped] by" (WL, 100). We who are "frail and infirm" thus find that, in contrast to Christ, we are infinitely "behind" in "every one of eternity's tasks" (WL, 102). Christ's "requirement and his criterion reduce [us] to nothing" (WL, 102). But, our damnation and our salvation coincide in this revelation. Kierkegaard indicates that, in Christ's life, we find the intersection of our infinite sin *and* our eternal hope. As the "fulfillment of the divine Law," Christ "fixes an everlasting cosmic abyss" between our love and the love commanded, but he also is, as the "fulfilling of the Law," the one whereby we become inextricably bound to God (WL, 101). Through Christ, as the law's "perfect fulfillment," the law as "require-ment" has been and is continually met (WL, 99). Only in this context of Christ's "perfect fulfillment" is the individual truly related to God and enabled to hear (but not fulfill) the command. Through Christ we know that "God is an eternity ahead" in God's love for us, and this sense of indentured gratitude is a key to how we are to love (WL, 102). It is at this juncture that we both find "humility" as the "essential expression of how we relate to God" and discover that God is the requisite "middle term" for all veritable intimacy (WL, 102, 107). It is only as we exist at the perilous intersection of our nothingness and Christ's grace that we may love. We will consider first the humbling effect of the law and then move to the effect of our indebtedness.[21]

The way of veritable love requires first that the Christian experience the profound perplexity occasioned by Christ's example. The secular version of moral vertigo experienced by Kierkegaard's characters has as its Christian counterpart the astonishment we must endure when we look up at the apex of Christian love revealed in Christ. God, through Christ, brings the requirement immediately close to the individual and, through Christ, infinitely elevates the requirement itself. The intended result is akin to our standing nose-to-wall with a high tower and gazing toward the upper limit. We are supposed to be thrown off balance. This profoundly disorienting encounter with Christ, Kierkegaard contends, is the only entry point for faith:

But when a person in the infinite transformation discovers the eternal itself so close to life that there is not the distance of one single claim, of one single evasion, of one single excuse, of one single moment of time from what *he* in this instant, in this second, in this holy moment *shall* do – then he is on the way to becoming a Christian. (WL, 90, emphasis in the original)

When we come literally face to face with the personification of love's ful-fillment, we must stagger. Due to its elevation and its proximity, Christ's law is to provoke the individual to stumble away from the moral assump-tions that have previously comforted him. As is the case in the story of the young lawyer who approached Jesus in order to justify himself, Christ undermines our presuppositions about the boundaries separating the just from the unjust, and addles our confident notions of moral adequacy. We are "grasped," "placed under the obligation to do accordingly," and forced to question the measly and muddled love we heretofore thought was adequate (WL, 96).

Moral confusion must prompt us to turn to Christ's law as the only gauge for human conduct, and open us up to the implications of our own guilt. Whether shuddering before Mount Moriah or before Christ, we are to know ourselves fraught with insurmountable error. Through Christ, God presents the "task as close as possible to the questioner," and the result is to be our realization that "right [where] we are," we stand as "nothing before God" (WL, 96, 365). Kierkegaard describes this effect as the result of Christ's activity and his command. In contrast to his perpetually loving work for others, we discover that "every previous moment is a wasted moment and more than just wasted time" and that "any other expression of love is procrastination and regression" (WL, 102, 95). Not merely missed minutes, in the light of Christ's life even our seemingly inadvertent evasions of the law indicate moral culpability. And Christ's command places the "middle term 'neighbor'" between the listener and every other beloved, determining that our love is rarely "conscientious" (WL, 142). Even though we count our passion, affection, and interest as evidence of our love, Christ's command exposes our arithmetic as spurious. Kierkegaard concludes that "to speak about love as the fulfilling of the Law is, of course," to "simultaneously acknowledge one's own guilt" (WL, 104). We who previously thought that we "had language usage on [our] side" are to find ourselves dizzy, speechless, and, most importantly, indicted (WL, 82).[22]

Before moving to our necessary turn toward Christ the redeemer, it is important to consider the impact of our indictment on the way we are to love. Entering intimacy through this bewildering, Christian route is to make the lover wary of self. The experience of self before Christ is to throw us sufficiently off balance to prompt our self-suspicion and cause us continually to question our motives and actions toward our neighbor. The "as yourself" spoken by and fulfilled in Christ "does not leave self-love the slightest little excuse" and is to result in the lover's "limping" (WL, 18). One way to interpret Kierkegaard's metaphor is to say that we who encounter Christ's judgment are slowed down; the requirement hinders our ready acceptance of what we immediately perceive as the truth about ourselves. Kierkegaard explains: "just as Jacob limped after having struggled with God, so will self-love be broken if it has struggled with this phrase [as yourself]" (WL, 18). This is not in order that the individual be left devoid of self-consideration, but that, having been "judged with the unshakableness of eternity," he is continually to check his immediate, default tendency to blur the boundary between self and other (WL, 18). We are prompted to peer as scrupulously at our self as do Kierkegaard's characters at the beloved, questioning the "feelings, drives, inclinations, and passions" that make up the potentially delusive "powers of immediacy" (WL, 25). The "earnest person" is never to "weary of tracking down the illusions," no matter how "cozy the arrangement is" or how "good the company." This "fear" of being "in error" is a key facet of Christian love (WL, 124).

While Kierkegaard most often speaks of this work as "self-renunciation" or "self-denial," the correction applies to A's submissive women as well as to the acquisitive poet or thief (WL, 3, 25, 52). Because the majority of Kierkegaard's characters jump the barrier between self and other in order to acquire, and because Kierkegaard often, in *Works of Love*, writes on the more obvious import of "self-denial," we may miss this less explicit facet of Christ's judgment in Kierkegaard's account. The determined "honesty" toward the self, the "earnestness of eternity," involves an individual's denial of herself, whether in her self-delusion she attempts to consume another or to fuse herself to another (WL, 25). The latter error is as grave as the former, in that she denies the true import of the phrase "as yourself" by denying, through submission to the other, that there are two selves involved. Cordelia, Margarete, William's wife, this author, and the reader must each "renounce" and "deny" our self-deluding interest in the "celebrated glory of poetry," which starkly contrasts with the "earnestness of the commandment" (WL, 25). The metaphor of moral vertigo thus also describes the proper effect of Christ's law on a duped and self-duping woman. She is to be thrown off the false balance she has achieved within an asymmetrical system. We are just as earnestly to become wary of self to the extent that we are taken in by the beguiling secular accounts of "abject" feminine love which encourage us to merge self with other, but, and this point is crucial, not in order that we may then turn toward the thief's error and blur the boundary the other way, welding other to self (WL, 126). Rather, we are, through Christ's judgment, to take note of the resilience of sin and of the impediment Christ's term "neighbor" places between two individuals in every engagement. Before the law we search ourselves for the many mutations of fallen love and discover the multiple ways we truly are "nothing" before God.

We must become sufficiently preoccupied with our own sin to avoid comparison. Just as our greatest opportunity to purloin or submit comes with intimacy, proximity brings with it occasion for what Kierkegaard calls the "loathsome rash" of comparison (WL, 186). This, love's "greatest torment" occurs as we attempt to avoid moral vertigo and evade indictment by stepping away from Christ as guide and peering suspiciously at the one closest to us (WL, 35). Kierkegaard terms this "the most disastrous association that love can enter into," and our experience before the law is to humble us sufficiently to preclude this dangerous form of preoccupation with the other (WL, 186). We will discuss below the effect of our indebtedness on our ability to forgive, but here, in the realm of Christ's judgment on us, we are in another way forced to forgo our tendency to count scrupulously the sins of another. When outside the context of Christ's command, we are often eager to "watch with a hundred eyes" in order to detect the faults of the one to whom we are committed (WL, 35). Before the infinitude of Christ's example and Christ's command, we are to remain in awe of our own utter inability to navigate love's terrain. As Kierkegaard insists, "there is always a new task" for those who would love well (WL, 188). The proximity and height of the command is to keep us intent on our own relation to the "shall" of scripture, and to curb our pitiful desire to watch, judge, and condemn the one whose error we have most opportunity to detect. To the extent that we do not sufficiently submit to the law and instead seek to "become better by comparison with the badness of others," we are to deem ourselves, again, as bad (WL, 183).

If we only knew ourselves "infinitely in the wrong before God," we might be tempted, like Constantin's guests, to revel in the rubble of human failure, and to create out of our malleable reality a malevolent but enjoyable system. Or, like the young poet or the Diarist, we might huddle alone, waiting for the thunderstorm to strike. But, while Christ's law does have the last word, Kierkegaard does not believe that God abandons us to the forces of human confusion and iniquity. There is a "very upbuilding thought" that undergirds Kierkegaard's account of faithful engagement and that enables the Christian to crack through the world of the pseudonymous texts. This is the "thought" that "love abides":

. . . we are speaking of the love that sustains all existence, of God's love. If for one moment, one single moment, it were to be absent, everything would be confused. But love does not do that, and therefore, however confused everything is for you – love abides. Therefore we are speaking of God's love, of its nature to abide . . . (WL, 301)

In the midst of the requisite confusion occasioned by Christ's law, we also receive the assurance that God's love abides. As we have noted before, Kierkegaard does not dwell on this fact, but rather presupposes it. Dealing in his "little book" with "human love" rather than with "God's love," Kierkegaard continues to focus on the task before us (WL, 301). But running throughout the text is Kierkegaard's assumption that God's grace is the "originating" source of "a person's love" (WL, 9). And in his description of the "upbuilding" that is to occur with faith, we may read Kierkegaard as assuming Christ's work in particular.

Through Christ's fulfillment of the law, the individual is bound to and dependent upon God. The confusion and guilt we experience before Christ as judge is bound up with our realization that he is the fulfillment of the law; he is God's absurd work of grace on our behalf. Unlike the characters of Kierkegaard's narratives, Christians must enter the strait of impending anarchy and receive Christ as their only hope. This strand twists through *Fear and Trembling* and the "Ultimatum" of *Either/Or*: the merman and we stand unarguably "in the wrong" before God, no matter how much we suppose ourselves to have accomplished, and the answer to our condition is therefore of a different order than the fine tuning of guilt and innocence, vice and virtue, doubt and determination. What is the case for righteous but supra-moral Abraham is also the case for immoral us. We who stand absolutely culpable before God require a third possibility outside the realm of the moral. Our lives require divine confiscation – that is, redemption. It is through Christ that we fallen and "botched" creatures are redeemed. Christ's fulfillment of the law is the radical gift to which none of us can lay "claim" but for which all of us are to remain stunned and grateful. It is in Christ that we know ourselves as "infinitely and unconditionally ow[ing] everything" to God (WL, 103). Kierkegaard contrasts this understanding of a Christian's relationship to God to other notions of freedom that miss "the infinite boundedness" that is a requisite result of faith (WL, 149). If our heart "is to be pure," we must know the gravity of our sin and the implications of Christ's extravagant work; our love must be "without limit bound to God" (WL, 148). Kierkegaard's construal of Christ's work leaves the one redeemed indebted to God, rather than let off the hook.[23] The individual's faith in the truth of Christ's work is to create a profound sense of humility and gratitude, and, importantly, a sense of being indentured now to God himself.

We may interpret much that Kierkegaard says about true love in the context of the individual's recognition of his debt and God's consequent claim on each of us. First, all relationships become a matter of "conscience," as Kierkegaard words it. Whenever two come together, God is present as the first and even "sole" claimant on the lover and the beloved (WL, 121). The one who would love truly must always keep in mind, "whatever else," that "God has first priority" (WL, 149). Loving "out of a sincere faith" thus requires a kind of "separation" insofar as the lover recognizes that, at each and every point, God comes between the two lovers as a "third party" to the relationship (WL, 153, 121). Kierkegaard links confidentiality to the "pure heart" that resides in the knowledge of both the lover's and the beloved's boundedness to God (WL, 153). This reinforces the law of which Christ is the fulfillment. The "as yourself" that the law uses to declare each person first and foremost "a neighbor," is, in a new way, enabled as the person of faith becomes aware of his and his beloved's primary relationship, each one of them, to God. True love must begin with and maintain, as an "eternal foundation," this acknowledgment of the beloved's prior commitment to God (WL, 141). As Kierkegaard explains, this is "beyond mutuality" and instead is something more akin to each individual loving God alongside of one another, supporting each other to the extent that each one can, but always cognizant that, as Kierkegaard so starkly puts it, God is truly "the wife's beloved" (WL, 121).

This goes against much of what we assume about intimate love, and Kierkegaard recognizes the difficulties. Should not truly intimate love countenance no intrusion or qualification and be, rather, "totally dependent" on the beloved (WL, 38)? Should not we feel that we would "lose everything by losing the beloved" (WL, 38)? Although Kierkegaard awkwardly suggests at one point that the truly faithful lover can lose a beloved here or there with little concern because we always have a new "neighbor" to love (WL, 65), he also acknowledges that one who loves another in particular always feels a "need" and in some sense is therefore "dependent" on the beloved (WL, 38). In this passage, Kierkegaard explains a second important implication of faith on our love. Because in faith we know that the beloved is first and foremost God's own, we must count as transgression any effort to "possess the beloved" (WL, 38). We may adore and need our beloved only "on one condition," and that is that we never "confuse love with possessing the beloved" (WL, 38). Again, faith enables my approximation of the law in that I know that my beloved is truly other than me; he is an individual confiscated by God and thus determinately *not* at my disposal. As Kierkegaard affirms, "a life without loving is [indeed] not worth living," but it is a dangerous "misconception" for me to suppose my life inextricably intertwined with my beloved's (WL, 38). Each of us must reserve our "infinite passion" for "the eternal" (WL, 40). To the extent that we instead "relate" ourselves "with infinite passion" for a "particular" person, we "make manifest" the "misrelation" in merely human love (WL, 40). While this implication of faith for love may make Christian intimacy sound overly cold or indifferent, Kierkegaard counters that a "cooling of the passions" is necessary for the sake of your own and your beloved's relationship to God (WL, 147). For one thing, you are otherwise tempted to fashion your beloved into a domesticated savior; for another, you otherwise tend to think of her as your pleasurable property; and, finally, you otherwise subtly or blatantly ignore her prior commitment to God. Or, to address the mistaken ardor of Dona Elvira, without this requisite cooling of human love, I break my own commitment to the eternal by fastening myself to a mere man.

But if our faith is in several ways to distance us from the beloved, our faith is also to add a resilience to our love when, left to our own devices, we would determine it scarcely worth the effort (WL, 141). This third aspect of faith on our love involves our ability to see mercifully our beloved as one whom "God has created" and "Christ has redeemed" (WL, 69). Knowing ourselves redeemed in Christ, we are also to recognize our "kinship" with the other, established through each person's "relationship to God in Christ" (WL, 69). By "deeply and forever memorably imprinting" on my mind our common predicament and salvation, God's work in Christ is to effect in me an ability to love (WL, 69). Kierkegaard writes on merciful love in at least two related ways: because we are, each one of us, damned and saved, we are all equally ill fitted and blessed to this task before us; and, because God has, through Christ, shown such infinite extravagance, we are in kind indiscriminately to love the uniquely (or so it seems) annoying one beside us. Given that "we human beings are all imperfect" (and that Christ's example reveals the imperfection to be extreme), we are to cultivate "the healthy, strong, capable love that is designed for loving the more imperfect persons, that is, the people we see" (WL, 167). With a "closed eye of forbearance and leniency," we are to love regardless of the multiple "defects and imperfections" we inevitably see if we peer closely enough at the one with whom we share our daily life (WL, 162). Or, to put the matter somewhat differently, having been shown a love that is "limitless," we are to love without limit (WL, 167). When, at any point, we think of love as a "claim" on which we are "entitled to collect" we are to be reminded, through faith, of the debt we instead owe Christ (WL, 163). We are to know ourselves, through Christ, as placed within an alternative context for love, one in which there is "an infinite quantity" of "boundless" love and in which, therefore, all attempts at miserly "calculation" are ruled "impossible" (WL, 178). For, as Kierkegaard concludes, to subtract or add from an infinite amount is pointless.

Beyond forgiveness, however, is the "presupposition of love" that Kierkegaard describes as another facet of indebted intimacy (WL, 217). This fourth effect of faith on our engagement is our ability not only to forgive the faults we cannot avoid noting, but also to assume love on the part of our beloved. By living within the context of our debt before God, our love for another is akin to a "gift," and thus, within this context, we cannot "be deceived out of [our] love" (WL, 242). If love is given out of a sense of gratitude and consequent generosity, we are able then not to look carefully for results. Through Christ, we are to learn that love involves bestowal, not investment, so one who counts the returns on love reveals himself outside the proper context of love (WL, 242). By presupposing "that love is in the other person's heart," we are able to focus on the (at times infinitesimal) potential for Christian reconciliation, rather than on the barriers to it; in this way we further "build up" love between us, even though that building up is seen only through the eyes of faith (WL, 217). Here Kierkegaard links our humility before the law with our ability to love in hope instead of mistrust. Given my predisposition to appraise another using the gauge of my own needs and desires (a predisposition exposed by Christ's command), I must suspect my own judgment of him (WL, 228). Kierkegaard explains that, "on the basis of the possibility of deception," we may conclude either that we should watch another scrupulously before loving him or, considering our own extreme potential for self-deception and false-judgment, we may presuppose love on the part of the beloved (WL, 228). If we are to love within the context of debt, we must choose the latter.

For Kierkegaard, faithful love has "the quality of giving itself completely," in trust, but not from the basis of our submission to the other that involves our willed ignorance of the other's transgressions (WL, 212, 228). It is important here that we again distinguish Margarete's duped love from faithful presupposing. The "ground" of love whereby we are enabled to love the other is our relationship to God in Christ, which requires our submission to God alone (WL, 217). And the route toward such a presupposition requires that we acknowledge our own and our neighbor's mortal frailty and sin. We are forbidden "a dream world" wherein we may cultivate "imaginary and exaggerated ideas" about a blameless beloved (WL, 161). For Kierkegaard, we know ourselves and our beloved as fallen and redeemed, and, even knowing our significant imperfections, we are to hope in the grace that will move us (at times imperceptibly) toward reciprocity. This hope is enabled precisely in our relationship to God in Christ, not in our lover's ability to achieve and maintain some image we have set for him or he has set for himself. True love is, according to Kierkegaard, in a certain way independent from the particular facts about the beloved herself. The one whose love has its "source" in the eternal is able to "bring love along" rather than seek what is lovable (WL, 157). It is our focus on God's work, our faith in God's grace, that enables Christian love to "give itself completely," without fear of the other's faults and without glancing continually at the other in order to gauge her response. And, because this context of presupposition and trust is itself grounded in faith in God, we must disbelieve and even distance ourselves from a lover like Margarete's (Faust) who claims himself to be a rightful object of faith and infinite passion. If the beloved's "idea of love" requires us to forgo our own prior commitment to God (as does Don Juan's and Faust's) the "love-relationship as such can be the sacrifice that is required" (WL, 130). The thin but infinite line between sacrificing such a relationship for God and doing so out of our own lack of faithful love is a distinction that anguishes the Diarist and tormented Kierkegaard. We who read him must become similarly troubled.

Which distinction brings us back around, a final time, to our relationship to the law. The salvation in Christ whereby we "have only God to deal with in everything" is "simultaneously the highest comfort and the greatest strenuousness" (WL, 377). It is the strenuousness itself that propels us into redemption. Our realization that, even with grace, we continue to transgress boundaries, calculate results, adore idolatrously, and detect defects, often in rapid succession, is to provoke us toward God. Realizing the extent to which we continue to escape our crises of guilt and innocence through false, irreligious routes, we are to flee, continually, to be with Christ. Kierkegaard contends that this is the only way we may "remain in God" (WL, 190). By residing consciously "in the debt," in the "infinitude of the debt," the Christian resides with God (WL, 190). And this is our only hope for approximating Christ's command. Not merely remembering but daily accepting God's redemptive work in Christ, we may be able to forgive and even love the fallen person we see before us (WL, 380). To the extent that we fail to do so, we fall away from God, fail to show mercy, and, Kierkegaard warns with foreboding, seal our fate

(WL, 380). In this journal entry, Kierkegaard characterizes the progress for which we are therefore to pray:

If I were to define Christian perfection, I should not say that it is a perfection of striving but specifically that it is the deep recognition of the imperfection of one's striving, and precisely because of this a deeper and deeper consciousness of the need for grace, not grace for this or that, but the infinite need infinitely for grace... (JP II 1482 [Pap. x.3 A 784 n.d., 1851]).

But this is a matter not for song or for text; "it must be believed and it must be lived" (WL, 8).

Notes

INTRODUCTION

1 George Lukács, "The Foundering of Form Against Life: Søren Kierkegaard and Regine Olson," in *Søren Kierkegaard*, ed. Harold Bloom (New York: Chelsea House Press, 1989), 5–18.

2 Karl Barth, *Church Dogmatics*, 4 vols. (Edinburgh: T. and T. Clark, 1967), IV:747. The entire passage by Barth on Kierkegaard is from this reference.

3 Sylvia Walsh, "Forming the Heart: the Role of Love in Kierkegaard," in *The Grammar of the Heart: Thinking with Kierkegaard and Wittgenstein*, ed. Richard H. Bell (San Francisco: Harper and Row, 1988), 234–56, 248. David Gouwens discusses Walsh's work as an answer to Barth in his *Kierkegaard as Religious Thinker* (New York: Cambridge University Press, 1996), 190.

4 I am indebted to John David Ramsey for suggesting "precarious" as an etymologically apt word to describe this stance.

5 A fuller description of the philosophical import of my reading of Kierkegaard must wait for another time, perhaps another interpreter. I here gesture toward possible implications for three current projects: (1) the attempt analytically to map human love in order more reliably to navigate the terrain, (2) the attempt to play fruitfully within our presently deconstructed existence, and (3) the attempt to reconstruct the world (and the word) by returning to the strength of Christendom.

6 George Pattison, "Friedrich Schlegel's *Lucinde*: a Case Study in the Relation of Religion to Romanticism," *Scottish Journal of Theology* 38, no. 4 (1985): 545–64.

7 Pattison, "Schlegel's *Lucinde*," 549.

8 I am in disagreement with Pattison on this; he reads William as Kierkegaard's answer to Schlegel.

9 Kierkegaard's depiction of loving speech thus coincides with Louis Mackey's evocative description of grace at the end of his essay, "Slouching Toward Bethlehem: Deconstructive Strategies in Theology," *Anglican Theological Review* 65, no. 2 (1983): 255–72. "The other side – the objective correlative – of faith is grace. And grace, at its signal advent in this world, did in fact (we believe) assume a mute and infant form" (270). I hope eventually to decipher further the relation of Kierkegaard's indebted Christianity to the work of those who are in debt to Derrida – Mackey and John Caputo in particular.

10 Pia Søltoft, *Svimmelhedens Etik* (Copenhagen: Gad Publishers, 2001).

11 Her Danish colleague, Anette Ejsing, also points to the necessity of receptivity in Kierkegaard's understanding of revelation. Anette Ejsing, "Revelation and Subjectivity: *The Book on Adler*," unpublished paper presented at the annual meeting of the AAR, November 2000.

12 M. Jaime Ferreira, *Love's Grateful Striving* (Oxford: Oxford University Press, 2001).

13 See Gene Outka, "Universal Love and Impartiality," in *The Love Command-ments: Essays in Christian Ethics and Moral Philosophy*, eds. Edmund N. Santurri and William Werpehowski (Washington, DC: Georgetown University Press, 1992), 1–103. For his discussion of conferral through redemption and through creation see especially p. 9.

1 THE CALL TO CONFESSION IN KIERKEGAARD'S WORKS OF LOVE

1 David Gouwens notes, "Kierkegaard's *Works of Love* presents an extensive grammar that examines and tests the quality of human love in light of divine love," David Gouwens, *Kierkegaard as Religious Thinker* (New York: Cambridge University Press, 1996), 197.

2 Mark C. Taylor, *Kierkegaard's Pseudonymous Authorship* (Princeton: Princeton University Press, 1975), 329.

3 Gouwens finds warrant in Kierkegaard's writings for the command in its third or guiding use. Ferreira and Walsh read the text as describing love as a graced virtue. See M. Jamie Ferreira, "Equality, Impartiality and Moral Blindness in Kierkegaard's *Works of Love*," *Journal of Religious Ethics* 25, no. 1 (1997): 65–85; and Sylvia I. Walsh, "Forming the Heart: the Role of Love in Kierkegaard," in *The Grammar of the Heart: Thinking with Kierkegaard and Wittgenstein*, ed. Richard H. Bell (San Francisco: Harper and Row, 1988), 234–56.

4 Paul Müller, *Kierkegaard's* Works of Love: *Christian Ethics and the Maieutic Ideal*, trans. and eds. C. Stephen Evans and Jan Evans (Copenhagen: C. A. Reitzel, 1993), 11. Bruce H. Kirmmse, *Kierkegaard in Golden Age Denmark* (Bloomington: Indiana University Press, 1990). In his "Christian humanist" rendering of the text, Müller ties Kierkegaard's account of both law and gospel more to the "creation order" than to our redemption in Christ. The designation "Christian humanist" is Stephen Evans's, x, xi.

5 Gouwens, *Kierkegaard as Religious Thinker*, 190.

6 I contend that this is a misuse of Luther given that Luther, even while praising marital relations, warns of the impediments to faith within marriage and that marital love exists "in the midst of demons." See Luther's *Sermon on the Estate of Marriage*, *On Marriage Matters*, or *Lecture on Psalm 128*.

7 And here I disagree with Gouwens's reading that "the passion of *eros* is not condemned as simply narcissistic, but is surrounded by a love for one's beloved as neighbor" (*Kierkegaard as Religious Thinker*, 192). I would

characterize the transformation Kierkegaard commends more as eros chastened and guided by than "surrounded by" *agape*. We will return to this distinction below, especially in the fourth chapter on Judge William's account of faithful passion.

8 Ernest B. Koenker notes in his article on Kierkegaard's use of Luther that Kierkegaard "can only distrust the spontaneity and freedom Luther identified with the life of faith." To "humiliation and exaltation" Kierkegaard "must add a third stage, the effort of thankfulness" (243). I believe that this effort requires that we be reminded of the debt that must be paid on our behalf. Ernest B. Koenker, "Søren Kierkegaard on Luther," *Interpreters of Luther: Essays in Honor of Wilhelm Pauck*, ed. Jaroslav Pelikan (Philadelphia: Fortress Press, 1968), 234–48. Also see footnote 5.

9 See, for example, Niels Thulstrup and Marie Mikulova Thulstrup, eds., "Kierkegaard's View of Christianity," *Bibliotheca Kierkegaardiana*, vol. 1 (Copenhagen: C. A. Reitzels Boghandel, 1978). See also Andrew Burgess, "Kierkegaard's Concept of Redoubling and Luther's *Simul Justus*," in Works of Love, vol. XVI of *The International Kierkegaard Commentary*, ed. Robert L. Perkins (Macon, GA: Mercer University Press, 2000), 39–55. Bruce Kirmmse reads Kierkegaard's emphasis on grace to be "well within the Pauline and Lutheran tradition" (*Kierkegaard in Golden Age Denmark*, 311). Because most of Kierkegaard's overt complaints against the misuse of Luther's theology are in his journals, it is important that we consider what he has written there. But a few methodological notes are in order. It is difficult to discern definitively the relation between Kierkegaard's thoughts on Luther and *Works of Love*, given that the book was published in 1847 and Kierkegaard states later that same year that he "never really read anything by Luther" (JP III 2463 [Pap. VIII.1 A 465 n.d., 1847]). We can reasonably read that sentence with an emphasis on the "really" rather than on the "anything," because Kierkegaard comments two years earlier, apparently while reading Luther, on Luther's writing style (JP III 2460 [Pap. VI A 108 n.d., 1845]). Regardless, scholars do agree that Luther's theology influences Kierkegaard's work from the beginning, if more generally, as a result of Kierkegaard's participation in the Danish church and Lutheran culture at large.

10 Gouwens, *Kierkegaard as Religious Thinker*, 128.

11 Ibid.

12 See also Louis Dupré, *Kierkegaard as Theologian* (New York: Sheed and Ward, 1963). Dupré spends more time on Kierkegaard's late journal entries in which Kierkegaard focuses on the necessity of a Christian's imitation of Christ's cruciform life and concludes that the "essence of the imitation" is humility itself (178).

13 This should become clearer in the section in this chapter comparing Luther's *The Freedom of a Christian* and Kierkegaard's section on debt.

14 Gouwens, *Kierkegaard as Religious Thinker*, 112.

15 The work of Christ as judge is an early and continual theme of Kierkegaard's journals; see for example, JP 1 287 (Pap. II A 261, Sept. 12, 1838) and JP IV 4804 (Pap. XI. 1 A 3 n.d., 1854).

16 Again, for a somewhat different read of Kierkegaard's interpretation of Christ as pattern, see Gouwens, *Kierkegaard as Religious Thinker*, 128 and following.

17 Koenker notes that Kierkegaard saw Luther's endorsement of marriage as representing an alliance with the world as opposed to a willingness to suffer; Luther established a "false bond with the world" that allowed for an easy alliance between civil culture and Christianity ("Søren Kierkegaard on Luther," 249).

18 Kierkegaard argues this point indirectly through the falsely confident Judge William in *Either/Or*, to which we will turn in Chapter 4.

19 Gouwens, *Kierkegaard as Religious Thinker*, 196.

20 The reference is to Pap VIII.2 B 45 n.d., 1847, and it continues "But love is devoutly oblivious of its works and the last thing it thinks of is having writers, and yet even the poorest work of love has the quality of being essentially indescribable, since it is speedier than any short-hand writer's pen and more deeply intimate than all the writings of the most prolix author" (WL, 427, Supplement). (Note the self-reflective reference to the relative worth of his authorship.)

21 Jeremy Walker explains this concept helpfully in two parts: first, "it is impossible that a man could ever be faced consciously with the objective truth about another man," and second, "although there may be the possibility of objective knowledge of others – up to a point – still, as ethical subjects we are not concerned with this sort of knowledge." Jeremy Walker, *To Will One Thing: Reflections on Kierkegaard's "Purity of Heart"* (Montreal: McGill-Queen's University Press, 1972), 158.

22 Kirmmse helpfully explains the import of this section, "Mistrustfulness errs in forgetting that [to choose between trust and mistrust] is a life question, that it concerns oneself in making such a judgement" (*Kierkegaard in Golden Age Denmark*, 314).

23 Müller softens such a reading when he explains that "it is only because there is no conception in paganism that eternity's demand for the self is self-denial that Kierkegaard can maintain that concerning love for one's neighbor there is 'not even a hint of paganism'" (*Kierkegaard's* Works of Love, 22). In his effort to find in Kierkegaard continuity between our natural and our graced loves, Müller at times under-represents Kierkegaard's emphasis that God's demand for self-denial makes a qualitative difference. Kierkegaard's insistence that there is "not a hint of paganism" in the Christian conception of love is to signal radical discontinuity between the self-denial of *Kjerlighed* and the default, self-centered love of the mere human.

24 Gouwens rightly reads in this section and others on forgiveness an account of Christian vision that draws upon a willed, continual cultivation akin to

what we usually think of as Christian virtue (205). Such loving vision is for Kierkegaard inextricably linked to one's ability to acknowledge and confess her own imperfections, and thus virtue itself is still dependent upon the theological work of the law.

25 This is a very different reading than Müller's, which sees Kierkegaard here explaining how Christian love is based on (rather than contrasted with) a human need to be loved (13).

26 These two sections (II.B and III) are crucial for our interpretation of *Repetition*, in Chapter 3.

27 Kierkegaard does not call here for the lover to endure abuse, verbal or physical, in the presence of another. The summons for the reader to lose herself in the hope that the other loves does not mean that she must remain physically with someone who repeatedly denies that she is also redeemed as God's own. (I use the female pronoun here advisedly.) But Kierkegaard does imply that the one abused should continue to hope for and believe in the possibility of love's triumph, from a safe distance. As Gouwens puts it, even while refusing to submit to "treachery" by colluding with evil, "one never gives up on another person" (204). The tension between abiding in hope and abiding physically with an abusive other will return in Chapter 4, the chapter wherein we discuss the idolatrous women of *Either/Or*.

28 At this point the Hongs suggest JP IV 4542 (Pap. VIII.1 A 165 n.d., 1847): "Most people are subjective toward themselves and objective toward all others . . . but the task is to be objective toward oneself and subjective toward all others" (WL, Supplement, 423).

29 As Daniel Barber put it in an (as yet unpublished) paper on this section, "When we have been sinned against and find ourselves unable, at the height of our mental powers, to create a mitigating explanation, then (and only then) are we referred to the task of forgiveness."

30 The emphasis is mine.

31 Gouwens, *Kierkegaard as Religious Thinker*, 196. George Pattison helpfully explains here, "In discovering our essential freedom in and through the realization of our nothingness before God we discover the 'divine equality' among humankind. It is only through such an absolute and inward 'leveling' that we realize the radical nature of the demand to see each and every one of our fellow human beings as a 'neighbor' in the Christian sense." George Pattison, *Kierkegaard and the Crisis of Faith* (London: Society for Promoting Christian Knowledge, 1997), 110.

32 My suggestion here that God's grace is the implicit subject of the entire text is consistent with Dupré's reading of Kierkegaard's theology as one constantly reliant on grace. See especially Dupré, *Kierkegaard as Theologian*, 170.

33 Dupré and Gouwens both explain that Kierkegaard's understanding of the work of God's grace is one of "attraction" (Dupré, *Kierkegaard as Theologian*, 170) or "elicitation" (Gouwens, using Gene Outka's distinction, *Kierkegaard as Religious Thinker*, 194). For Kierkegaard, the will is always necessarily an element in the work of God on an individual. It makes rhetorical sense, then,

for Kierkegaard to turn again to the individual's task of recognizing the need for grace rather than dwelling in this text on the work of grace.

34 He insists that Christianity "teaches that money in itself smells bad" (WL, 321).

35 Kirmmse, *Kierkegaard in Golden Age Denmark*, 328.

36 Kierkegaard deleted the line "– to say it jestingly (and jest truly has its justification also in earnestness) before God, we are not merely all Jutlanders, but we are all robbers." See WL, Supplement, 464.

37 Kirmmse notes that Kierkegaard ultimately "leaves one confronted with the problem of the book, which has nothing to do with whether or not another person (even the author of *Works of Love*) acts out of love, but whether one is oneself, at every moment, loving" (*Kierkegaard in Golden Age Denmark*, 318).

38 Luther makes lovely use of Aesop's fable. A dog, running along the stream with a big steak in its mouth, sees the reflection of the steak in the stream, and snaps at the reflection. In so doing, the silly dog drops the meat, the water ripples, and he loses both the meat in his mouth and the reflection of the meat. By snapping at the reflection of Christ's righteousness, the benefits, the "works," we lose both the righteousness of Christ and the works that issue forth from our union with the righteous Christ. We "lose faith and all its benefits." We may read this little fable as the telling transition between Luther's section on our marriage to Christ and his section on the outward benefits that this marriage conveys. Martin Luther, "The Freedom of a Christian," in *Martin Luther's Basic Theological Writings*, ed. Timothy F. Lull (Minneapolis, MN: Fortress Press, 1989).

39 Regarding *Works of Love*, Kirmmse writes, "SK takes the notion of equality and ethics up into a sphere that is distinctively Christian and that stands in extraordinarily painful relation to the temporal world with its ordinary ethics and politics" (*Kierkegaard in Golden Age Denmark*, 308).

40 While there are other examples of Kierkegaard's rhetorical (but not merely rhetorical) use of Christ's life, I will concentrate on these related stories.

41 The sentence is a paraphrase from Kierkegaard's conclusion (WL, 382).

42 I believe that there are other valid interpretations of this exchange in Luke 22:60–62. Nonetheless, I do not consider Kierkegaard's use of the story to be irresponsible.

43 Gouwens, *Kierkegaard as Religious Thinker*, 117.

44 Müller notes that "God educates the person by steadily drilling his eyes into the person's conscience in such a way that the person is forced to look at God all the time" (*Kierkegaard's* Works of Love, 34).

45 See also WL, 76, 122, 133, 202.

46 See for example his thinly veiled self-exaltation in WL, 109: "See, worldly wisdom has a long list of various expressions for sacrifice and devotion. I wonder if among them this is also found: out of love to hate the beloved, out of love to hate the beloved and to that extent oneself, out of love to hate the contemporaries and to that extent one's own life?" In his journal, Kierkegaard contends that what Denmark most needs is not Luther's

corrective to asceticism, but one who "could say . . . 'to defy Satan, the public, the newspapers, and the whole nineteenth century, I cannot marry'" (JP III 2537 [Pap. x A 324 n.d., 1857]). There are traces of this self-righteous self-elevation in the pseudonymous texts (from the knight of resignation to the Diarist), as well as signs that Kierkegaard himself knows that this is a warped version of spiritual confidence.

47 The danger about which I am warning is quite different, I believe, from a third strand of the text wherein the reader is advised to keep God as her witness against those who would undermine her resolve to live first with faith. This "proper" self-love, as Kierkegaard describes it, is not an elevation of the self above others but a counting of oneself as also judged by God and saved by Christ. See Gouwens on the necessity of suffering with patience, and the distinction between avoidable and unavoidable suffering in our approximation of Christ's love (*Kierkegaard as Religious Thinker*, 164, 170). Kirmmse also gives a helpful account on apt and delusive suffering (*Kierkegaard in Golden Age Denmark*, 319–22).

48 The italics are mine, but the emphasis is Kierkegaard's: "To be able to love a person despite his weaknesses and defects and imperfections is still not perfect love, but rather this, to be able to find him lovable despite and with his weaknesses and defects and imperfections." Yet again, Gouwens phrases this well when he explains that love "hides" sin in that sin is seen "in light of a larger imaginative vision of the other person" (*Kierkegaard as Religious Thinker*, 206). Walsh nicely considers the possibility of a "second immediacy" whereby one's dulled love is not transformed merely through duty but through a passionate commitment to see differently ("Forming the Heart," 244).

49 Gouwens quotes Simone Weil on this idea of humble vision, "The soul empties itself of all its own contents in order to receive into itself the being it is looking at, just as he is" (*Kierkegaard as Religious Thinker*, 204). I believe this is similar to Kierkegaard's insistence that true love requires an abiding awareness of potential transgression.

50 Frederick Sontag, "The Role of Repetition," in *Concepts and Alternatives in Kierkegaard*, vol. III, of *Bibliotheca Kierkegaardiana*, eds. Niels Thulstrup and Marie Mikulova Thulstrup (Copenhagen: C. A. Reitzels Boghandel, 1981), 285; quoted in David Cain, "Notes on a Coach Horn: 'Going Further,' 'Revocation,' and *Repetition*," in Fear and Trembling *and* Repetition, vol. VI of *The International Kierkegaard Commentary*, ed. Robert Perkins (Macon, GA: Mercer University Press, 1993) 335–58.

2 PROVOKING THE QUESTION: DECEIVING OURSELVES IN *FEAR AND TREMBLING*

1 I am grateful to Vanessa Rumble for pointing me to Mark C. Taylor's and Louis Mackey's readings of *Fear and Trembling* as a text about silence, sin, and deception. See Mark C. Taylor, "Sounds of Silence," in *Kierkegaard's* Fear and Trembling: *Critical Appraisals*, ed. Robert Perkins (University, AL:

University of Alabama Press, 1981), 165–87; and Louis Mackey, *Points of View: Readings of Kierkegaard* (Tallahassee: Florida State University Press, 1986).

2 Here my argument coincides with C. Stephen Evans's assessment that the text is to muddy our moral certainty: "[the ethical answer] assumes that one understands the good and has the power to will it. The religious life [to which we are indirectly called in *Fear and Trembling*] begins with the discovery that this tidy, rational assumption is contradicted by experience; it begins with the discovery that actual existence is 'incommensurable' with the demands of ethics." C. Stephen Evans, "Faith as the Telos of Morality: a Reading of *Fear and Trembling*," in Fear and Trembling *and* Repetition, vol. VI of *The International Kierkegaard Commentary*, ed. Robert Perkins (Macon, GA: Mercer University Press, 1993), 9–27; 19.

3 The reference provided in the supplement to FT is from a letter by Johann Georg Hamann to Johannes Gotthelf Lindner: "When the son of Tarquinius Superbus had craftily gotten Gabii in his power, he sent a messenger to his father asking what he should do with the city. Tarquinius, not trusting the messenger, gave no reply but took him into the garden, where with his cane he cut off the flowers of the tallest poppies. The son understood from this that he should eliminate the leading men of the city" (FT, Supplement, 339).

4 Mark C. Taylor writes of the Third Problem, "Kierkegaard relentlessly probes the ambivalence and ambiguity of silence's sources" ("Sounds of Silence," 177).

5 Evans, "Faith as the Telos of Morality," 20.

6 See in particular Kierkegaard's chapter "Our Duty to Remain in Love's Debt" with which he closes the first series of *Works of Love*. His account of loving indebtedness leads into and informs the second series wherein he describes God's command that we humbly rely on God and forgive our neighbor.

7 See Ronald M. Green, "Enough IS Enough! *Fear and Trembling* Is NOT about Ethics," *Journal of Religious Ethics* 21, no. 2 (1993): 191–210, 192. See also Gene Outka, "God as the Subject of Unique Veneration: a Response to Ronald M. Green," *Journal of Religious Ethics* 21, no. 2 (1993): 211–16.

8 Green, "Enough IS Enough!" 192.

9 The first quote is from Green, "Enough IS Enough!" 199, and the second is from Outka, "God as the Subject," 211.

10 The phrase is Gene Outka's, but I use it here to highlight our difference ("God as the Subject," 211). I argue below that we are not to recognize Abraham's predicament as our own, but rather to see ourselves mirrored by the contrasting merman. I agree with Outka that Green's reading of Abraham does not take sufficient account of de Silentio's assertions that Abraham is not a sinner (212). However, given that we *are* sinners, I suggest that we approach Mount Moriah with more ethical confusion and fear than Outka's proposal of universalizability affords (214).

11 Kierkegaard spells this out explicitly in his chapter in *Works of Love*, "Love is a Matter of Conscience."

12 Outka, "God as the Subject," 213.

13 Louise Carroll Keeley, "The Parables of Problem III in Kierkegaard's *Fear and Trembling*," in Fear and Trembling *and* Repetition, vol. VI of *The International Kierkegaard Commentary*, ed. Robert Perkins (Macon, GA: Mercer University Press, 1993), 127–54, 130.

14 I suggest that this is the prevailing pedagogical tactic after teaching many graduate students who learned it thus in college and after having discussed the text with other professors who teach the text. I should here thank Vanessa Rumble, who, blessedly, did not teach the book in this way. See her articles "The Oracle's Ambiguity: Freedom and Original Sin in Kierkegaard's *The Concept of Anxiety*," *Soundings* 25 (Winter 1992): 605–25 and "Eternity Lies Beneath: Autonomy and Finitude in Kierkegaard's Early Writings," *Journal of the History of Philosophy* (January 1997): 83–103. For a discussion of these preliminary sections as "a set of *false starts*," through which we must read in order to understand the import of the Problems, see Edward F. Mooney, "Art, Deed, and System," in Fear and Trembling *and* Repetition, vol. VI of *The International Kierkegaard Commentary*, ed. Robert Perkins (Macon, GA: Mercer University Press, 1993), 67–100; quote from 77, emphasis in original.

15 Mooney, "Art, Deed, and System," 78.

16 Mackey, *Points of View*, 67.

17 From the Hongs' notes: "Approximately three years before the publication of Fear and Trembling (1843), the first omnibuses (horse-drawn) were put into use in Copenhagen" (FT, 340n). Denmark's confidence in this new means of transportation serves as a metaphor for their duped confidence in the progress afforded by Hegel's system.

18 Mooney, "Art, Deed, and System," 83.

19 This seems to be an issue for Kierkegaard, as the young man in *Repetition* is relieved in the end not to have to be called to dinner. It is a daily example perhaps of the necessity of patience with finitude.

20 This call to sleeplessness returns in the Third Problem wherein the individual is to "scrutinize in sleepless vigilance every single secret thought" (FT, 100).

21 De Silentio makes the point less radically later about the worth of the rich young man's charity: "for if he were to give away his possessions because he is bored with them, then his resignation would not amount to much" (FT, 49).

22 The musical metaphor is Evans's; "Faith as the Telos of Morality," 26.

23 Kierkegaard repeats this theme of leeched suffering in *Repetition*, as the young man who has fled the girl likens himself to Job, who has genuinely been deprived of his loved ones. The young man states without embarrassment that he is like one who imagines himself ill while reading about someone else's malady (R, 206). For a similar reading of Kierkegaard's intentionally

deceptive stretching of scripture in these two texts, see Mark Lloyd Taylor, "Ordeal and Repetition in Kierkegaard's Treatment of Abraham and Job," in *Foundations of Kierkegaard's Vision of Community*, eds. George B. Connell and C. Stephen Evans (Atlantic Highlands, NJ: Humanities Press, 1992), 33–53.

24 De Silentio describes "infinite resignation" as "that shirt mentioned in an old legend" wherein "the thread is spun with tears . . . but then it also gives protection better than iron or steel" (FT, 45).

25 Because Kierkegaard's interpreters have been drawn, almost exclusively, to Problems I and II, I will not spend a great deal of time on these sections.

26 Outka calls Kierkegaard's "vindication of a direct relationship to God" the "center" that governs the revolving accounts of "obedience to God, the ethical, sin, and so on" ("God as the Subject," 211).

27 "Queen Elizabeth sacrificed to the state her love for Essex by signing his death decree. This was a heroic act, even though there was a little personal resentment involved because he had not sent her the ring. As is known, he had in fact done so, but a spiteful lady-in-waiting had held it back. It is said, *ni fallor*, that Elizabeth learned of this and sat for ten days with one finger in her mouth, biting it and not saying one word, and thereupon she died" (FT, 93–94).

28 Mark Lloyd Taylor interprets this passage as crucial for understanding Kierkegaard's aim in *Fear and Trembling*, and he helpfully links the brevity of de Silentio's treatment of sin to the efforts of *Repetition*'s young man hastily to liken himself to Job rather than to Cain ("Ordeal and Repetition in Kierkegaard's Treatment of Abraham and Job," in *Foundations of Kierkegaard's Vision of Community*, eds. George B. Connell and C. Stephen Evans. Atlantic Highlands, NJ: Humanties Press, 1992).

29 This theme of our refusal to repent and disclose returns in full force with *Stages on Life's Way*, to which we will turn in Chapter 5.

30 Keeley, "The Parables of Problem III," 136.

31 Ibid.

32 Mackey, *Points of View*, 65.

33 Keeley's essay is again very helpful here. She finds in this section Kierkegaard's insistence that "religiousness is not a lingering in the darkness of human evil but an entrance into the light of God's grace" ("The Parables of Problem III," 147).

34 Evans, "Faith as the Telos of Morality," 26.

35 The full quote is, "Nor could Abraham explain further, for his life is like a book under divine confiscation and never becomes *publice juris* [public property]" (FT, 77).

36 Edward F. Mooney, *Selves in Discord and Resolve* (New York: Routledge, 1996), 49. He writes more hopefully than I do about the possibility of our being well shaped for moral discernment by this pseudonymous text.

37 Mooney, "Art, Deed, and System," 96.

38 Outka, "God as the Subject," 215.

3 THE POET, THE VAMPIRE, AND THE GIRL IN
REPETITION WITH *WORKS OF LOVE*

1 Joakim Garff, "'My Dear Reader!' Kierkegaard Read with Restrained Affection," *Studia Theologica* 45 (1991): 127–47; 130.

2 Louis Mackey, *Points of View: Readings of Kierkegaard* (Tallahassee: Florida State University Press, 1986), 95.

3 For what I believe may be an invitation to play, see Sylviane Agacinski, "An Aparté on Repetition," *Feminist Interpretations of Søren Kierkegaard*, eds. Céline Léon and Sylvia Walsh (University Park, PA: Pennsylvania State University Press, 1997), 131–45.

4 Frederick Sontag, "The Role of Repetition," in *Concepts and Alternatives in Kierkegaard*, vol. III of *Bibliotheca Kierkegaardiana*, eds. Niels Thulstrup and Marie Mikulova Thulstrup (Copenhagen: C. A. Reitzels Boghandel, 1981) 285; quoted in David Cain, "Notes on a Coach Horn: 'Going Further,' 'Revocation,' and *Repetition*," in Fear and Trembling *and* Repetition, vol. VI of *The International Kierkegaard Commentary*, ed. Robert Perkins (Macon, GA: Mercer University Press, 1993), 335–58.

5 See Supplement to R, 276; JP, IV B 97:2 n.d., 1843.

6 George Pattison explains, "the situation becomes downright disastrous when an engagement is announced, since the real possibility of marriage confronts him with the need to break the spell of his dream world and come to terms with the reality of another person and his responsibility towards her" (369). George Pattison, "The Magic of Theater: Drama and Existence in Kierkegaard's *Repetition* and Hesse's *Steppenwolf*," in Fear and Trembling *and* Repetition, vol. VI of *The International Kierkegaard Commentary*, ed. Robert Perkins (Macon, GA: Mercer University Press, 1993), 359–77. Pattison's perceptive skepticism of the young man's and Constantin's relation to the other is heightened by using *Works of Love* as a contrasting text.

7 Cain notes that "freedom as sagacity," of which Constantin is an example, "develops strategies seeking to outwit repetition as tiresome and make it interesting" ("Notes on a Coach Horn," 351).

8 I respectfully disagree with Stephen Crites, who discusses the Berlin passage as "a comic counterpoint to Nameless's ordeal" without noting the problem of the others on whom Constantin feeds (237). Stephen Crites, "'The Blissful Security of the Moment': Recollection, Repetition, and Eternal Recurrence," in Fear and Trembling *and* Repetition, vol. VI of *The International Kierkegaard Commentary*, ed. Robert Perkins (Macon, GA: Mercer University Press, 1993), 229–45. Mackey calls Constantin's trip a "parody" without noting the menacing aspect of his perusals (*Points of View*, 76). While I take their point that Constantin provides a contrast to the young man's seeking, neither Crites nor Mackey notes the mutual collusion of both quests.

9 Pattison explains that, at the theater, Constantin is "completely secured against the disturbing contingency and other-relatedness of life" ("The Magic of Theater," 368).

10 Mackey misses the furtively predatory nature of Constantin's work, even while noting that he "requires novelty and variety" (*Points of View*, 77). He construes Constantin more as a seducer than as a voyeur. I believe that there are relevant differences between Constantin and the seducer of *Either/Or*, although both characters exhibit vices to which most of us can, albeit more subtly, relate.

11 Crites notes that Constantin's "ecstasy of the moment is hostage to momentary disruption that explodes it as wholly as it has taken form" ("The Blissful Security of the Moment," 239).

12 This passing and oblique biblical reference, to the speck in his eye, is one of several biblical or liturgical references in the Berlin passage. At two points, Constantin refers to, and then eschews, the idea that he is actually part of a larger body (R, 151, 161). He arrives in Berlin on the "Universal Day of Penance and Prayer," but misses the significance (R, 153). Finally, he refers to Jonah's story, without reconsidering his own story accordingly (R, 166). These are just a few of Kierkegaard's pseudonymous examples of revelation mishandled by one incapable of true hearing.

13 While their reading of the young man's advance is guarded, both Crites and Gouwens see him as going beyond Constantin, toward "the absurdity of the coincidence of eternity in time present that is inexpressible" (Crites, "The Blissful Security of the Moment," 246) or by exploring "the question of his own guilt and innocence." David Gouwens, "Understanding, Imagination, and Irony in Kierkegaard's *Repetition*," in Fear and Trembling *and* Repetition, vol. vi of *The International Kierkegaard Commentary*, ed. Robert Perkins (Macon, GA: Mercer University Press, 1993), 290–310, 296.

14 Mackey warns that we should not, like the young man, "misread nervous apoplexy as divine intervention" (*Points of View*, 90).

15 And here Gouwens is certainly correct that the young man is able to "conjure up how his actions have affected the girl" (Gouwens, "Understanding, Imagination, and Irony," 294). The young man merely glimpses this, however, and does not at any point choose his course of action out of concern for her.

16 Gouwens and Mark Lloyd Taylor note that the young man views his guilt as a "temporary position" (Gouwens, "Understanding, Imagination, and Irony,"304), a "category" that can be resolved in an instant. Mark Lloyd Taylor, "Ordeal and Repetition in Kierkegaard's Treatment of Abraham and Job," in *Foundations of Kierkegaard's Vision of Community*, eds. George B. Connell and C. Stephen Evans (Atlantic Highlands, NJ: Humanities Press, 1992), 33–53.

17 Mackey, *Points of View*, 95.

18 Ibid.

19 Cain, "Notes on a Coach Horn," 352.

20 John Caputo, "Kierkegaard, Heidegger, and the Foundering of Metaphysics," in Fear and Trembling *and* Repetition, vol. vi of *The International*

Kierkegaard Commentary, ed. Robert Perkins (Macon, GA: Mercer University Press, 1993), 210–23.

21 For what I believe to be the best discussion of Christ's work and our hope, see David Gouwens, *Kierkegaard as Religious Thinker* (New York: Cambridge University Press, 1996), although I do see grace as effecting a more radically discordant change in the individual than does Gouwens.

22 Pattison, "The Magic of Theater," 372.

23 Thank you, Margaret Farley, for this phrase.

24 Pattison, "The Magic of Theater." 110. The forgiveness Kierkegaard describes does not require us to remain in proximity to another who physically or verbally abuses us, however. In *Either/Or* Kierkegaard implies and in *Works of Love* he insists that were I to remain with another who so fundamentally refuses to acknowledge my selfhood before God, I would myself be in error. This does not preclude God's call that I love and forgive the abuser as my neighbor, but I must do so from a considerable distance.

25 David Cain notes another apt metaphor for loving truly from Kierkegaard's journal, of building a "nest upon the sea" (JP I, VIII 1023 A [Pap. II 612 n.d., 1837]).

26 Gouwens aptly suggests that "perhaps one could go even further, reading and understanding *Repetition* as the young man read and understood the book of Job" (Gouwens, "Understanding, Imagination, and Irony," 308).

4 THE MARRIED MAN AS MASTER THIEF IN *EITHER/OR*

1 Wanda Warren Berry, "Judge William Judging Woman: Existentialism and Essentialism in Kierkegaard's *Either/Or*," in Either/Or, vol. IV of *The International Kierkegaard Commentary*, ed. Robert Perkins (Mercer GA: Mercer University Press, 1995), 34.

2 Wanda Warren Berry, "The Heterosexual Imagination and Aesthetic Existence in Kierkegaard's *Either/Or*," in Either/Or, vol. III of *The International Kierkegaard Commentary*, ed. Robert Perkins (Mercer, GA: Mercer University Press, 1995), 201–28; and "Judge William Judging Woman," 34.

3 Céline Léon, "(A) Woman's Place is Within the Ethical," in *Feminist Interpretations of Søren Kierkegaard*, eds. Céline Léon and Sylvia Walsh (University Park, PA: Pennsylvania State University Press, 1997), 119.

4 Louis Mackey, *Kierkegaard: a Kind of Poet* (Philadelphia, PA: University of Pennsylvania Press, 1971), 45, 48. I otherwise agree with and am grateful for Mackey's close, skeptical reading of Judge William.

5 Léon, "(A) Woman's Place is Within the Ethical," 107.

6 Even when scolding A for his "egotism," William puts the matter in terms of reciprocal "enjoyment." A errs to the extent that he does not allow others to "enjoy" him (EO, II:25).

7 Kierkegaard continues, "We say of a seducer that he steals a girl's heart, but of all purely human love, even when it is the most beautiful, we must say that it has something thievish about it, that it really steals the beloved's perfections . . ." (WL, 173).

8 Mackey, *Kierkegaard: A Kind of Poet*, 61. See also David Gouwens, *Kierkegaard as Religious Thinker* (New York: Cambridge University Press, 1996), 103.

9 While Louis Mackey well notes that Constantin Constantius and Johannes the Seducer share particular, seedy characteristics, he misses this chance to link William's and Constantin's patterns toward women (Mackey, *Kierkegaard: A Kind of Poet*, 24–27).

10 See R, 159 and following.

11 Mackey, *Kierkegaard: A Kind of Poet*, 90.

12 Ibid.

13 Ibid., 89, 91.

14 In his treatise in *Stages on Life's Way*, William directly addresses the problem of comparison and appraisal in a way closer to Kierkegaard's position in *Works of Love*.

15 Gouwens, *Kierkegaard as Religious Thinker*, 109.

16 Ibid., 117.

17 Ibid., 121.

18 Berry, "The Heterosexual Imagination," 57. We consider this further in the last chapter by noting the futility of William's method for women.

5 SECLUSION AND DISCLOSURE IN *STAGES ON LIFE'S WAY*

1 Drawing upon French feminism, Céline Léon offers another reading of *Stages* as a text on the negation of otherness in her essay, "The No Woman's Land of Kierkegaardian Exceptions," in *Feminist Interpretations of Søren Kierkegaard*, ed. Céline Léon and Sylvia Walsh (University Park, PA: Pennsylvania State University Press, 1997), 147–73. Reading *Stages* with *Works of Love* allows us not only to indict Kierkegaard for his own painful evasions (as does Léon) but, more to the point, to find *ourselves* implicated in the multiple narratives of *Stages*. We may use Kierkegaard's own critique, in *Works of Love*, of the deception, use, and avoidance of the other to crack open this fraternal text. To do so also allows us to hear in *Works* Kierkegaard's call to a Christian alternative only glimpsed through the fissures of *Stages*.

2 The idealistic Young Man, William the Married, and the Diarist are less ape-like than the others, but, as Kierkegaard asserts, "To become better or seem to be better by means of comparison with the badness of others is, after all, a bad way to become better" (WL, 286).

3 I say "largely" because William the Married also has intimations of the truth in his passages against comparison. This truth slips through his hands, however, when he suggests that love can be based on his admiration of the maternal and sustained by woman's inherent goodness.

4 Although these men's divergence from Kierkegaard's norm in *Works of Love* is obvious, the nuances of their distortions are worth attention. For a much more in-depth look at misogyny in this portion of the text, see

Robert L. Perkins, "Woman-Bashing in Kierkegaard's '*In Vino Veritas*': a Reinscription of Plato's *Symposium*," in *Feminist Interpretations of Søren Kierkegaard*, eds. Céline Léon and Sylvia Walsh (University Park, PA: Pennsylvania State University Press, 1997), 83–102.

5 We should note that the Young Man shudders at the thought that he might find a woman who likewise understood the dangers involved in intimacy, for this would "betray alarming foreknowledge" and thus taint "her lovableness" (SLW, 47).

6 For a different interpretation of the narrative transition from "*In Vino Veritas*" to Judge William's treatise, see Perkins, "Woman-Bashing." Perkins understands Kierkegaard here to underscore the extent to which "the Judge and his wife are far closer to the ethical" than the banqueters (100).

7 N.B.: I say "our condition" rather than merely "his" in order to involve us all in this critique. If at any point in Kierkegaard's poetics we find ourselves peering in self-righteously at others, we have missed (and also illustrated) his point. While Kierkegaard satirizes patriarchal domesticity by use of William, the allegation implied is more generally applicable than merely to the oblivious, married man. Relationships among men, women, and children may be fraught with assumptions similar to William's.

8 WL, 228, 139, 36.

9 Remember that Victor chides William for a related error in his preface to *Either/Or*. He notes that William's math is off in his figuring that "ninety-nine are saved by woman" in that William "gives no place to those who are actually lost" (EO, I, 11).

10 Indeed, William notes that, if she refuses to cohere to these wishes, he may by law "go out to the forest and cut the switches white" (SLW, 85).

11 For a more in-depth discussion of the difference between the Young Man and the Diarist, see again Léon, "The No Woman's Land of Kierkegaardian Exceptions."

12 This distinguishes the Diarist also from the young man of *Repetition* and Constantin's banquet. It is not incidental either that the Young Man is at the banquet or that he chooses Constantin as his confidant. The Young Man, unlike the Diarist, maintains his own purity and innocence in both texts. We will further discuss the necessarily prior step of guilt and confession below.

13 In "The No Woman's Land of Kierkegaardian Exceptions," Céline Léon judges the Diarist more harshly than do I, reading his break with the girl as evidence of his fear of her rather than as evidence of his fear of his own potential for harming her or of his fear of the rough road ahead of them.

14 Yet, as we will relate, the Diarist does, to some extent, believe himself to be one and a half to her one.

15 See Judge William on this: "neither of us is anything by oneself, but we are what we are in union" (SLW, 93).

6 ON THE WAY

1 See the "Ultimatum" of *Either/Or*, II:345.

2 Kierkegaard almost subtitled *Repetition* "A Fruitless Venture"; R, 276.

3 To say that the merman, Johannes and Constantin *miss* an earnest walk is somewhat misleading. We note below that they, unlike the others, recognize that they are in grave sin, but decide to remain in the sea.

4 Even the most perspicuous calculation of our own or another's good deed and error, when performed with the slightest glance toward self-justification, betrays our confusion. As the Jylland pastor continues, "How could a person ever gauge his relationship with God by a more or a less, or by a specification of approximation?" (EO, II:352).

5 The quote is from a passage wherein Kierkegaard imagines writing on the further exploits of Johannes the Seducer.

6 WL, 110 and supplement to WL, 464.

7 See the quote opening this section regarding the exploits of Johannes.

8 The voice is that of A, interrupting William's treatise.

9 From a journal entry on *Works of Love* and the distinction between deliberations and discourses; JP 1 641 (Pap. VIII.1 A 293 n.d., 1847). See introduction to WL, xi.

10 While in these pseudonymous texts the rupture is not explicitly caused by the juxtaposition of Christian revelation and human love, the narratives of those who become baffled have religious relevance inasmuch as they intimate our own fissures.

11 Several of the characters (de Silentio, the Diarist, William) try out multiple methods, and, at the risk of losing the reader, we here describe the patterns rather than maintaining the textual flow of character degeneration. We will also at this point leave behind Johannes and his unapologetic cronies, given that they apparently do not seek moral clarity but instead fashion the chaos for their own pleasure. Their happy amorality indicates the danger we face if, rather than moving toward faith, we remain blithely within a context of moral deconstruction.

12 As de Silentio notes, it is at this point that the knight loses the princess.

13 This is a pattern for William who, prior to this story, relates his admiration for another mother on the street. He tellingly explains that he was "walking steadily at [his] businesslike pace from the other end of the city to the court-house to render a verdict" when he espies a mother patiently caring for her dawdling toddler. Always the judge, he renders his favorable verdict on her maternal care (SLW, 137).

14 He insists "mother's milk" is "lifesaving," and through his wife, he "absorbs" sufficient "peace and contentment" to resolve his "vexation of spirit" (SLW, 130).

15 Here I refer to Gene Outka's apt retrieval of Kierkegaard's concern that in Kant's system God becomes something akin to metaphysical caulking, providing coherence to our moral lives. See Outka's "God as the Subject

of Unique Veneration: a Response to Ronald M. Green," *Journal of Religious Ethics* 21, no. 2 (Fall 1993): 211–16.

16 What William dismisses as a matter of "insufficient comprehension," (that is, the "differences" in ethical performance) de Silentio, the young poet, A, and the Diarist take as an indication of their own ignorance and inability to perform (EO, II:265).

17 This, one of the Diarist's longer stories, is of a man who thinks himself perhaps to have sired a child on one irresponsible night. The man routinely paces the street in a futile but symbolic effort to find his potential child and becomes a financial benefactor to the children of the city, telling himself that this latter gesture is truly nothing in comparison with his debt (SLW, 276–84).

18 It makes some rhetorical sense for Kierkegaard to resist shifting the story from the active lover to the submissive beloved. For the key to the characters' and the reader's misunderstanding is, in many cases, their preoccupation with the thoughts and behavior of the other, which deflects self-scrutiny.

19 Recall William's advice to A: "After all, you are not supposed to give birth to another human being; you are supposed to give birth only to your-self" (EO, II:206) and "Through the individual's intercourse with himself the individual is made pregnant by himself and gives birth to himself" (EO, II: 259).

20 Or, what is perhaps worse, William may be only imperceptibly headed to hell. This is Kierkegaard's fear, I believe, for his fellow Danish citizens. Given Kierkegaard's skepticism regarding the coherence of worldly success and spiritual rectitude (and his correlation between vice and worldly fame) he may have surmised that William's house, even though built on shaky sand, would remain standing until the eschaton.

21 Here it bears repeating that Müller reads Kierkegaard differently as do, to some extent, Ferreira, Berry, and Walsh. To a greater or lesser extent, these critics interpret *Works of Love* as being more about God's role as creator than Christ's work as redeemer. While theirs is a plausible reading, I believe that much of what Kierkegaard writes on true love and our obligation to God depends on our sense of great indebtedness after our realization of our sin and faith in Christ's intercession. This problem, of grave human sin and confusion, appropriately preoccupies Kierkegaard, and his account of the answer to our predicament thus relies heavily on our redemption.

22 The reference is to Kierkegaard's passage on the self-supposed philanthropist who discovers that, given Christ's parable of the wedding banquet, his own carefully chosen guest list is an indication of his sin (WL, 82).

23 It is not clear whether Kierkegaard here has in mind a critique of Danish Lutheranism, but this concern corresponds with many of his journal entries on the need for us to recall the immensity of the debt paid. The thought that we are "let off the hook" so to speak by Christ's work would be, I believe, a misconstrual of Luther's ethics.

Works cited

(*See List of Abbreviations on p. viii for Primary Works*)

SECONDARY WORKS

Agacinski, Sylviane. "An Aparté on Repetition." *Feminist Interpretations of Søren Kierkegaard*. Eds. Céline Léon and Sylvia Walsh. University Park, PA: Pennsylvania State University Press, 1997. 131–45.

Barth, Karl. *Church Dogmatics*. 4 vols. Edinburgh: T. and T. Clark, 1967.

Berry, Wanda Warren. "The Heterosexual Imagination and Aesthetic Existence in Kierkegaard's *Either/Or*." *International Kierkegaard Commentary*, volumes III–IV: Either/Or. Ed. Robert Perkins. Macon, GA: Mercer University Press, 1995. III:201–28.

"Judge William Judging Woman: Existentialism and Essentialism in Kierkegaard's *Either/Or*." *International Kierkegaard Commentary*, volumes III–IV: Either/Or. Ed. Robert Perkins. Macon, GA: Mercer University Press, 1995. IV:33–57.

Burgess, Andrew. "Kierkegaard's Concept of Redoubling and Luther's *Simul Justus*." *International Kierkegaard Commentary*, volume XVI: Works of Love. Ed. Robert L. Perkins. Macon, GA: Mercer University Press, 2000. 39–55.

Cain, David. "Notes on a Coach Horn: 'Going Further,' 'Revocation,' and *Repetition*." *International Kierkegaard Commentary*, volume VI: Fear and Trembling *and* Repetition. Ed. Robert Perkins. Macon, GA: Mercer University Press, 1993. 335–58.

Caputo, John. "Kierkegaard, Heidegger, and the Foundering of Metaphysics." *International Kierkegaard Commentary*, volume VI: Fear and Trembling *and* Repetition. Ed. Robert Perkins. Macon, GA: Mercer University Press, 1993. 210–23.

Crites, Stephen. "'The Blissful Security of the Moment': Recollection, Repetition, and Eternal Recurrence." *International Kierkegaard Commentary*, volume VI: Fear and Trembling *and* Repetition. Ed. Robert Perkins. Macon, GA: Mercer University Press, 1993. 229–45.

Dupré, Louis. *Kierkegaard as Theologian*. New York: Sheed and Ward, 1963.

Ejsing, Anette. "Revelation and Subjectivity: *The Book on Adler*." Unpublished paper presented at the annual meeting of the American Academy of Religion, Nashville, Tennessee, November 2000.

Evans, C. Stephen. "Faith as the Telos of Morality: a Reading of *Fear and Trembling*." *International Kierkegaard Commentary*, volume VI: Fear and Trembling *and* Repetition. Ed. Robert Perkins. Macon, GA: Mercer University Press, 1993. 9–27.

Ferreira, M. Jamie. "Equality, Impartiality and Moral Blindness in Kierkegaard's *Works of Love*." *Journal of Religious Ethics* 25, no. 1 (1997): 65–85.

Love's Grateful Striving. Oxford: Oxford University Press, 2001.

Garff, Joakim. "'My Dear Reader!' Kierkegaard Read with Restrained Affection." *Studia Theologica* 45 (1991): 127–47.

Gouwens, David. *Kierkegaard as Religious Thinker*. New York: Cambridge University Press, 1996.

"Understanding, Imagination, and Irony in Kierkegaard's *Repetition*." *International Kierkegaard Commentary*, volume VI: Fear and Trembling *and* Repetition. Ed. Robert Perkins. Macon, GA: Mercer University Press, 1993. 290–310.

Green, Ronald M. "Enough IS Enough! *Fear and Trembling* is NOT About Ethics." *Journal of Religious Ethics* 21, no. 2 (1993): 191–210.

Keeley, Louise Carroll. "The Parables of Problem III in Kierkegaard's *Fear and Trembling*." *International Kierkegaard Commentary*, volume VI: Fear and Trembling *and* Repetition. Ed. Robert Perkins. Macon, GA: Mercer University Press, 1993. 127–54.

Koenker, Ernest B. "Søren Kierkegaard on Luther." *Interpreters of Luther: Essays in Honor of Wilhelm Pauck*. Ed. Jaroslav Pelikan. Philadelphia, PA: Fortress Press, 1968. 234–48.

Kirmmse, Bruce H. *Kierkegaard in Golden Age Denmark*. Bloomington, IN: Indiana University Press, 1990.

Léon, Céline. "The No Woman's Land of Kierkegaard's Exceptions." *Feminist Interpretations of Søren Kierkegaard*. Eds. Céline Léon and Sylvia Walsh. University Park, PA: Pennsylvania State University Press, 1997. 147–73.

"(A) Woman's Place is Within the Ethical." *Feminist Interpretations of Søren Kierkegaard*. Eds. Céline Léon and Sylvia Walsh. University Park, PA: Pennsylvania State University Press, 1997. 103–30.

Léon, Céline and Sylvia Walsh, eds. *Feminist Interpretations of Søren Kierkegaard*. University Park, PA: Pennsylvania State University Press, 1997.

Lukács, George. "The Foundering of Form Against Life: Søren Kierkegaard and Regine Olson." *Søren Kierkegaard*. Ed. Harold Bloom. New York, NY: Chelsea House Press, 1989. 5–18.

Luther, Martin. "The Freedom of a Christian." *Martin Luther's Basic Theological Writings*. Ed. Timothy F. Lull. Minneapolis, MN: Fortress Press, 1989.

Mackey, Louis. *Kierkegaard: A Kind of Poet*. Philadelphia, PA: University of Pennsylvania Press, 1971.

Points of View: Readings of Kierkegaard. Tallahassee, FL: Florida State University Press, 1986.

"Slouching Toward Bethlehem: Deconstructive Strategies in Theology." *Anglican Theological Review* 65, no. 2 (1983) 255–72.

Mooney, Edward F. "Art, Deed and System." *International Kierkegaard Commentary*, volume VI: Fear and Trembling *and* Repetition. Ed. Robert Perkins. Macon, GA: Mercer University Press, 1993. 67–100.

Selves in Discord and Resolve. New York, NY: Routledge, 1996.

Müller, Paul. *Kierkegaard's* Works of Love: *Christian Ethics and the Maieutic Ideal*. Trans. and eds. C. Stephen Evans and Jan Evans. Copenhagen: C. A. Reitzel, 1993.

Outka, Gene. "God as the Subject of Unique Veneration: a Response to Ronald Green." *Journal of Religious Ethics* 21, no. 2 (1993): 211–16.

"Universal Love and Impartiality." *The Love Commandments: Essays in Christian Ethics and Moral Philosophy*. Eds. Edmund Santurri and William Werpehowski. Washington, DC: Georgetown University Press, 1992. 1–103.

Pattison, George. "Friedrich Schlegel's *Lucinde*: a Case Study in the Relation of Religion to Romanticism." *Scottish Journal of Theology* 38, no. 4 (1985): 545–64.

Kierkegaard and the Crisis of Faith. London: Society for Promoting Christian Knowledge, 1997.

"The Magic of Theater: Drama and Existence in Kierkegaard's *Repetition* and Hesse's *Steppenwolf*." *International Kierkegaard Commentary*, volume VI: Fear and Trembling *and* Repetition. Ed. Robert Perkins. Macon, GA: Mercer University Press, 1993. 359–77.

Perkins, Robert L. "Woman-Bashing in Kierkegaard's '*In Vino Veritas*': a Reinscription of Plato's *Symposium*." *Feminist Interpretations of Søren Kierkegaard*. Eds. Céline Léon and Sylvia Walsh. University Park, PA: Pennsylvania State University Press, 1997. 83–102.

Rumble, Vanessa. "Eternity Lies Beneath: Autonomy and Finitude in Kierkegaard's Early Writings." *Journal of the History of Philosophy* (January 1997): 83–103.

"The Oracle's Ambiguity: Freedom and Original Sin in Kierkegaard's *The Concept of Anxiety*." *Soundings* 25 (Winter 1992): 605–25.

Sontag, Frederick. "The Role of Repetition." *Concepts and Alternatives in Kierkegaard*. Eds. Niels Thulstrup and Marie Mikulova Thulstrup. *Bibliotheca Kierkegaardiana*, vol. III. Copenhagen: C. A. Reitzels Boghandel, 1981.

Søltoft, Pia. *Svimmelhedens Etik*. Copenhagen: Gad Publishers, 2001.

Taylor, Mark C. *Kierkegaard's Pseudonymous Authorship*. Princeton: Princeton University Press, 1975.

"Sounds of Silence." *Kierkegaard's* Fear and Trembling: *Critical Appraisals*. Ed. Robert Perkins. University, AL: University of Alabama Press, 1981. 165–87.

Taylor, Mark Lloyd. "Ordeal and Repetition in Kierkegaard's Treatment of Abraham and Job." *Foundations of Kierkegaard's Vision of Community*.

Eds. George B. Connell and C. Stephen Evans. Atlantic Highlands, NJ: Humanities Press, 1992. 33–53.

Thulstrup, Niels and Marie Mikulova Thulstrup, eds. "Kierkegaard's View of Christianity." *Bibliotheca Kierkegaardiana*, vol. 1. Copenhagen: C. A. Reitzels Boghandel, 1978.

Walker, Jeremy. *To Will One Thing: Reflections on Kierkegaard's "Purity of Heart."* Montreal: McGill-Queen's University Press, 1972.

Walsh, Sylvia. "Forming the Heart: the Role of Love in Kierkegaard." *The Grammar of the Heart: Thinking with Kierkegaard and Wittgenstein.* Ed. Richard H. Bell. San Francisco, CA: Harper and Row, 1988.

Living Poetically: Kierkegaard's Existential Aesthetics. University Park, PA: Pennsylvania State University Press, 1994.

Index